Introduction to Business

Marvelle S Colby

Selig Alkon

Tony Bushell

HarperCollins*Publishers*

This edition first published in 1995 by
HarperCollins College Division
An imprint of HarperCollins*Publishers* Ltd, UK
77–85 Fulham Palace Road
Hammersmith
London W6 8JB

Tony Bushell asserts the moral right to be identified as the author of the
adapted material.

British Library Cataloguing in Publication Data
A catalogue record for this book is available from the British Library

ISBN 0–0–499015–3

Typeset by Harper Phototypesetters Ltd, Northampton, England
Printed and bound by Scotprint Ltd, Musselburgh, Scotland
Cover design: The Senate

Contents

Preface   vii

Part 1: The Challenge of Business

1	Foundations of Business: Understanding Basic Economics	1
2	Business and Social Responsibility	12
3	The Role of Government	20

Part 2: Business Formation

4	The Legal Forms of Business	25
5	Small Business, Entrepreneurship and Franchising	33
6	Business Law and Ethics	39

Part 3: Management of the Enterprise

7	Management Fundamentals	48
8	Organisational Structure	61

Part 4: Managing People and Production

9	Human Resource Management	69
10	Labour-Management Relations	77
11	Producing Goods and Services	82

Part 5: Marketing Management

12	The Marketing Concept	93
13	Products and Pricing Strategies	101
14	Placement/Distribution Strategy	115
15	Promotional Strategy	128

Part 6: Management Tools

16	Accounting and Financial Statements	139
17	Management Information and Statistical Analysis	156
18	Computers and Computer Systems	167

Part 7: Financial Management

19   Money, Banking and Credit   179
20   The Securities Market   187
21   Financial Strategies: Short and Long-Term Financing   198
22   Risk Management and Insurance   204

Part 8: The Challenge of the Future

23   International Business   213
24   Careers   221

Glossary   233
Index   247

International Edition Preface

This book has been written to meet the needs of students, teachers and business-people for an introductory guide to the many and varied aspects of business management. The book is not intended to support any particular examination syllabus and therefore it is free to follow any exciting aspects of business which can only add interest to a subject such as financial aspects and the derivatives market, the role of insurance in business, how to choose a career in business, and how to manage a small business. This has been done without forgetting the building blocks of business management.

The author of this International Edition has made a particular study of the needs of owners/managers in small businesses and where possible this book addresses these specific issues without detracting from issues important to students and those employed in larger businesses. Owners/managers of small businesses need to know how to communicate their plans – financial, marketing and organisation – to others, especially bank managers. This book will provide the framework for developing the skills necessary to do this.

The International Edition has been 'translated' from the original US Edition and the English author is totally responsible for those parts of the text which specifically refer to UK practice.

I hope you find this book fun to read, and that it whets your appetite to examine more closely, what is erroneously referred to by many (probably unsuccessful businesspeople!) as a commonsense subject.

Tony Bushell
Norwich, England (May 1995)

Acknowledgements

The English author would like to thank:

- Caroline Bushell for completely retyping the whole US edition of this book.
- Mike Allen, lately of Proctor & Gamble, for putting the author right on the names of P & G's UK products.
- Sedgwick Group plc for information on insurance for business.
- Philip Gunn and Malcolm Surridge, the author's co-authors on *Business Explained*, published by HarperCollins.

Part 1

The Challenge of Business

1   Foundations of Business: Understanding Basic Economics

What is 'business'?

A *business* is an organised effort of individuals to produce and sell goods and services for a profit. Businesses vary in size, as measured by number of employees or by volume of sales. Large companies such as Exxon and General Motors count their employees in the hundred thousands and their sales revenues in the billions. Most (98 percent) of the businesses in Europe and the United States are small businesses – independently owned and operated with fewer than twenty employees. The key people responsible for creating businesses as a result of their original ideas are called *entrepreneurs*.

Whether a business has one employee working at home, 100 working in a retail store, 10,000 working in a plant or factory or 100,000 working in branch offices nationwide, all businesses share the same definition and are organised for the same purpose – to earn profits. Profit is the money that remains after the costs of a business (expenses and taxes) are subtracted from the revenue received from the sales of goods and services.

Goods and Services

The sources of a business' revenues, and therefore of its profits, are its *goods and services*. Goods are tangible items, such as cars, shoes, radios, computers and can openers. Services are intangible items, such as the professional advice and assistance provided by lawyers, doctors, electricians, accountants and hairdressers.

Consumers will buy only those goods and services they need or want. Therefore, to be successful, businesses must provide goods and services that satisfy consumers' needs and wants. Consumers need shoes and will buy shoes. Consumers may not need expensive high-tech shoes, but they may purchase them if they want them. Thus, identifying consumers' needs and wants are key factors in business success.

Factors of Production

All goods and services are produced from five specific resources, namely land, labour, capital, information resources and entrepreneurs. These resources, known as the *factors of production*, are the basic elements a business uses to produce goods and services.

- **Land:** includes not only real estate but the resources associated with land – water, minerals and timber.
- **Labour:** sometimes called human resources, labour refers to the mental and physical skills and abilities of employees. Labour includes all the employees, from top-level executives to truck drivers, who produce and distribute the goods and services a business sells.
- **Capital:** all businesses require capital (money) to operate. Businesses need capital to buy buildings, machinery and tools, all of which are also considered capital. In addition, they need capital to hire labour, distribute finished products and so on.
- **Information Resources:** these supply the facts, intelligence and knowledge needed to manage and operate a business. Because information resources enable managers to control (and to use effectively) all other resources, its value as a factor of production has greatly increased in recent years.
- **Entrepreneurs:** these are the risk-takers who create businesses; the people who assemble all the other factors of production in an effort to start and operate a profitable business. Entrepreneurs have vision. Recognising consumers' needs and wants for certain goods and services, they will risk their time, gather capital and apply their information resources to create and manage a profitable enterprise.

Availability of Resources

Economics is the study of how goods and services are produced, distributed and consumed. In any society, the resources that are available are limited and economics is concerned with:

- How businesses use those limited resources to create and distribute goods and services.
- How individuals and society consume those goods and services.

Economics can be divided into two fields: macroeconomics and microeconomics. Macroeconomics deals with the broader, wide-scale picture; it studies the behaviour of the nation's economy. Microeconomics has a narrower focus; it studies the behaviour of individual organisations or people, in particular markets.

Business is applied economics. Because resources are limited, businesses consider factors related to resource limitations, namely scarcity and opportunity cost.

Scarcity

All resources, those related to humans as well as those related to nature, are limited in some way.

For example:

(i) skilled labour may not be plentiful in a particular location; (ii) capital is not free; and (iii) some natural resources, such as time, are renewable, whilst others, such as oil, are nonrenewable. The *scarcity of resources* forces us to make choices.

Opportunity Cost

The term *opportunity cost* is applied to attempts to measure the value of the best alternative way to use a particular resource. For example, one pound can be spent in many ways, but when that pound has been spent, it can no longer be used for another purpose. A business that will purchase, for instance, new production-line equipment instead of hiring additional employees, must consider the opportunity cost (the value) of that alternative use for that particular resource. Opportunity cost, therefore, shapes every choice. It is the loss in profit that occurs by not undertaking the most profitable alternative.

Economic Systems

Every society must answer these three economic questions:

1 What will be produced? (What goods and services will be produced and in what quantity?)
2 How will these goods and services be produced? (Who will produce these goods and services and which resources will be used to produce them?)
3 For whom will these goods and services be produced? (Who gets what?)

How a society answers these economic questions determines its economic system; its methods for distributing resources to meet the needs of its people.

An economic system deals with the production and distribution of goods and services, while the political system deals with the organisation of government, ideology, conduct of public affairs and the pursuit of national interest. The three most common economic systems are the market economy, the planned economy and the mixed economy.

In a *market economy*, individuals control all or most of the factors of production and make all or most of the production decisions. The market economy is also called the free-market or the free-enterprise system.

In a *planned economy*, the government controls all or most of the factors of production, and makes all or most production decisions.

In a *mixed economy*, as its name clearly tells, the system shares some of the features of both market economy and the planned economy. Most countries do not rigidly follow one economic system, but instead tend to 'mix' (to varying degrees) some features of communism, socialism or capitalism. For example, the UK, France, India and other free-enterprise societies have a degree of socialism, whilst some communist societies have incorporated elements of free-enterprise systems into their economies.

Capitalism

Capitalism is a market economy. It relies on free markets, not on government, to determine what, how and for whom goods and services will be produced. In a market economy, businesses are owned by individuals and are controlled by the owners, or by managers who are accountable to the owners. The profits flow to the owners and investors. Market economies are driven by the profit motive (the desire to maximise profits), and therefore place a high premium on entrepreneurship.

Socialism

In a socialist economy, the government controls key industries such as transportation, communication, banking utilities and major natural resources such as oil. Private ownership of businesses that are not in vital industries is permitted to varying degrees, depending on the country. The government establishes national goals for utilising the country's resources. Countries with a socialist government place a high priority on achieving an equitable distribution of income, and on providing a high level of social and medical services.

The public welfare programmes underwritten by socialist governments such as that in Sweden are financed by high taxes. In the last ten years, however, many socialist governments have encouraged privatisation – the selling of government-controlled industries to private investors.

Communism

Communism is both a political and an economic system based on the doctrine of Karl Marx, whose goal was to achieve a more equitable distribution of wealth than found in capitalist systems. Communist governments control economic decisions through their centralised state planning committees, which set, for example, wages and prices. Communist economic systems emphasise producing capital goods such as machinery, rather than consumer goods.

Today, more than half the world's population live in communist societies, notably in the former Soviet Union, the People's Republic of China, Cuba, North Korea, and some countries in Eastern Europe.

Economic Forces

A number of forces and conditions interact to determine the price of goods and services in the market. The theory of supply, demand and equilibrium helps explain the interaction of these forces and their effects on the economy.

Supply

Economists define *supply* as the amount of output of a good or service that producers are willing and able to make available to the market at a given price, at a given time. The law of supply states that producers are willing to produce and offer for sale more goods at a higher price than at a lower price.

Demand

Demand is the willingness of purchasers to buy specific quantities of a good or service at a given price, at a given time. The law of demand states that people will buy more of a product at a lower price than a higher price.

Equilibrium

According to the laws of supply and demand, the lower the price, the more consumers will buy – but the less producers will be willing to supply. If the price is so low that producers cannot make a profit, they will cease to produce and the supply will drop to zero. The satisfaction of both the buyer and the seller will balance at some point called the *equilibrium*. At the point of equilibrium, demand (the number of units consumers are willing to buy at a given price) equals supply (the number of units the producer is willing to produce at that price). The point of equilibrium, in theory, is the market price.

If the supply is greater than the demand, there is a surplus and the price will fall. If the supply is less than the demand, there is a shortage and the price will rise. It is important to note that supply and demand work simultaneously. As the price of a product goes up, suppliers produce more whilst at the same time consumers buy less. As the price goes down, suppliers produce less, and consumers then demand more.

Competition

Competition describes the degree of rivalry among businesses for sales to potential customers. At the same time, it describes the constant effort on the part of a business to operate efficiently so as to keep its costs low, develop new and improved products and make a profit.

The intensity of competition varies from one industry to another. Economists have identified four basic degrees of competition: pure competition, monopoly, monopolistic competition and oligopoly.

Pure Competition

Pure competition describes a situation in which a large number of small firms are producing identical, or nearly identical, products. Because consumers consider the product identical from company to company, and because both consumers and producers know the price in the marketplace, no one firm has the power to affect the price. As a result, the price is set by supply and demand. In pure competition situations, producers can enter or leave the business very easily.

Except for the fact that it enjoys government price supports, the agricultural industry is a good example of pure competition. Corn from one farm is the same as corn from another farm, and both producers and buyers are aware of the market price.

Monopoly

A company has a *monopoly* when it is the only producer in a market, an industry or an area. Because of its absolute control, the company can set prices as it wishes and prevent other companies from competing. The company's only constraint on pricing is how much consumer demand will fall as prices rise.

In the UK, businesses, or businesses acting together (known as a cartel), with more than 25 per cent of the market are investigated by the Monopolies and Mergers Commission to see if they act against the public interest. The European Community has produced legislation under Article 85 of the Treaty of Rome, which also prohibits unfair domination by a monopolistic business.

Monopolistic Competition

Monopolistic competition exists when (i) there are many buyers and few sellers and (ii) the sellers' products appear slightly different from their competitors'. In such situations, product differentiation and brand names give sellers some control over the price. The market for light bulbs is an example of monopolistic competition.

Oligopoly

In an *oligopoly* a small number of very large firms has the power to influence the price of the firms' products. Would-be competitors are restricted from entering the market because doing so requires huge amounts of capital. The car, steel and aircraft manufacturing industries are examples of oligopolies.

The actions of one firm in an oligopoly are usually copied by the other firms. For example, when one steel company lowers its prices, the others also lower their prices; when one petrol company offers a significant price reduction, the other petrol companies usually follow suit. Since substantial price reductions adversely affect profits, the competition is usually based on product differentiation.

The Free-Enterprise System

A capitalistic economy thrives on competition. It is based on a system of voluntary association and exchange, and is called a *free-enterprise* (or a free-market) *system*. The voluntary nature of association and exchange in the marketplace depends on individuals having the freedom and power to make their own choice, both in what they produce and what they buy.

Basic Freedoms

The free-enterprise system, as its name implies, offers a number of *freedoms*, including the freedom of choice, the freedom to own property, the freedom to earn a profit and the freedom to go out of business. Although such freedoms are written into the American Constitution, they more often form part of the 'common law' in long established democracies such as the United Kingdom.

Freedom of choice is every individual's right to choose his or her occupation and place of employment. Freedom to own property permits a business or an individual to buy or sell land, machines or buildings and to use these assets to generate income. Freedom to earn a profit allows individuals to (i) to decide what to make, how to make it and how to sell it and (ii) to keep the profits that result from their risk–taking. Freedom to go out of business cannot be restricted by the government. If a business cannot make a profit, the government cannot prevent it from going into liquidation. Businesses have free exit from the market.

Entrepreneurs and Profits

The factors of production can yield rewards in various forms:

- Land and material resources earn rent.
- Labour earns wages.
- Capital earns interest.
- Entrepreneurs earn profits.

Entrepreneurs enjoy a special place in the business world. While lenders receive interest and stockholders receive dividends, only entrepreneurs receive profits. Profit is the difference between the selling price of a good or service, and the cost of producing and marketing that good or service. For example, if the total cost of producing and marketing a toy is £2.50, and the manufacturer sells that toy for £3.15, the profit is £0.65 for each toy.

Profits are entrepreneurs' rewards for their risks, their work and their investment of time and money – in other words, for their success in creating and operating a business.

The Development of the Modern Economic System

Over the years, the economy in the UK has changed significantly, and it is important to understand those events which have instigated these changes.

The Industrial Revolution

The Industrial Revolution refers to a series of events and inventions that dramatically changed the way people worked, moved their workplace, improved their work efficiency and raised their standard of living.

The first key event occurred around 1750 in England as a result of Sir Richard Arkwright's development of a water-powered spinning machine to replace the hand-operated spinning wheel. In the United States, the effects were felt later, early in the nineteenth century, when textile mills began using Arkwright's invention to spin cotton.

As the new machinery gained in use, the workplace shifted from the home to the textile mills and factories where all the materials, machinery and workers were assembled. At the same time, the factories began dividing manufacturing procedures into separate tasks, with each task being assigned to different workers. This division of labour, known as specialisation, not only changed the way people worked, but improved their productivity.

Thus, the Industrial Revolution was characterised by these three key changes:

● The replacement of human labour with newly invented machines (mechanisation).
● A shifting of the workplace from home to factory.
● The division of labour into smaller work tasks (specialisation).

Many early factories in England were established in the Midlands, where labour, coal, waterpower and capital were available. The new principles worked so well that they spread from textiles to other products. More inventions followed, increasing mechanisation of work.

The Information Sector

The information sector is a specialised (and a very fast growing) part of the service sector. The information sector includes people employed in the computer and information-processing technologies.

All businesses value highly any information that improves production and distribution, and increases efficiency and profitability. Thus, the accumulation, manipulation and dissemination of customer credit histories, financial data, sales statistics and similar information is essential to business. These tasks fall into the information sector. The information sector now claims a substantial segment of the labour market.

Economic Goals and Performance

Several performance indicators provide key methods for measuring how well an economy has achieved its goals and how much it has grown. Nearly all economic systems share the same goals: stability, full employment and growth.

Stability

Stability is a condition in which the relationship between money, goods, services and labour remains constant. Major threats to stability are inflation and rising prices. Other threats are recession (which decreases employment, income and production) and depression (which is a severe, prolonged recession characterised by high unemployment).

Full Employment

Full employment, meaning that everyone who wishes to work has a job, is an ideal, never a reality. Realistically, even in the best of times, some workers will be unemployed for a variety of reasons:

- Frictional unemployment describes workers who have left one job but have not yet found another.
- Seasonal unemployment includes all seasonal workers; those employed in agriculture and other seasonal industries.
- Structural unemployment identifies people who lack skills or are retaining for other jobs.
- Cyclical unemployment includes workers who are temporarily unemployed due to a downturn in business activity.

Thus, the realistic goal is not full employment but minimal unemployment.

Measuring Growth

Growth is an increase in the amount of goods and services produced by the total economy in a given period as compared to another period. With specific measurement tools, businesspeople can evaluate economic performance. Among the most useful economic measurement tools are gross national product, productivity, the balance of trade, economic growth and inflation. These are discussed below.

Gross National Product

Gross National Product (GNP) is used to measure the country's economic growth. GNP is the total value of all goods and services produced in a particular economic system during a one-year period.

GNP is an especially useful indicator because it enables businesspeople to trace the performance of the economy over a period of time, and to compare specific years. In addition, GNP provides measurements by industry which are particularly helpful in identifying business sectors that are, or are not, growing.

Productivity

Productivity measures efficiency by comparing how much is produced against resources used. For example, if Company A produces a certain engine for £2,000 and Company B can produce the same engine (that is, use the same resources) for £1,850, then Company B has a higher rate of productivity.

Balance of Trade

Each country exports goods and services, for which it receives money, and imports goods and services, for which it pays money. The term *balance of trade* is a country's total exports minus its total imports. A positive balance of trade, or trade surplus, is favourable: it indicates a flow of money into the country. A negative balance, or trade deficit, is not favourable: it indicates a flow of money out of the country.

Inflation

Inflation is a rise in the general prices of goods and services. One cause of inflation is the relationship between productivity (output per worker) and wages. When workers' wages increase faster than their productivity, the cost per unit produced increases. So, although consumers (which include workers) have more money available, the price of goods has risen. When the new cost of goods exceeds the increase in wages, a new wage demand emerges and the cycle repeats itself. Stopping consumers borrowing money to defer payment for goods by increasing interest rates, and encouraging more efficient methods of production are the major tools of curbing inflation. However, international trading and financial speculation do not allow governments to effect easy solutions.

The most commonly quoted measurement of inflation is the Retail Price Index (RPI) which measures the effect of price increases and inflation on the cost of a 'typical basket' of a householder's purchases and expenses.

Government Deficits

Government deficits measure the excess of money spent over the amount of money received by the government, which in turn, affects interest rates. The government finances its deficits by borrowing money – that is, by issuing and selling treasury bonds. The more money the government borrows, the less money is available for businesses. To compete for these reduced funds, businesses must bid higher, raising the cost of credit and causing higher interest rates.

Higher interest rates, in turn, make it more difficult (and more expensive) for businesses to borrow money for new factories or machinery. Thus, government deficits provide an important means of measuring the economy.

SUMMARY

This chapter has presented the development of the business environment and has described the different economic systems. Basic economic principles, types of businesses and utilisation of resources will serve as the beginning as we continue to examine the foundations of business.

SELECTED READING

Maunder, Peter et al. 1987. *Economics Explained.* Collins Educational.
Ricketts, Martin. 1994. *Economics of Business Enterprise.* Harvester Wheatsheaf.
Powell, Ray. 1993. *Economics for Professional and Business Studies.* DPP.
Worthington, Ian & Britton, Chris. 1994. *The Business Environment.* Pitman.

2 Business and Social Responsibility

The survival of a company depends on how well it reacts to change, and the 1990s will witness the greatest economic, social, technical and political changes since the Industrial Revolution – changes that will challenge the business world.

The Changing Business Environment

Companies do not exist in a vacuum. They exist within many environments, for example, political, social and natural environments. These environments exert pressures on companies to change; whilst at the same time companies exert pressure on these environments to change. The result is a complicated interaction of business and society, and the key to understanding this interaction is the systems theory.

The Systems Theory

A system is a group of elements acting as one. The elements in the *systems theory* are inputs, processes, outputs and feedback.

Inputs are resources that a business takes from the environment. Inputs include the factors of production such as the material, human, financial and information resources. These inputs are transformed into outputs as a result of technological or managerial processes.

Outputs are the products or services that a business sells to generate a profit. As consumers react to the outputs, that is, as they buy or use the output products or services, they provide feedback – information that re-enters the system as input.

This process can be represented as follows:

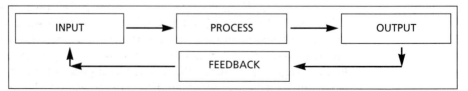

Figure 2.1

Open and Closed Systems

There are two types of systems: open and closed.

Open Systems

A system is open when the business interacts with its environments. Examples of interaction include: government legislation leading to a company changing its hiring practices; technological advances convincing a company to change its manufacturing processes; and changes in consumer tastes which tell a company to alter its marketing strategies. Interaction provides feedback, and feedback provides a business with information that is critical to its future. A business that does not interact with its environments does so at its peril.

Disregarding feedback has led to the demise of many once-powerful companies. Chrysler, for example, neglected to respond to environmental demands for smaller, fuel-efficient cars. Therefore, for business, the lesson is clear: feedback helps to evaluate the input/process/output cycle. Consumers' feedback informs the business whether its products or services are acceptable.

Closed Systems

A system is described as closed if it does not interact with the environment. In closed systems, most of the factors influencing the organisation are internal and therefore controllable. In theory, the standardised procedures, specialisation and property controls of closed systems lead to success. Changes in the external environment (that is, social, economic, political and technological changes) do not significantly affect the business' internal operations.

The Need for Balance

The ultimate survival of an organisation, and therefore its success, depends on its ability to adapt to the demands of its environment. To survive, a business must achieve a balance between inputs, processes and outputs. Achieving a balance requires business managers to be sensitive to all the elements in their particular environment, and to understand how those elements influence the business.

Elements of the Business Environment

The elements of a business environment include employees, shareholders, directors, suppliers, government officials at all levels, managers of competitors, customers, clients and the 'general public'. Because all these people have an interest or stake in the organisation, they are collectively known as *stakeholders*.

A stakeholder is anyone who wants the organisation to behave in a way that will benefit him/her and satisfy his/her wants and needs for goods, services or profits. The wants and needs are different, of course, for each group of stakeholders: they are not necessarily compatible. For example: employees want higher wages, but shareholders want a higher return on their investment; customers want lower prices, but businesses want higher profits. Stakeholders can be separated into two groups:

- **Internal Stakeholders:** these are people inside the business, for example, shareholders, directors, managers and employees.
- **External stakeholders:** these include customers, clients, suppliers, vendors, special interest groups (such as consumer advocates or environmentalists), the media, labour unions, financial institutions, competitors, and European, national and local governments.

Forces of Change

The major external forces or variables that influence the way businesses function are economic, social, technological and political. Businesses cannot control these variables, which make up the ever-changing environment within which business decisions have to be made.

Economic Variables

Economic variables are (i) the economic conditions and trends that affect the cost of producing goods and services and (ii) the market conditions under which they are sold. Economic variables include raw material costs, sales and government fiscal policy.

Economic changes greatly affect the profitability of industries and of individual business firms: economic change is constant. The difficulty lies in distinguishing between cyclical changes and structural changes.

Cyclical changes are periodic swings (upward or downward) in the general level of economic activity. Cyclical changes affect, for example, interest rates, inflation and housing starts.

Structural changes are major alterations, permanent or temporary, in the relationships between different sectors of the economy. The shift from an industrial to a service company, or the rise in energy costs relative to the cost of raw materials, are examples of structural changes.

Social Variables

The three social variables are demographics, lifestyles and social values.

Demography, the statistical study of the characteristics of human populations, offers valuable business information: including general population increase or decrease; specific segments that are most affected by the increase or decrease; changes in the makeup of specific age groups; and geographic shifts within the total population.

Demographic studies show the changes in population size: the makeup of the population into different cultural and racial groups; the changes in age group sizes, especially the increasing number aged over 65 due to rapid improvements in health care; and also shifts in population location within Europe to warmer places, emulating the population movements in the US to California in the post-War period.

Thus, demographic studies offer businesses a wealth of important information about their future customers.

Lifestyle, an individual's way of living, affects the composition, location and expectations of business' labour supply and of its customers. For example, people are showing an increased emphasis on physical fitness and sound nutrition. The number of working women is rising, and as a result, the number of two-salary households and the number of women managers are also rising steadily. A greater percentage of Europeans have attended and have graduated from universities and colleges than ever before. The proportion of 'traditional' families is shrinking. Fewer households are now made up of married couples. Instead, more households are comprised of single adults and one-parent families. Businesses 'read' such information to analyse their products and services and determine how well they fit the needs of the marketplace.

Social values reflect the attitudes and beliefs of a society, and these values too are subject to change. For example: as people have become more and more concerned about environmental issues, their attitudes toward companies that abuse the environment have had an impact on many businesses; and as attitudes toward civil rights have broadened from a national to a global focus, companies doing business with 'aggressive' governments have faced the wrath of a concerned public. Thus, in this way, social values also make up the ever-changing business environment.

Technological Variables

Technological variables include new developments and advances in science and manufacturing, all of which affect business activities. The level of technology in a society or in a particular industry determines to a large extent which goods or services will be produced, what equipment will be used, where and how many people will be employed, and what tasks these people will do.

The first step in technological advancement is research and development (R& D). *Basic research* is aimed at discovering new knowledge. This is research purely for the sake of learning. While the results of basic research may lead to the improvement of products or processes, the original objective is pure research. *Applied research* is aimed at discovering new knowledge that has some specific potential use. *Development* is aimed at putting new or existing knowledge to use in producing goods or services.

Technological advances are responsible for vast changes in the proportion of the population now working in the service sector. Specifically, fewer people are now employed in manufacturing and more people are employed in service jobs. In the UK in 1901, for example, approximately 80 per cent of the work force was found in manufacturing and related industries (including agriculture) and 20 per cent in service jobs. By 1951, the service sector accounted for approximately 30 per cent of the overall working population, continuing to grow rapidly to 75 per cent by 1993.

Technology is also responsible for changing the tasks performed and the skills needed in service positions. Traditional service positions were found in restaurants, hotels and repair businesses. Technological advancements have brought about a shift to service industries that provide information for a fee.For example, thanks to computers, many new service jobs were created in data-processing and work-processing.

Political Variables

The *political process* and the *political climate* are two variables that influence business. The political process involves competition among interest groups seeking to advance their own values and goals. Thus, environmentalists battle against road constructors nuclear power station constructors and waste disposal organisations.

The political climate toward business depends upon the administration in power and, of course, the point of view of the observer. In the 1970s and 80s, UK Prime Minister Margaret Thatcher strongly advocated the importance of 'market forces'. Today, however there is in the UK a rejection of some of the extreme market forces, especially in the area of senior executive pay when many below this level are facing redundancy.

Social Responsibility

Every business has an obligation to make a profit for its shareholders. Clearly, it also has an obligation to operate within the law. While there is widespread agreement on these two business obligations, a third, *social responsibility*, is subject to debate.

Social responsibility refers to a business' obligations to society. Many businesses recognise that their activities and decisions have an impact on employees, the environments, minority groups and their local communities. As a result, they feel a responsibility to contribute positively by adopting policies that go beyond their own narrow concerns of making a profit and growing.

But while being socially responsible is admirable, it is also costly. There are opponents to the idea that business has a social responsibility. Economist Milton Friedman, winner of the Nobel Prize, summarised the opposition's viewpoint: 'There is one and only one social responsibility of business – to use its resources and engage in activities designed to increase its profits so long as it stays within the rules of the game, which is to say, engages in open and free competition without deception and fraud'.

Strategies Concerning Social Responsibility

Companies adopt different strategies to meet, or to limit, their social responsibilities, depending on their policies. Some of the most common management strategies are:

● **Denial strategy:** this claims that the 'problem' does not exist. Tobacco companieś, for example, tend to adopt a denial strategy when they try to refute the evidence that smoking is a health hazard.

- **Reaction strategy:** this is when a company offers a deliberate response to a perceived problem. The UK nuclear power industry' reaction strategy to public opinion towards safety was to promote an on going 'open day' campaign to attract all members of the family to a 'day out' at the nuclear power station.
- **Defence strategy:** such a strategy, often utilised by trade associations, attempts to use legal manoeuvering or public relations to avoid additional obligations. Businesses involved in the transportation of live animals to the European continent have utilised the law, and hence the police forces, to defend their activities against considerable public displeasure.
- **Accommodation strategy:** this is often a company's response to external pressure or a lawsuit threat. When one of its ships, the *Exxon Valdez*, spilled vast amounts of oil in Alaska, Exxon tried to placate the public outcry by adopting an accommodation strategy. Exxon then paid a record $1 billion fine for the clean up.
- **Proactive strategy:** this strategy is prompted by internal desires within the company, not by external pressures or threats of any kind. A proactive strategy indicates a company's voluntary commitment to social responsibility. Examples of proactive strategies are: Apple Computers' donation of computers to schools; the 'adoption' by some big businesses of inner-city schools; and Johnson & Johnson's voluntary withdrawal of unsealed medicines that might have been tampered with by outside sources.

Areas of Responsibility

A business' social responsibility spans environmental, consumer and employee issues.

Environmental Issues

Concern for the environment is receiving global attention, and so are the companies that meet, or flaunt, their responsibilities to maintain the environment. Pollution, toxic waste, the ozone layer, climatic changes, the depletion of natural resources – all are of growing concern worldwide.

Pollution (the contamination of water, air or land) now threatens human, animal and plant life around the globe. As a result of the concerns of individuals, organisations and governments worldwide, pollution has become a major business issue. Many laws have been enacted to protect the environment:

- The Environmental Protection Act, 1991, is aimed at the total pollution system and puts the responsibility of control onto the polluter. This act covers most forms of pollution including car exhaust, effluents, waste disposal and industrial emissions.
- The European Community has passed many regulations relating to all aspects

of the environment, including the classification of beaches for safe bathing.
- International agreements on pollution are aimed at minimising the problems of global warming and reducing the risks of nuclear accidents such as that at Chernobyl in 1986.

While these laws address past damages and try to prevent further damage, they do not address the costs of repair and prevention– and in particular, who should pay those costs. For environmentalists, the answer is clear: business should pay. Environmentalists claim that proper treatment and disposal of industrial wastes are part of the expense of doing business. For business leaders, the answer is tax money. They argue that business is not the sole source of pollution and that tax money, therefore, should be used to pay for cleaning up the environment and preventing further damage. In either case, whether through higher prices or higher taxes, the public will indirectly bear the burden of the costs. For example, the use of new chemical gases to replace CFCs for aerosols has increased manufacturing costs significantly.

Consumer Issues

There are many laws in the UK which have been passed to protect the consumer of products and services. The main ones are:

- The Sale of Goods Act, 1979, which stipulates that goods must be of merchantable quality, fit for the purpose and are as described on the package.
- The Supply of Goods and Services Act, 1982, extends the Sale of Goods Act to services which must be delivered with care and skill within a reasonable time.
- The Trade Descriptions Act, 1968, protects consumers from misleading claims about a product's content and performance.
- The Consumer Protection Act, 1987, stipulates the safety standards expected from a product and service, in addition to other measures regarding pricing.
- The Consumer Credit Act, 1974, ensures that customers are fully aware of their commitment before buying goods or services on credit.

Employment Issues

There is extensive EC legislation within the Social Chapter of the Treaty of Rome which has not yet been fully accepted by a number of individual countries, including the UK which argues that its own current legislation is more than adequate. Current UK legislation to protect employees and potential employees include:

- The Race Relations Act, 1976, The Equal Pay Act, 1970, and the Sex Discrimination Act, 1986. These make it unlawful to discriminate against any person on the basis of race, gender, religion or marital status.
- The Disabled Persons Act, 1958, encourages employers to employ a quota of registered disabled persons.

- The Employment Act, 1990, makes it unlawful to discriminate against members of a labour union when advertising for staff.
- The Employment Protection Act, 1978, sets out the fundamental rights of employees concerning their contract of employment, which must be supplied to them within eight weeks from the start of employment. This contract contains details of sick pay, holidays, pension schemes, pay rate, hours of work and disciplinary procedures which could lead to dismissal. Disagreements between employers and dismissed employees are resolved by industrial tribunals which comprise one legal representative and two lay members; one generally representing employers' interests and the other generally representing employees' interests.
- The Health and Safety at Work Act, 1974, was passed to set minimum standards for health and safety for all employees. The Act covers a wide range of activities, from identifying and eliminating hazards at work (for example, electrical safety) to the design of cutting equipment. The Act is constantly updated to accommodate new industrial practices and emerging hazards. Health and safety officials have great powers to stop processes which they think are likely to become dangerous.
- Increasingly, attention is being given to health and welfare problems within the workforce, such as the early identification of cancer. The Control of Substances Hazardous to Health Regulations, 1988, insists that businesses undertake a comprehensive study of the health effects of substances used within the business. EC health and safety regulations have been agreed by all member states.

SUMMARY

The rapid development of all types of communication systems has made a lot more people aware of the many diverse consequences of business activities, such as pollution, financial rewards and unemployment. People with an interest or stake in a business expect to be better informed about it, and demand that businesses are socially responsible. Business is becoming more and more complex at the same time that social factors are also changing at a high rate. The result is that business, once regarded as a 'common sense' activity, now demands the very highest standards and skills from its staff and management.

SELECTED READING

Buono, Anthony & Nichols, Larry. 1985. *Corporate Policy, Values, and Social Responsibility.* Praeger.
Drucker, Peter. 1992. *Managing for the Future.* Heinemann.
Hugo, Ian St.John. 1991. *Practical Open Systems: A Guide for Managers.* Data General/Ncc Blackwell.

3 The Role of Government

In a free-market economy, the role of government in business affairs is extremely complex. Basically, the government, whether national (UK), regional (England, Wales, Scotland and Northern Ireland) or local government (e.g., Norfolk County Council), plays four key business roles of regulator, consumer, supplier and supporter.

Government in a Free Market System

The Role of Regulator

In its role as regulator, the government attempts to provide a balance among all the forces in the economy, a stable environment, and a level playing field. Toward this end, the government:

- Supervises and enforces a vast network of laws and regulations enacted to encourage some, and to limit other, business activities and policies.
- Establishes environmental and safety regulations.
- Defines property rights.
- Encourages competition and at the same time limits unfair practices.
- Establishes fiscal (tax collecting) and monetary policies which profoundly affect business.

The Role of Consumer

The government is one of the largest consumers of goods and services in the UK, and much of its spending serves as a catalyst to the economy. Using revenues raised through taxation, the government re-channels money by injecting vast amounts back into the economy through its spending. Its purchases range from paper clips to computers to aircraft carriers. It pays for the building and maintenance of roads. It provides services of all kinds and makes direct payments to pensioners, the sick and the disabled. It funds research at universities and other organisations.

The Role As Provider

The government provides most essential transport, health care and educational services. However, the government is nowadays very much aware that in a free-market economy, excessive subsidy to support such services cannot be sustained without high and unpopular taxation levels. Nor, in general, can such businesses be run as efficiently as desired. Hence, in the UK, the Conservative government has an ongoing policy to privatise many publicly owned (government owned) businesses. The debate between Conservative and Socialist parties is often centred on the degree of public ownership.

The Role As Supporter

In its role as business supporter, the government provides direct help (e.g., farm subsidies) and indirect support through organisations such as the Department of Trade and Industry and the Department of Employment (e.g., advice for small businesses). The government collects vast amounts of information, much of which is collected and collated by the Central Statistical Office, and makes it available to industry at little or no cost.

Government Regulation

Over the years, there has been a movement in the capitalistic-based economies to introduce legislation to guard against monopolies. However, in the UK, because of the history of public ownership of monopolies (such as rail transport) there has been a more cautious approach to the introduction of anti-monopolistic legislation than there has been, for example, in the US where antitrust laws are well established. This cautious approach has resulted in legislation which generally has to be applied on a specific basis as a result of a complaint by another party.

Antitrust Legislation

The following are the main legislations introduced in the UK to ensure a certain amount of competition within business:

- **The Monopolies and Restrictive Practices Act, 1948:** a general statement of 'not acting in the public interest' embodied in the Act, led to a great deal of difficulty in interpretation by the Monopolies and Restrictive Practices Commission set up to apply the Act. The commission comprised mostly 'lay' persons, who had difficulty in deciding outcomes on issues which could only be given to them by the government itself in the guise of the Board of Trade.
- **The Restrictive Trade Practices Act, 1956:** as a result of evidence collected by the Monopolies and Restrictive Practices Commission, this Act was introduced to require businesses to register any trading agreements. This allowed public inspection and required each business to prove that the agreement was not contrary to public interest. The Act considered not only

distribution agreements, but also price agreements between suppliers and customers at any point in the distribution chain.

● **The Resale Price Act, 1964:** this Act stopped any efforts to fix a minimum resale price except on specially approved grounds.

● **The Monopolies and Mergers Act, 1965:** following a proposed takeover bid for Courtaulds by ICI, which would have resulted in one company dominating the plastics industry, the government passed the Monopolies and Mergers Act. This Act required all proposed mergers, which would result in one business controlling more than one-third of the market, to be referred to a commission for prior approval.

● **The Fair Trading Act, 1973:** this Act gave some teeth to the new appointment of a Director General of Fair Trading who was asked to report any unfair practices to the government. These unfair practices related to restrictive practices, monopolies and mergers, and consumer protection. This Act for the first time tried to establish a working partnership between the needs of competitive business to be profitable and the interests of the public.

● **The Competition Act, 1980:** the Office of Fair Trading was further empowered by this Act to receive complaints about anti-competitive activities, to examine these complaints, to seek a voluntary change by the business concerned and, if necessary, to recommend an order prohibiting the activity. The range of businesses included most nationalised industries, except those of an international nature (airlines), and small businesses with a turnover of less than £5 million and less than 25 per cent of the market.

Government and Taxation

Government fiscal policy determines how tax money is raised, how much is raised and how funds are used. Tax serves two purposes. The first is to raise revenue to pay for the costs of government. The second is to supply a disincentive, such as the high taxes on alcoholic drink and tobacco. This is not to suggest that if alcohol and tobacco were banned, the total tax income would fall! The money required to run government would have to be raised by taxing other products or services. The principal taxes paid by business and by individuals in the UK are discussed below.

Personal Income Tax

Individuals must pay personal tax on their income to the Inland Revenue. There are certain minimum levels of income on which no tax is paid, and higher levels of income on which a higher tax (above the standard rate) is paid. In addition, tax is due from individuals on capital gains, inheritances and certain benefits. There are also a large number of tax allowances which can reduce the net income on which tax is paid, the most important ones being a personal allowance, married persons' allowance and mortgage interest. Personal taxes increase the expenses of businesses in recording dividends to shareholders, and also reduce the savings of individuals into banks, building societies and other savings or investment opportunities. This also has an effect on business growth.

Corporation Tax

Corporations pay tax on profits in much the same way as individuals pay tax on income. How much tax is paid by a large organisation is a complex calculation especially if there is a degree of international trading involved. The rate of tax charged starts at 35 per cent, but smaller businesses are charged at a lower rate.

National Insurance Charge

Each employee has to pay a percentage of income to the government at the rate of approximately 10 per cent; the employer has to pay a similar amount. Actual percentages, like income tax and corporation tax percentages, are fixed each year by the annual Finance Act which confirms the intentions of the government published within the Budget. Income from this 'charge' is used to pay social benefits. As far as the employer is concerned, the National Insurance Charge is similar to a high payroll tax.

Property Tax

Businesses have to pay local rates, the Business Rate, to support the activities of local government. These rates have to be paid on all business premises and are in addition to the property rates paid by individuals on private property. There is a significant degree of government subsidy on local government spending and, therefore, central government has a high degree of leverage on local issues (such as local spending on education).

Value Added Tax

Value Added Tax (VAT) is used throughout the EC as a tax on the added value, the difference between the selling price of a product or service, and the cost of the materials and services used to produce the product or service. Different VAT rates operate in different member states, although there is pressure for uniformity. Essential basic commodities, such as food for home consumption, public transport, printed matter and housing, escape VAT which is currently charged at 17.5 per cent in the UK. Domestic fuel has a lower rate of 8 per cent. VAT is collected by the Customs and Excise.

Customs Duties

The Customs and Excise collects duty on many products imported from outside the EC. GATT (the General Agreement on Tariffs and Trade) is an international body which endeavours to harmonise customs taxes throughout the world, to prevent unfair discrimination between large trading groups and to promote world trade.

SUMMARY

In the UK, as in most West European countries, the Government is balanced between free-market and socialistic strategies, and between centralised and decentralised control. The Conservative Party tends to promote a centralised free-market economy, whereas the opposition tends to promote a decentralised socialist economy. Business has to develop strategies which exist within both types of economies since the democratic system can change an economy from one type to another fairly quickly. Business must try to forecast government activities and, if possible, to work with government to produce socially acceptable, and yet profitable practices.

SELECTED READING

Board of Trade. 1994. *Competitiveness: Helping Business to Win*. HMSO.
Beesley, M.E. 1992. *Privatization Regulation and Deregulation*. Routledge.

Part 2

Business Formation

4   The Legal Forms of Business

A business is a legal entity, and as legal entities businesses can be organised in a variety of legal forms. The three most common types of business organisations are sole traders, partnerships and limited companies. Each of these three forms of business ownership have advantages and disadvantages that business owners must consider at the time the business is organised. These advantages and disadvantages, as well as the features of these different forms of organisation, are detailed below.

Sole Traders

Sole trader is by far the most widely used business form in the world. Nearly 75 per cent of all businesses are sole traders, and many of the largest companies began as sole traders. Although owned and managed by one person, the sole trader may have numerous employees. Many local neighbourhood businesses are sole traders – owned by people who are 'self employed' – retail, gift, floral and shoe repair shops, for example.

Advantages of Sole Traders

One advantage of a sole trader is the ease of starting the business. Unless the business requires a licence, as some professions (doctors and lawyers) do, sole traders can usually be established simply by opening the door and doing business. Other advantages include the cost of organisation, tax considerations and the ease of dissolution.

Sole traders are the easiest and least expensive form of business to start. They demand no legal or organisational expenses. Frequently the main investment is the labour and ability of the sole proprietor. As long as the proposed activity is legal, anyone can start as a sole trader.

The sole trader directly receives any profits the business makes, and absorbs any loss that the business may experience. The business pays no taxes, but all of the income from the business is considered the owner's personal income and is taxed accordingly. Thus, the owner has no obligations to reveal financial information to anyone other than the Inland Revenue. He or she can make all business decisions independently.

To dissolve a sole trader, the owner can sell the business (remember: it is his/her personal property) or simply close the doors and stop doing business.

Disadvantages of Sole Traders

The disadvantages of being a sole trader are several fold. The owner has complete liability for the business. His/her personal assets (home, car, personal savings and so on) are considered part of the business. Therefore, the owner's personal assets are not protected from creditors.

Sole traders have limited ability to borrow money. When sole traders borrow money, they do so as individuals, using their own personal assets to finance personal loans. Therefore, borrowing power is directly dependent on the credit standing of the proprietor. Thus, the owner of a successful business may not be able to borrow money for business expansion if he or she, for example, has large personal debts from a home mortgage.

Ownership of the business does not continue automatically with others. The sole trader business has a limited life; namely the life of the sole proprietor. With the death of the owner, the sole trading business ceases to exist.

Sole trading businesses offer few career opportunities to employees. Since the business is generally small and career advancement is limited, recruiting and retaining good personnel can be difficult.

Finally, the demands on management are great. Because a sole trader is usually owned by a single individual, that person must have a multitude of abilities, skills and experience in management, bookkeeping, sales, marketing, production skills and so on.

Partnerships

A partnership is defined in the UK by the Partnership Act, 1890, as the relationship between persons carrying on business in common with a view to sharing profits. Partners not only share profits, but also share all losses. Each partner has unlimited responsibility for any debts incurred by any other partner unless a Deed of Partnership has been agreed. This means that different partners may receive more profits or others may be freed from debt responsibility since they contribute capital but not expertise to the partnership (so called 'sleeping partners'). In the absence of any Deed, partners are assumed to be equal in all respects. Partnerships are limited by law to operate within the range two to 20 partners unless dispensation has been given under the Companies Act, 1980.

Advantages of Partnerships

Unlike sole traders, partners within a partnership can concentrate on different aspects of the business or, like a law practice, on different parts of the law. More expertise is available within the business. Moreover, since more than one person is involved with the ownership, more capital is available to the business, thus permitting expansion without loss of control.

Because a partnership is like joining two or more sole traders, a partnership shares some of the advantages of a sole trader. The formation of a partnership does not require complicated or expensive organisation. The major element is the partnership agreement, which a solicitor can easily draw up.

A partnership is neither singled out for government regulation nor subject to special taxes. The partnership's profits are not taxed but treated instead as personal income of the partners, whether or not the profits are distributed to them.

Since more than one person owns the business, the financial resources of the partners is increased along with the borrowing capacity.

When a partner wishes to leave the partnership or dies, that partner's share of the business can be sold to the remaining partner(s). An alternative solution is to sell the partner's share to an outside person; someone who is acceptable to the remaining partners. In this way, partnerships have continuity.

Since there are at least two partners, in theory the partnership has greater management skills and other business talents available to it. Frequently in fact, partnerships are formed by people of complementary skills. For example, a sales expert who works 'outside' bringing in business, and an operational professional who works 'inside', managing and supervising the day-to-day operation of the enterprise. Finally, partnerships have an added incentive for job applicants and talented employees alike - the opportunity to become a partner.

Disadvantages of Partnerships

The major disadvantage of partnerships is the degree of liability of the partners. Each general partner is liable for the full debts of the partnership. Within partnerships there is potential for disagreement and conflict. Managerial difficulties may arise when two or more partners cannot agree. And even when there is agreement, control is divided, making operations very difficult. It is easy to enter into partnerships but often difficult to withdraw with the full original investment. It is not easy to sell one's share of the partnership. A partnership is dissolved every time a new member is added or an existing member ceases to be a partner either, through withdrawal or by death.

Limited Companies

The *limited company*, or business corporation, is clearly the dominant element in the UK economy in terms of total sales, profits and number of employees. Limited companies employ millions of people and are owned by millions of investors. Although it is not a real person, a limited company can conduct business, own and sell property, borrow money, sue and be sued. In fact most laws that apply to people also apply to limited companies.

A limited company means that the owners of the business (the shareholders) are only liable to the amount invested in the business. If Mr A buys 100 £1 shares in a business, Mr A cannot lose more than £100 (or whatever he paid for the shares if they were already owned by another person) if the business is declared bankrupt. An exception to this is where the owners have given a personal guarantee to cover any loans from a bank or other institution. This often happens when the business is a small private limited company and the owners often work in the business.

Forming a Limited Company

Anyone wishing to form a company in the UK will find that the law requires them to follow a set procedure. The people involved in setting up a company have to apply for registration to the Register of Companies. The Registrar will require details regarding the nature of the business, how it will be organised and the rules governing its methods of operation. The two main documents are the Memorandum of Association and the Articles of Association.

The *Memorandum of Association* is concerned with the reasons for the business being in existence. The following information must be included:

- The proposed company name.
- The company's registered address.
- The amount of capital employed.
- The company's objective in trading.
- A statement that the shareholders' liability is limited.
- For public companies, a statement that shares are available to the public.

The *Articles of Association* of a company consist of a series of regulations governing the conduct of the company's business and the internal management of the company. These rules form an agreement between the company and its members, defining their rights and duties. The areas covered by this agreement are:

- The face value of the shares to be issued (nominal capital).
- The directors' names.
- The frequency and procedures for shareholder meetings.
- The distribution of profits.
- Shareholder voting rights.
- Directors' duties and responsibilities.
- Appointment of directors.

● Rules over transfer of shares.

Company Framework – Shareholders, Directors and Management

The limited company has a clearly identified framework, consisting of shareholders, a board of directors and management.

The nominal capital of a company is usually issued as £1 or 25p shares. The owner of each share has a corresponding share in the ownership of the company. Owners of shares are called shareholders. Each share of 'ordinary' stock carries with it the right to cast one vote in electing members of the board of directors. The number of directors is established in the Articles of Association. Exceptionally, some shares do not carry voting rights, but these are clearly identified as such. If Mr A owned 25 per cent of the shares in a company, he would own 25 per cent of the company. He would hold 25 per cent of the votes at a shareholders' meeting where the election of directors, and decisions about the distribution of dividends, would be decided. Since only a small percentage of shareholders attend the shareholders' Annual General Meeting, Mr A's 25 per cent vote may well be enough to dominate the proceedings and consequently control the company.

Shareholders also vote on any changes in the Articles of Association and on the appointment of professional accountants to audit the firm's books. When shareholders cannot attend the limited company's annual meeting, they can vote by proxy. A proxy is a statement that authorises someone else to vote for the shareholder.

The *board of directors* represents the shareholders, sets corporate policy and distributes dividends. It has the final authority for all corporate actions. The board of directors, under a chairman, meets regularly and is required to hold an annual meeting which is open to all shareholders. Within the board, there are committees that deal with the company audits, the compensation of the chief executive officer (CEO or often called the Managing Director), long-term strategy and other important issues. An inside director is an employee of the limited company; someone engaged in its day to day operations. Usually, the chairman of the limited company serves as an inside director on the board.

A *non-executive director* is not an employee but someone outside the limited company – frequently a banker, a supplier, someone representing a group of shareholders or someone with a special skill. In most cases, a non-executive director only attends board meetings with other directors, although this would be on a regular basis.

The board of directors selects and hires the limited company's *senior managers* in charge of day to day operations, including the CEO.

Types of Limited Companies

There are two types of limited companies in the UK: the private limited company and the public limited company.

The *public limited company* (plc) must have a minimum of two directors, a minimum of two shareholders, a minimum amount of authorised share capital and the right to offer its shares and debentures (loans) for sale to the general public. The company must include the initials 'plc' in its name and allow the public access to summary financial accounts.

A *private limited company* is one which cannot, or does not wish to, meet the conditions of a public limited company. Shares cannot be offered to the public at large, but the company must have a minimum of two directors. Private limited companies have the initials 'Ltd' after the company name. The accountants of private limited companies have to submit copies of their summary annual financial accounts to the Registrar of Companies. Therefore these accounts are available for inspection by members of the public.

Other types of limited companies are created by combinations or associations of several companies. A *holding company* is a limited company organised to own stock in, and manage, another company or companies. Holding companies are frequently found in banking or public utilities. A *joint venture* is a separate limited company owned by two or more limited companies. The limited companies form the joint venture to work on a specific project or in specific markets. They agree to share the profits and losses in proportion to their contribution. The joint venture is limited to that one project. A *subsidiary* is a limited company that is: (i) owned by another limited company (50 per cent or more of its stock is owned by that other limited company) and (ii) operated as a separate entity. A *syndicate* is a group of firms operating together, usually on a large project. For instance, a syndicate developed the Alaska pipeline. Although the companies in a syndicate work together, they retain their separate identities.

Advantages of Limited Companies

A major advantage of the corporate form is that limited companies have limited liability. Owners of the limited company (shareholders) are not personally liable for the acts or debts of the limited company. Owners' losses are limited to their individual investments in the shares they own.

Another advantage of a limited compant is its ability to borrow. When a limited company is formed, it raises capital by selling shares in the business to individuals, who then become shareholders. At its formation, a limited company's shares may sell for pennies, enabling virtually everyone to invest and to own a tiny portion of the company. Once formed, a limited company can then raise money in two basic ways: (i) by issuing more shares, a process that increases ownership in the limited company and (ii) by issuing fixed interest securities or bonds, a process that increases the indebtedness of the limited company.

A limited company has an unlimited life. Its existence is not dependent on the life of any individual or group. The owners are the shareholders, and as shares are bought and sold, ownership changes and continues into the future.

Employees generally have a wider range of opportunities in a limited company, especially if the limited company is large. Employees can benefit from the potential for growth and promotion that limited companies offer, and perhaps even take a share of the ownership.

Disadvantages of Limited Companies

Compared to traders or partnerships, limited companies are more expensive and complex to form and operate. Corporations must pay legal and filing fees, and must file numerous tax and regulatory reports.

Limited companies face legal restrictions. Corporate activities are limited to the purposes stated in the Memorandum of Association, and are restricted by laws that specifically cover the corporate form.

Limited companies are required to submit detailed reports to government agencies and shareholders, reports that include details of the limited company's financial operations. Because these reports are public, they are available to all, including competitors.

Mergers, Acquisitions and Takeovers

Limited companies are grown in a variety of ways, among them, by merging with, acquiring or taking over other limited companies.

Combining two companies in related industries is called a merger. Often a new limited company is formed as a result of the merger. There are two main types of merger:

- **Horizontal merger:** a merger is horizontal when the acquired company is a direct competitor. If one newspaper acquired another, or if two tyre manufacturers merged, each would be an example of a horizontal merger.
- **Vertical merger:** a merger is vertical if the acquired company is in the same chain of supply - for example, when a tyre manufacturer acquires a rubber company that supplies it with raw material or when it acquires a retail chain that sells tyres.

An *acquisition* is the purchase of a controlling share in a limited company by another limited company. The acquired company might still be managed separately. When a company acquires another company in an unrelated business to increase its size or profits, or because it feels the acquired company is undervalued and a bargain, the new, enlarged company is called a *conglomerate*.

Most mergers and acquisitions are friendly, but *hostile takeovers* are not. Because of the frequency of hostile takeovers, businesses have developed strategies to avoid an unwanted takeover. The three main defence have colourful names: the poison pill, the white knight and the leveraged buyout (LBO).

- **Poison pill:** The poison pill describes a situation in which the target company adds large amounts of corporate debt through borrowing. The additional debt then makes the target less attractive, since the buyer will have to assume the debt.
- **White knight:** A second defence is to find a white knight; a friendly purchaser who will buy the company and rescue it, much as medieval white knights rescued damsels in distress. A friendly takeover avoids the cost of a prolonged battle and leaves the company, along with its management, intact.
- **Leveraged buyout:** In a leveraged buyout, 'LBO' for short, the management of

the target company borrows money, using the company itself as collateral. The management then purchases the company. This defence is also known as 'going private'.

SUMMARY

Each of the forms of business organisation has its own set of advantages and disadvantages. The choice of the best form for any given enterprise is not always clear and must be carefully considered. Many businesses start as sole traders or partnerships. As they grow and financial and management needs increase, they may choose to incorporate to increase their ability to borrow funds. As a company, additional funds for purchasing new equipment or developing new products can be obtained by selling additional shares of stock.

SELECTED READING

Phipps, Rosemary. 1994. *Start A Successful Business*. BBC Publications.
Hempshell. M. 1994. *Your Own Business in Europe*. International Venture Handbooks.
Willett, Rodney. 1995. *Right Way to Start Your Own Business*. Elliot Right Way Books.
Longenecker, Justin & Moore, Carlos. 1991. *Small Business Management*. South-Western Publishing.

5 Small Business, Entrepreneurship and Franchising

An Overview of Small Business

Small business serves many roles in the economy, including the roles of employer, supplier, purchaser of goods and services, and tax-payer. In just one of its roles, that of employer, small business makes a significant contribution to the economy: more than 99 per cent of businesses employ fewer than 100 people, yet they account for over half of the total work force. But the contributions of small business to the economy do not end there. Even large corporations benefit greatly from small business, because most of the products made by large corporations are distributed to and sold by small business. It is also a major supplier of parts and components to large manufacturers.

Independent, unencumbered by corporate bureaucracy and free to make quick decisions, small business owners aggressively seek new opportunities and technologies and as a result, they are responsible for many major innovations and breakthroughs. Small business can more easily fill the needs of 'niche' markets not covered by others. Many products with small initial demand, not suited for mass production or for specialised markets would never be available were it not for small business.

What is a 'Small' Business?

In recent years, small business has experienced a major revival fuelled by: the entry of women into the work force; the advent of new technologies such as software design; the restructuring of business during the late 1980s and the subsequent release or redundancy of many staff from a wide range of skills levels; the positive attitude of government, 'high street' banks and charities (e.g., The Prince's Youth Business Trust) to support small business; and ease of entry in most markets. Small business is indeed a major force in the economy. But what is a 'small' business?

In the US, the Small Business Administration (SBA) goes to some detail to define a small business, but this detail is missing in the UK and Europe. Different institutions have different definitions, depending on the degree of help they wish to define. Less than 500, 200 or 50 employees have been quoted as definitions, or less than £5 million, £2 million, or even £50,000 annual turnover. Definitions differ greatly for different types of businesses such as construction, manufacturing and retailing. In order to be eligible for support by the Department of Industry, a 'small business' must have less than 500 employees. Whatever the definition chosen, the best is probably where the owner of the business thinks that it is *small*!

Advantages of a Small Business

Almost every list of advantages for small business begins with the opportunity to be one's own boss. The independence, creative freedom and challenges of managing a small business are appealing to people who enjoy innovating, adapting to change and making and executing decisions quickly. They take risks but keep the profits. They develop close relationships with customers and employees. They can control the work environment, which for many means working at home. They can often keep overheads (rent, utilities and other expenses) low, making more capital available for productive purposes and raising profitability.

Disadvantages of a Small Business.

The small business owner cannot always afford to hire others to perform tasks. Thus, he/she is often sales manager, production manager, chief financial officer and secretary, and as a result, usually puts in long hours and works hard. Also, because raising capital is difficult for small business, the owner must often put his/her personal resources at risk.

Types of Small Business

Most small businesses are independently owned and are local operations, not part of another business. There are several types of small business; most fall into the category of lifestyle, high-growth venture, niche or cottage business.

- **Lifestyle business:** this is a modest operation with little growth potential, such as a neighbourhood grocery, restaurant or small retail store. It is intended to provide the owners with a comfortable living. Lifestyle businesses are often 'family' businesses.
- **High-growth venture:** this is an operation that tries to introduce new products or services. Thus, its goal is to grow and become a large company, and has the potential for great success. High-growth ventures may require considerable capital. Many large, major companies in the computer industry started as small high-growth ventures.
- **Niche business:** this is a business that fills a small need in the market place, a need or niche not addressed by other companies.
- **Cottage business:** this is the term used to describe an individual who works in his/her home (thus 'cottage'). Many computer-related jobs can be performed

just as well in the home, because electronic technology permits data transmission over telephone networks, allowing more and more people to work at home or anywhere else. Among the most obvious benefits are the lack of commuting, flexible hours and the ability for parents to work while they mind their children.

Entrepreneurs - The People Behind the Business

An *entrepreneur* (the word is derived from a French word meaning 'to undertake') is that person who undertakes the responsibility to bring together the idea, the money, the organisation, the materials and any other resources required to start a business. Entrepreneurs are the small business owners we have been discussing.

The term *entrepreneurial spirit* is reserved for those businesspeople, whether they literally own a business or not, who exemplify the characteristics common among entrepreneurs: the desire to create a new business, the freedom to determine one's own destiny, the need for independence and the willingness to meet a challenge. Entrepreneurs are highly motivated and have great determination and perseverance. No wonder they form the back-bone of small business.

Entrepreneurs generally continue to manage the businesses they have created. They tend to choose risks over certainty and hard work over a life of ease, all in an effort to make money. For some, the independence that owning and operating their own business affords far outweighs the financial return. Thus, they will continue in their businesses even if they might earn more by working for someone else. However, there is a category of 'habitual entrepreneur' which defines that special person who gets maximum satisfaction from setting up successful businesses rather than maintaining them.

Immigrants often take advantage of the opportunity to start their own small businesses. They often succeed by initially meeting the special ethnic needs among their fellow immigrants. Further, they are not uncommonly willing to work long hours.

Popular Industries

With the exception of industries that require extensive resources (for example, the steel and the car industries), small business thrives in every industry, in every business segment. Some industries, however, have a greater concentration of small businesses.

Service Business

The fastest growing area of small business is the service business. The reason is that most service businesses do not require extensive financial investment and huge resources. The range of service businesses is enormous, ranging from dog walking, beauty parlours, house painting, garden services to interior decorating and management consulting. The list seems endless. Service businesses are frequently based on the owner's special interest, knowledge or skills.

Retail Business

Another very popular industry group is retail business. Because of the enormous range of merchandise sold to consumers, the variety of retail businesses is very broad. Many are speciality shops that have limited stocks, selling a narrow range of merchandise, such as Belgian chocolates, permitting the owners to focus on their areas of expertise and to limit their investments.

Wholesale Business

Wholesaling consists of buying products in bulk from the manufacturer and storing them in quantities and locations convenient for the retailers. Most small wholesalers enter the business with some expertise in the industry, since success is based on relationships with both manufacturers and retailers.

Manufacturing Business

The manufacturing industry is dominated by big business, partly because of the economies of scale and the high investment needed for manufacturing equipment and raw materials. However, small business thrives in industries where innovation is important, such as construction, electronics, toys and computer software. Apple Computers and Microsoft, once small, are now well-known large businesses. Such success stories are common in the computer industry.

Government and Small Business

Recognising the far-reaching impact of small business on the UK economy, the government tries to support small business in a number of ways. Some are discussed below.

The Department of Trade and Industry (DTI)

In 1994 the DTI supported the launch of a large number of regional One Stop Shops, Business Links, which provides a full range of services for small businesses, from 'start up' advice through to growth and maturity. Initially funded by the government these Business Links will eventually charge for their services.

Training and Enterprise Councils (TEC)

TECs have been set up by the DTI to provide and support local initiatives for all types of business, including small ones. The TEC Business Development Centre provides information on all types of government support for small businesses. Business Growth Training is available to small, established businesses and takes the form of a 50 per cent subsidy on the costs of qualified consultants to advise on innovation, financial management, marketing and so on.

Government Loans

Since 1981, the government has underwritten loans to approved small businesses advanced by 'high street' banks. The borrower pays a premium on the normal interest charges applied to the loan. Borrowers are given up to seven years to repay the loan. In general, such loans are expensive because of the high risks involved.

Tax Concessions

The government supports the Business Expansion Scheme (BES) whereby individuals can invest income in approved small businesses free of personal income tax. Thus, a higher tax of 40 per cent can be avoided by high income earners. Invested funds have to remain in the business for a period, usually five years, and the investor must not be involved in the management of the business. At the end of the time period, the investor may withdraw the funds which may have increased in value. Tax will only be paid on any capital gain. The saving of income tax at source is a significant attraction. BES schemes are constantly under government review in order to ensure that the main objectives of the scheme are met and that loopholes are not being provided for unplanned tax avoidance.

Franchising

Franchising, a growing and popular route to establishing a small business, presents an alternative way to start a new business or buy an existing one. A franchise is a licence to sell another company's products, to use another company's name, or both. A franchisor is the company that sells a franchise, that is, the company that sells the licence to use its name or products. The franchisee is the person who buys the franchise and with it acquires the rights to a name, a logo, methods of operation, national advertising, products and other elements of the franchisor's business. The appeal of franchising includes the expertise and training that franchisors provide, and helping franchisees to avoid many of the start-up pitfalls and risk of starting a new business.

Franchise agreements vary from one franchisor to another. Generally, the terms require the franchisee to pay a flat fee initially, plus a monthly or an annual percentage of sales or profits. The amount of the initial fee (which depends on the type of franchise, the success of the franchisor and other factors) can vary from a few hundred pounds to over £100,000.

Franchises are most commonly found in retail and service businesses. Among the best known are McDonalds, Bennetton, Holiday Inn and Hertz. Nearly all car dealerships are franchises.

Advantages of Franchising

There are a number of advantages to franchising. Most franchises have national recognition among customers, thanks to each franchisor's advertising and promotion. As a result, a franchisee who purchases a Domino Pizza or Kentucky Fried Chicken or Tupperware franchise has a recognised name on the first day of business.

Some franchisors operate elaborate training programmes and facilities for their franchisees. They can provide management training, prepare business systems and procedures and provide operation plans. They can also assist in location selection, store layout and employee training.

Many franchisors supply almost everything needed to do business. The financial advantage of large-scale purchasing is passed on to the franchisee, and uniformity of product quality throughout the system is passed on to the consumer. The customer who buys a KFC chicken leg in London knows that it will taste the same as one bought in Manchester.

Disadvantages of Franchising

The initial high cost of buying a quality franchise is a disadvantage. On the other hand, however, it also prevents the common pitfall of trying to start a business with insufficient capital. Profits must be shared with the franchisor, who may already be making a generous profit on the supplies sold to the franchisee. A franchise limits the owner's independence and control of what to buy, from whom, how to operate and so on. Also, each badly operated franchise reflects on the acceptance of all other franchisees. But the major potential disadvantage is that success or failure depends so strongly on the franchisor - on product quality, on quality and quantity of advertising, and other factors controlled by the franchisor.

SUMMARY

All businesses start as small businesses. Some became worldwide organisations, others withered and died, other reached a certain size and stayed there or collapsed. Small businesses are such important providers of employment that the government in the UK, and elsewhere in Europe, has provided significant funds and help to aid small business development. The paradox is that many small business owners started the business to be independent and free from government attention, and therefore much of the government effort is wasted. However, many opportunities exist for successful small business start-up and growth, providing that the owner/manager has been trained to operate the business efficiently.

SELECTED READING

Surridge, Malcolm et al. 1993. *People, Marketing, and Business.* Collins Educational.

Business Law and Ethics

Sources of the Law

Law is a body of principles, rules of behaviour and standards used to settle disputes in an orderly way. In other words, law is what makes civilization civil. Every individual is subject to the law, and every business or organisation is subject to special laws that apply to business.

The impact of the legal system on business relates essentially to establishing the organisation, acquiring resources, business operations and selling output for consumption.

Understanding business law requires a brief overview of the categories of law and the judicial system.

Categories of Law

Law in the UK derives from a number of sources, including custom, judicial precedence and legislation from regional, national, European and international bodies. English law relates to England and Wales but some legislation applies only to Scotland and/or, Scotland and Northern Ireland.

Custom

Early society developed many laws, or customs, which have now been accepted as social norms. Many of these customs have been incorporated within a body of legal principles known as *common law*. Much common law has itself been included within statutes or case law (precedent established by the courts), but some common law remains especially in the area of land and property usage.

Judicial Precedent

Judicial precedence is based on the rule that decisions taken in a higher court on a previous occasion, sometimes many years previously, are binding on a lower court at any time in the future. Legal argument centres on whether the legal issues in a current case are the same as a previously determined case or if significant differences exist.

Legislation

A significant proportion of current law, especially laws governing the operation of business, derives from statute or an Act of Parliament. Acts of Parliament represent the supreme law of the land unless they are overridden by European Community Law. Statutes are used not only to introduce new legislation but also to change existing legislation.

Some legislation is passed to consolidate a number of individual statutes to eliminate any ambiguities which may have arisen in interpretation in the courts. Other legislation is passed to enable specific individuals, such as a Secretary of State, to make regulations as is deemed fit, although some powers are sometimes hotly disputed by opposition MPs. Sometimes a high court may decide that individuals have gone beyond their statutory powers and decisions are then cancelled or reversed.

European Community Law

European Community legislation is becoming an important factor as regards business throughout the Community, and the final result will be the eventual harmonisation of legislation. EC law is contained within the Treaty of Rome (1957), the Single European Act (1987) and the Maastricht Act (1992). Although the main treaties represent primary legislation, the EC institutions can make regulations, directives and decisions which are aimed either at individual states or at individuals. In general, these activities are enforceable in national courts if there is a financial obligation. Regulations apply to all states; directives apply to member states and not individuals; and decisions apply to specified member states, organisations or individuals.

The Courts

The courts are a central element of the country's legal system and have a responsibility for interpretation and administration. All political and governmental activity takes place within this legal framework.

The Legal System

In the UK there is a hierarchy of courts and two distinct branches: the Civil Division and the Criminal Division. The High Court is the major court for civil actions and the Crown Court is the major court for criminal actions. Decisions from the High Court can be appealed against at the Court of Appeal (Civil Division) and decisions from the Crown court can be sent to the Court of Appeal (Criminal Division). Appeals from both of these Appeal courts may be allowed to be heard at the House of Lords, the ultimate authority for domestic legislation.

The High Court

The High Court comprises three divisions: the Family Court (e.g., divorce, adoption, ward of court), the Chancery (e.g., trusts, property and taxation) and the Queen's Bench (e.g., business contracts, negligence and defamation).

The Crown Court

The Crown Court has the right to try all indictable offences and hear appeals from lower courts, County Courts and Magistrates Courts where trial by jury is not required.

County Courts

County Courts deal only with civil matters and are concerned only with statute law. County Courts deal with small claims between supplier and consumer, and conflicts between landlord and tenant. The system is relatively quick and inexpensive.

European Court of Justice

The European Court of Justice deals with issues of a supranational dimension. The Court is required to ensure that the application and interpretation of the Treaty of Rome is observed. Individuals can appeal to the European Court if they feel that their rights have been abused by a member state. Usually, such an appeal is supported by a 'pressure group' which is trying to establish a precedent and endeavouring to have national laws changed as a consequence of a successful appeal.

Contract Law

A contract is a legally enforceable agreement, written or oral, between two or more parties. A contract must meet a number of requirements to make it legally enforceable. These elements are discussed below.

Offer

An offer is a declaration by the offeror to be legally bound by the terms stated in the offer if it is accepted by the offeree. Such a declaration would relate to performance, price and possibly time. That is, what will the product or service do, how much will it cost and when will it be delivered? Offers are given in writing, orally or by implication by the conduct of the parties. Advertisements and goods on display are not offers but 'invitations to treat' and require a formal offer to be made. Offers can be terminated at any time up to acceptance or by failure of a condition. For example, an offer to purchase a business property 'subject to the sale of another property'.

Acceptance

Just as an offer must be clear and unambiguous, so the acceptance must be clear and unambiguous. Therefore, there is an advantage in having both offer and acceptance written up by legal experts in major contracts, even though oral acceptance and appropriate subsequent conduct are also binding. Silence cannot be assumed to mean acceptance. Postal acceptance is universally used by business, but it must be properly addressed and placed in the hands of an authorised delivery service such as the Royal Mail in the UK.

Consideration

Offer and acceptance are the basis of an agreement and both parties must be quite clear on the issues involved. In commercial contracts one party supplies a product or a service and the other party supplies some form of cash payment. However, in some contracts, bartering goods for goods is acceptable.

Intention to Create Legal Relations

In commercial contracts there must be a clear intention that both parties intend to make a legally binding contract and, therefore, it is not necessary for parties to include contract terms.

Capacity

Capacity deals with the competence of one party to make a contract with another party. In general, contracts with minors (under 18 years of age), mentally ill people and wards of court cannot make contracts. As regards commercial contracts, both parties must have the legal authority to undertake the contract.

Lawful Purpose

To be enforceable at law, a contract must be legal and must be entered into voluntarily. Consequently, contracts based on mistakes may be void. The deliberate or accidental non-disclosure of information may also make a contract void, as in the case of not giving full medical information for a personal insurance policy.

Property Law

Property defines anything which can be owned. Property can be 'real' as in bricks and mortar, machinery and land, or it can be intangible such as debts and investments. A special category of property is called intellectual property which includes the ownership of copyrights, patents, design rights and trade marks.

Intellectual Property

Intellectual property reflects the skills within a business and relates to design, marketing, information and production processes. Innovative applications of these skills can be protected by law, providing that the correct procedures are strictly followed. The innovator can therefore prevent a competitor from copying ideas for gain, or can seek reward for allowing the competitor to copy. Significant fines can be imposed after conviction of infringements of intellectual property (for example, the unauthorised photocopying of this book!).

Patents

A patent grants exclusive rights for a machine, process or other useful invention for a period of 20 years. During this period no one may copy the design without the innovator's permission.

Copyright

A copyright grants exclusive rights to publish, perform or sell an original book, article, design, illustration, computer program, film or other creation for a period of 50 or 75 years after the creator's death. Holders of copyright can sell or licence the use of their creations within the periods of exclusivity. Copyright protection is cheap and is granted immediately to a 'work of art' or a 'work of artistic crafts-manship'. Since it is a cheap process, many businesses copyright manuals and drawings as an alternative means of protection (as opposed to seeking a patent).

Trademarks

Trade marks, brands registered with the Trade Marks Registry at the Patent Office in London, can be renewed indefinitely. Example of trade marks are Kleenex brand tissues and the symbol 'IBM' used by International Business Machines.

Tort Law

A tort is a civil wrong concerned with those situations where one party threatens the interests, or actually harms the interests, of another party. The most common torts relate to negligence, nuisance, defamation and trespass. The injured party is entitled to compensation when an action is successfully brought in a court of law.

Intentional Tort

An intentional tort results from a deliberate action. Deliberately failing to rectify a dangerous error in a product is an intentional tort. Sexual harassment in the workplace is an intentional tort.

Negligence

Negligence, failure to exercise reasonable care and caution, can be the basis for a tort suit. For example, failure to mark properly an excavation would be grounds for a negligence action.

Product Liability

Product liability holds a company responsible for harm caused by a product it makes or markets, whether the oversight is intentional or the result of negligence. The Consumer Protection Act, 1987, deals with the obligations of producers to consumers.

The Law of Agency

The agency-principal relationship is rich in potential problems, many of which can be avoided by executing a written contract that specifies the conditions and limitations of the agency. The relationship between agent and principal varies depending on the specific situation.

Agents

An agent is a person who acts for, and in the name of, a second person who is known as the *principal*. Sales representatives, representatives of performers or athletes, solicitors, and brokers often act as agents. Loosely interpreted, business partners, company officers and, in some cases, employees are agents of the business.

Agents should be compensated for their work and for expenses incurred, warned of any dangers, and have limits of authority clearly stated. Agents owe their principals loyalty. This loyalty requires that agents should turn profit opportunities over to the principals, exercise due care and skill, preserve confidentiality of trade secrets and internal company information, and keep and render accurate accounts.

In law, the agent has a duty to act on behalf of a principal to effect a contract between the principal and a third party. When this contract has been established, the agent withdraws and usually has no further rights or duties.

Principals

The principal is liable for the acts committed by his/her agent, providing these acts are within the agent's authority.

Insolvency

At one time, those who could not pay their debts went to debtor's prison. Today, bankruptcy is not a criminal offence, and individuals or companies who cannot pay their debts may seek relief by petitioning for bankruptcy (individuals) or liquidation (companies).

Bankruptcy is court-granted permission not to pay some, or all, of an individual's debts. Bankruptcy serves two purposes: (i) it assures fair treatment of creditors (those who are owed money); and (ii) it permits the debtors, those who owe, to make a fresh start after three years.

The Insolvency Act, 1986, is the current act in the UK that deals with bankruptcy. The treatment of persons or companies which are insolvent is a balancing act between the prosecution of fraudulent behaviour, and sympathetic treatment of the persons or company caught by no mistake of their own in a hostile commercial environment. The 1986 Act represents the current social attitudes towards this balance.

Corporate Insolvency

Insolvency is defined as the inability to repay debts as and when they fall due, or when liabilities exceed assets. There are various corporate procedures in the UK which may be followed in the hope of rescuing the business and repaying all debts. These are administrative receivership, administration order and, if all else fails, liquidation and the selling of assets.

Administrative Receivership

A major creditor (usually a bank with a floating charge over the assets of a business – that is a general unspecified security for a loan) may appoint an administrative receiver through the courts if the business defaults on a loan repayment. The receiver, working on behalf of the major creditor, takes immediate control of the business and has the alternative of selling assets to repay the secured creditor, or operating the business to get it back to a profitable position with a view to selling the business and hopefully protecting jobs.

Administration Order

If there is no major creditor willing to appoint a receiver, a court may appoint an administrator who has similar powers to an administrative receiver. For the duration of the administration, the business cannot be put into the hands of a receiver or a liquidator. During the administration, the court will be looking for survival of all or part of the business, approval of a voluntary arrangement, or a better realisation of assets than liquidation. A 50 per cent majority of creditors is required to support an administration.

Voluntary Arrangement

A voluntary arrangement occurs when a business, together with a qualified insolvency practitioner puts up proposals for a compromise to a meeting of its creditors. If 75 per cent of the creditors agree, the proposals are put into effect and the nominee, the insolvency practitioner, supervises the business until settlement has been reached.

Liquidation

There are three types of liquidation, or winding up, of the business. All lead to the dissolution of the business under a liquidator (a qualified insolvency practitioner).

- **Members Voluntary Liquidation:** if the directors of the company make a declaration that all debts can be paid within 12 months, the liquidator is appointed by the company shareholders and the creditors have no involvement.
- **Creditors Voluntary Liquidation:** a creditors voluntary liquidation is initiated by the company directors who decide that the company is insolvent and convene a meeting of shareholders to put it into liquidation. Creditors may approve the shareholders' liquidator or appoint one of their own.
- **Compulsory Liquidation:** this is ordered through the courts following a creditor's petition. The official receiver, a Department of Trade officer, becomes the liquidator. A meeting of the creditors will be held to appoint a licensed insolvency practitioner to conduct the liquidation, unless there are no assets.

 # Business Ethics

Closely related to law is the study of 'right' and 'wrong'; of the morality of individual choices as judged by some standard of behaviour. Business ethics is the application of moral standards to business decisions and actions.

Unfortunately, there are all too many examples of unethical actions of individuals and companies, including stock market insider-trading scandals, overcharging, and bid-rigging by major contractors. Newspapers provide examples almost daily, pointing up the need to review business ethics and prompting business schools to offer courses in ethics.

Business ethics involves all relationships among people involved in a business, both inside and outside (e.g., employees, investors, customers, creditors, competitors and so on). Each group has a responsibility in its dealings with the firm in an effort to remind employees of their specific responsibilities.

SUMMARY

The subject of business ethics is rapidly becoming of interest to many people (especially consumers) as a result of media attention and public education into health and safety issues; social awareness especially as regards gender and religion, and also the increasing public investment in business through ownership of shares. The law in the UK has been slow to respond to public concern basically because of its long tradition of 'careful thought' and minimisation of possible backlash through hasty legislation. In business, the law has been reactive rather than proactive, such as the unethical use of employee pension investments.

SELECTED READING

Hilder, P. 1994. *Essential Business Law.* Collins.
Pearson, Edward. 1994. *Law for European Business Studies.* Pitman.
Redmond, Peter. 1993. *Introduction to Business Law.* Pitman.
Kelly, David & Holmes, Ann. 1995. *Business Law.* Cavendish.

Part 3
Management of the Enterprise

7	# Management Fundamentals

What is 'Management'?

Management can be defined as 'working with and through people and other organisational resources to achieve the organisation's goals and objectives'. Basically, management involves all business decisions - what to do, how to do it, who is to do it, where to do it, when to do it, and perhaps most important of all, whether to do it. The principles and processes can be applied to all organisations, even to managing our homes.

To begin with, let us look at the basic functions and activities that all managers perform: planning, organising, directing/leading and controlling.

- **Planning** involves deciding what has to be done and determining the goals to be met.
- **Organising** involves deciding how to utilise the organisation's resources - land, labour and capital - and determining which people will do the work that has been planned.
- **Directing/leading** involves putting the plans into action by motivating people to do the work.
- **Controlling** involves monitoring the people and the work to ensure what has been planned is being done.

Theories of Management

Management theories first emerged during the early 1900s. Knowing some of the 'classical' theories is both interesting and helpful.

Scientific Management

Frederick W. Taylor is considered the founder of scientific management, an approach that studied jobs and broke them down into smaller tasks, determining the 'one right way' of accomplishing those tasks. Taylor pioneered the piece-rate system, whereby each worker received the same wage for each piece of work produced.

Other contributors to the theory of scientific management were Frank and Lillian Gilbreth, who further refined time-motion studies to improve worker productivity through job simplification. Henry Gantt, an associate of Taylor, is best known for the Gantt chart, a chart that made significant contributions to scheduling and controlling work and improving productivity. Gantt also developed the concept of a production bonus for producing above the daily quota.

Scientific management, despite its name, was concerned with worker and production efficiency, not with 'management'.

Classical Organisation Theory

Henri Fayol and Max Weber were two key contributors to classical organisation theory.

Guidelines for managing complex organisations (such as factories) originated in France with *Henri Fayol*, founder of the classical management school, who attempted to identify principles and skills that underlie effective management. Fayol made four major contributions to management theory:

- He distinguished between managers and supervisors at the operating level of organisations.
- He defined five functions of management: planning, organising, commanding, coordinating and controlling.
- Fayol developed his Fourteen Principles of Management, which included division of labour, unity of command, chain of command, mechanisms to insure communications and specialised groups.
- Fayol maintained that flexibility was needed in applying his principles, and that managers could learn to manage.

We now take Fayol's 'total organisation' approach for granted, but Fayol's work on the subject was not translated into English until 1945 and was considered revolutionary at the time.

Max Weber, a German sociologist, addressed the issue of organisational administration from a different perspective. His ideal organisation (a bureaucracy) emphasised order, system, rationality, uniformity and consistency, thus ensuring equitable treatment of employees by management. According to Weber, technical competence should be emphasised, and performance evaluation made entirely on the basis of merit.

The Behavioural School

The classical approach focused on the work, not the worker. The worker was considered the economic man, driven by rational economic motives. In the 1920s, managers experienced difficulties and frustrations because people did not follow predicted or expected patterns of behaviour. The behavioural school was developed by management scholars trained in social sciences; scholars who used their knowledge of social science and applied it to understanding and improving organisation management.

Elton Mayo and his associates, through their Hawthorne studies, established the field of human relations. They found that work productivity was related to psychological and social variables, and as a result, they introduced the concept of the *social man*, motivated by the desire to form relationships with others. Thus, behavioural scientists - sociologist, anthropologist and psychologists (such as Abraham Maslow) - shifted the focus from the workplace to the worker.

Management Science

A quantitative approach to management called *operations research* (OR), was developed in Great Britain at the beginning of World War II. OR brought together teams of mathematicians, physicists and other scientists to use mathematical models to simulate management problems and generate potential solutions to the problems. With the development of the computer, OR procedures were formalised into what became known as *management science*.

The Systems Approach

Whereas the quantitative approach of management science neglects the behavioural side of an enterprise, the systems approach views the organisation as one unified, directed system of interrelated parts, where changes at one point may result in significant changes at another point. For example, the introduction of new working practices in order to improve efficiencies in one department may result in a lowering of efficiencies in another department, with the result that the overall result is a financial loss to the organisation. In one particular manufacturing organisation, the introduction of personal identity badges to improve security measures prevented the common practice of movements between sections by key personnel. Not only did this result in a lowering of the transfer of information since alternative methods were needed, but also caused the operators to consider the introduction, without proper consultation, to be an infringement of their accepted rights. Subsequent industrial unrest and lowering of productivity resulted in the withdrawal of identity badges pending more effective consultations. The systems approach tries to anticipate such behaviour by widening the planning activities.

Contingency Approach

According to the contingency approach, a manager's task is to identify which technique will best contribute to the attainment of management goals in a particular situation, under particular circumstances, and at a particular time. This approach is sometimes called 'situational' and is characterised by the phrase 'it all depends'.

Management Resources

To achieve its goals, management must utilise the organisation's resources. These resources are the organisation's assets; the factors of production that are available to produce the company's products or services. Land includes buildings, raw materials and equipment; labour includes the people, the human resources who work for the company; and capital is the funds needed to operate the enterprise. Managers assemble these resources and use them to create goods or services, and they are evaluated by how well they do so. Two criteria for judging managers are *effectiveness* and *efficiency*. Effectiveness measures the manager's ability to accomplish the company's goals. Efficiency measures the manager's ability to minimise the use of resources - to get the most output with the least input. A good manager must be both effective (do the right things) and efficient (do things right).

Levels of Management

Every organisation has several levels of management. The responsibility of each manager depends on his/her level in the organisation. The chief financial officer and the supervisor of the purchasing department are both managers, but their duties and responsibilities are quite different.

Authority versus Responsibility

Authority is the power to command and can be delegated. A manager can assign a task to another person and delegate the authority needed to accomplish it. Responsibility is the obligation to perform, and the manager's responsibility cannot be delegated. The ultimate responsibility always remains with the manager.

One way to categorise managers is to separate them into three levels: top, middle and first-line managers. In most organisations, there are a small number of top managers, a larger number of middle managers, and an even larger group of first-line managers. (See Figure 7.1). Top management has the most authority, first-line management the least, and the middle management's authority lies between the two. The CEO, or chief executive officer, has the most authority and, therefore, the most responsibility.

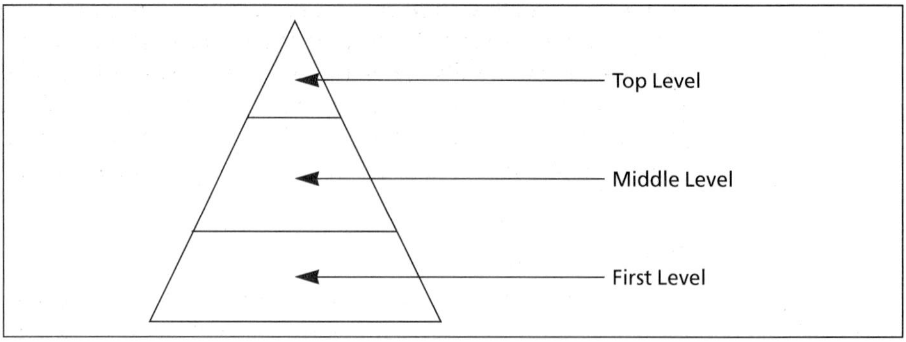

Figure 7.1

Top Management

Top management, the relatively small group at the top of the pyramid, is made up of the chairman, chief executive officer and senior executives, and is responsible for the overall management of the organisation. They are general managers, responsible for all activities, or for an entire company or subsidiary. They set the corporate objectives, policies and strategies. They also deal with government relations and the external economic environment.

Middle Management

Middle management is made up of the managers who are not part of top management or first-level management. They act as liaison between the top management and the first-level management (whom they supervise). They are charged with coordinating and carrying out the policies set by the top management. They are often functional managers, responsible for a single function such as sales, marketing or production.

First-Line Management

Supervisors, department managers and team leaders at the base of the pyramid make up first-line management; the largest management group in an organisation and the group responsible for getting the work done. First-line managers supervise only non-management personnel, who report directly to the first-line managers. They oversee the scheduling of work, maintenance of equipment and work routines on a day-to-day basis. They have considerable responsibility for seeing that tasks are accomplished.

Management Skills

The successful manager requires basic technical, human and conceptual skills. Although the 'mix' of these skills will vary from one level of management to another, every manager must be skilled in all three areas. In general, however, all managers at all levels need human skills because, by definition, managers get things done through people. Because first-line managers are closest to the process, they generally spend more time using technical skill, and their technical skill, will have a greater effect on their success. Top-level managers, by comparison, must have keen conceptual skills because they are responsible for company planning. Middle-level managers will need a mixture of all three skills.

Technical Skill

Technical skill is the ability to use specialised knowledge about the mechanics of a job such as tools, procedures and techniques. A manager does not have to be the most proficient person in the production process, but he/she must know the process well enough to perform his/her responsibilities and make decisions.

Human Skill

Human skill is the ability to work with and motivate people, utilising one's personal and interpersonal skills. Personal skills involve self-awareness, knowledge of how one is perceived by others, time management and stress management. Interpersonal skills involve interaction with others, such as communicating, listening, leading, motivating and resolving conflict among people.

Conceptual Skill

Conceptual skill is the ability to see how parts function as a whole. A manager must see how different departments and divisions of an organisation are interrelated; how they work together. A manager must recognise that, and know how, a change in one element can affect other elements.

The Management Process

The management process can be discussed by function. A manager frequently performs more than one function at any given moment. These functions mentioned earlier, are planning, organising, directing and controlling.

Planning

Planning is the process of establishing objectives, then setting policies, procedures and a course of action to accomplish these objectives. It is a complex process and consists of several steps discussed below.

Planning begins with a *purpose*, a reason for establishing the organisation. The purpose may be to make a profit for the owners. In the case of a university, it may be to develop and transmit knowledge; or in the case of a hospital, to provide health care.

Once an organisation establishes its purpose, it states how it will accomplish this purpose – that is, it states its *mission*. A company's mission describes the path it will take to achieve its goals. General Motors' purpose is 'to make a profit', and its mission is 'to manufacture automobiles'. Within the car industry, other firms may adopt variations of the same mission. Ferrari's mission, for example, may be 'to manufacture high-performance sports cars'.

The next planning step is to develop *objectives*, statements of how the organisation plans to achieve its mission. Objectives are generally expressed in more specific terms and provide a definite time frame. While a business will have a singular purpose and a singular mission, it will usually have several objectives. Objectives usually include goals – measurable steps that provide guides to help accomplish the objectives (e.g., specific sales revenues, growth rates and profits).

Broad objectives must be converted to specific actions, usually stated in terms of an action plan. An action plan may be classified as either strategic or tactical.

A *strategic plan* describes the objectives and actions of a company over a long-term period, frequently five to ten years. In other words, it describes a long-term strategy. Strategic plans are prepared by the top level of management and approved by the board of directors.

A *tactical plan* is specific, detailed and current, and focuses on present operations. Tactical plans, which typically cover a one-year period, are prepared by middle management and implemented by first-line management.

Managers use three *planning tools*:

- **Rules:** a rule is a planning tool that precisely designates a specific required action. It indicates what an organisation member should or should not do. 'All employees must begin work by nine o'clock' is an example of a rule.
- **Policies:** whereas a rule is specific, a policy is general. A policy furnishes broad guidelines for making decisions and taking action. A policy gives, in general terms, the kind of actions needed to achieve goals.
- **Budgets:** a budget is a financial plan that covers a specific period of time. It details how funds will be obtained and how the factors of production will be allocated. In addition to showing how money will be spent, a budget sets limits on how much will be spent for each expense.

Organising

Once objectives and plans have been established, the organising function comes into play. Management must design and staff the organisation to carry out its purpose: it must specify the people, the process, the equipment, the time and the material. Management must establish clear lines of authority and communication. Precisely how the company will be organised depends on its objective. For example, in a car plant, management will organise the personnel of the assembly line differently from the personnel in the engineering department, as would management in a retail store. Organisation will be discussed in more detail in Chapter 8.

Leading/Directing

Key to management success is the process of influencing people so that they are motivated to behave in ways that meet the firm's objectives. This process, whether it is called leading, directing or motivating, always involves influencing people. For the purpose of this discussion, we will use the word *leading* or *leadership.*

Leading is guiding the actions of organisation members toward the attainment of the organisation's goals and objectives. Managers have the authority to request and require performance and hold people responsible, but the most effective leaders get employees to perform tasks willingly. It is possible to be a manager without being a leader, and it is possible to be a leader without being a manager. If management is 'the art of getting things done through people', then we may call leadership 'the art of getting people to perform'.

Controlling

Controlling is the process of evaluating the organisation's performance and taking corrective action as necessary to keep the firm on track. The controlling function ensures that the organisation is performing according to, and accomplishing, the company's goals, as identified in its plan. Controlling and planning are inseparable functions.

After establishing performance standards, the controlling process consists of four steps:

1 Measure the performance.
2 Compare the performance to the established standards and the objectives of the plan.
3 Identify deviations from the plan and their causes.
4 Take corrective action.

The management tools for this process are described in Part VI, Chapters 16 to 18.

Aspects of Leadership
Leadership Styles

While there is a wide range of leadership styles, they all stem from three basic approaches: autocratic, participative and laissez-faire. Managers may adopt and use one style consistently or they may use different styles in different situations (i.e., situational leadership).

- Autocratic leaders: autocratic describes leaders who make decisions without consulting employees, then announce their decisions and expect (perhaps demand) compliance.
- Participative leaders: participative describes leaders who share their decision-making with others. They may gather information from others and make their own decision based on the information. In group situations, they may allow the group they are leading to make the decisions.

- Laissez-faire leaders: laissez-faire describes leaders who allow employees to make decisions. Their attitude is based on the idea that the people performing the job are best qualified to make decisions that concern their jobs. Laissez-faire tends to be more popular in situations where employees have greater technical knowledge than managers.

Situational Leaders

Situational leadership recognises that leadership success requires using a style that is appropriate to the specific situation and to the specific kinds of people involved in that situation. Situational leaders do not limit themselves to one style. As changes occur, they adopt the appropriate leadership style.

Leadership Behaviour

Two aspects of leadership are job-centred and employee-centred behaviour:

- **Job-centred behaviour:** job-centred leaders practise close supervision so that performance can be strictly monitored and controlled. Their primary interest is in production and in meeting production goals.
- **Employee-centred behaviour:** employee-centred behaviour demonstrates concern for the well-being of employees. The leader who practises employee-centred behaviour is interested in developing a cohesive work group and ensuring that employees are satisfied with their jobs.

Leadership and Motivation

Effective leadership depends strongly on a manager's ability to motivate employees to perform tasks willingly and to the best of their ability. Thus, motivation is the stimulation and energising of an individual to take those actions necessary to accomplish a desired goal or task. Motivational issues require a manager to be concerned with keeping workers challenged, productive and using their capabilities fully. Many of the same theories detailed earlier in this chapter pertain to motivation. Taylor's view is of the worker concerned with the economic necessities of working, while the behaviourists' view is of the worker motivated by the social aspects of work. The theories directly related to encouraging high performance from employees are grounded in the work of Abraham Maslow.

Maslow's Hierarchy of Needs

Early theories claimed that needs were the basis of motivation, but no one formally classified those needs until 1943, when Abraham Maslow, a psychologist, published his theory of motivation based on a hierarchy of human needs.

Maslow organised human needs into five different levels. (See Figure 7.2). In Maslow's theory, the prime source of motivation is unfulfilled needs. The needs at any level do not have to be fully satisfied before the needs at the next level come into play.

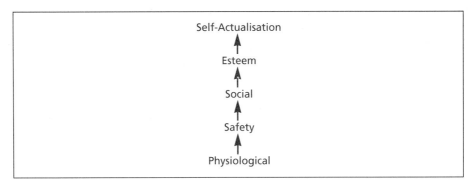

Figure 7.2 Maslow's hierarchy of needs

The lower-level needs, according to Maslow's hierarchy, are the most *basic needs*, our physiological needs, such as our requirements for food, water, shelter and sleep. In a business environment, these needs are usually met by adequate wages. The next level is *safety needs*, which include physical and emotional security. These needs are met by health insurance, pension plans, safe working conditions and job security. Next 'up' the hierarchy are *social needs*, such as the need for friendship, companionship and the need to belong. Friends, relatives and co-workers help satisfy these needs. On the next level are *esteem needs*: our needs for status, recognition and self-respect, which are satisfied by awards, promotions and job titles. The highest level of needs is *self-actualisation* needs: our need to grow and develop and to realise our full potential, to become all we are capable of being.

In essence, Maslow's theory states that normally humans will try to satisfy a particular level of needs only when needs on the level below have first been satisfied. Thus, according to Maslow, the primary source of motivation is unfulfilled needs.

Maslow's hierarchy has had a profound effect on various areas of motivation, management and communication theory.

Theory X and Theory Y

Douglas McGregor, a psychologist, presented an approach to understanding motivation called Theory X based on sets of assumptions that underlie management's attitudes and beliefs regarding worker behaviour. This approach adopted a rather pessimistic view of employees as people who can be motivated only by fear (e.g., job loss). He also postulated a more optimistic approach called Theory Y which offered a humanistic approach. According to Theory Y, workers could be motivated by better challenges, personal growth, improved work performance and productivity.

Knowing the theories on what motivates workers is not solely sufficient. The skills to put them into practice, to apply them, are also necessary. One of the best programmes to accomplish this is Management by Objectives (MBO).

Management by Objectives

Management by Objectives (MBO), first described by Peter Drucker in his 1954 book, The Practice of Management, is a set of procedures that starts with setting performance targets and continues through to performance review. It features involvement at every level of management and staff; the setting of goals and the clear definition of every individual's areas of responsibility in terms of expected results or 'objectives', with periodic reviews and performance appraisals. MBO programmes can vary greatly, but most contain the following elements:

- **Commitment to the programme:** time, effort and commitment at every level are required in setting objectives and reviewing results for an MBO programme to be effective.
- **Top-level goal setting:** the process begins with top managers setting measurable preliminary goals, such as '7 per cent increase in sales next quarter'. This furnishes managers and employees with a clear idea of what it is hoped will be accomplished.
- **Individual goals:** each manager and employee needs to have a clearly defined responsibility and objective or goal. The objectives for each individual are set collaboratively between the individual and his/her superior.
- **Participation:** the extent of employees' participation in setting objectives varies widely. As a general rule, the greater the participation of both managers and employees, the more likely realistic goals will be set and met. Individual goals linked to the organisation and the overall goals need to be worked out cooperatively, not assigned.
- **Autonomy in implementation of plans:** Once the objectives have been set and agreed upon, the individuals need to be free to choose the means of accomplishing the objectives and implementing the programme.
- **Review of performance:** managers and employees meet periodically to review progress made toward the objective. This review reveals any problems that exist, zeros in on what can be done to resolve them and allows for modification of goals if necessary. It is important that the review and feedback be based on measurable performance rather than subjective criteria.

MBO has proved to be an effective motivation tool, enhancing communication and understanding in many companies. In order for it to be effective, the process must begin at the top level of the firm and include all levels. The disadvantages of MBO are that it is time-consuming and can involve a considerable amount of paperwork and meetings.

Decision-Making

Managers are continuously involved in decision-making, and they are evaluated by their organisations on the basis of the quality of their decisions. Decisions taken by managers range from minor and relatively unimportant to major and potentially life-threatening to the organisation. They decide whether to buy another company, which overnight delivery service to use, how to price the company's goods and services and so on.

Information gathering is an integral and continuing part of the decision-making process. Successful decision-making utilises this information effectively. Decision-making goes beyond choosing among options; it is based on a number of clearly defined steps.

Define the Problem

The first step in decision-making is to define the problem. Many managers skip this step because they assume they know what the problem is or because they mistakenly conclude that the symptom is the problem. For instance, a high level of rejects in a manufacturing process is a symptom, but the problem may stem from a variety of factors.

Identify Alternatives

Business problems seldom have just one solution. It is the manager's role to identify a range of creative solutions – a complete list of potential alternatives.

Evaluate all Alternatives and Choose One

Managers use several methods to screen and choose from a selection of alternatives. One method is to eliminate, in a series of evaluations, the less satisfactory alternatives until only one or two remain. Another method is to evaluate and score each alternative, much as a teacher grades papers, then choose from the top-scoring alternatives.

Implement the Decision

The decision process does not end with making the decision. There are two more steps, of which the next is to implement the decision. After managers have selected the most effective solution to the problem, they must implement their decision, thus taking the necessary actions to do so.

Monitor Decision Outcomes

The final step in decision-making is to monitor and control the outcome of the implemented decision. Evaluation performed after implementation is part of management control, and may call for corrective action and follow up. Are the steps being implemented working according to plan? Does the plan need to be adjusted or altered? Should another alternative be considered, and if so, what other alternatives are available?

SUMMARY

Management is a subject for study (just like languages or mathematics) but its theory changes in response to social and political factors. Leadership styles, once so autocratic, are now more cooperative, whilst businesses, once so bureaucratic, now try hard to respond to individual problems. The basic issues which motivate people in general (both as consumers and suppliers) have not changed, and it is important that these factors are clearly understood. But the degree of importance of these factors depends greatly on the characteristics of each individual, which in turn can change with time. Management is therefore an evolving activity requiring constant reflection and updating.

SELECTED READING

Drucker, Peter. 1986. *The Practice of Management.* Heinemann.
Peel, Malcolm. 1993. *Introduction to Management.* Pitman.
Dewhurst, Jim. 1993. *Small Business Management.* Macmillan Press.
Schein, Edgar. 1985. *Organisational Culture and Leadership.* Jossey-Bass.

8 | Organisational Structure

After organisational goals are established and strategies for meeting them have been planned, organisational structure (the delineation of jobs and reporting relationships) indicates the way work is arranged and the manner in which people and other resources are allocated.

An Overview of Organisational Structure

The Components of an Organisation

A company may have, for example, sales, production, design, shipping, human resources, advertising, public relations and finance departments. Each department is one component, one part of the whole organisation. Each component has its own specific purpose and its own set of goals, yet each component must fit in with all the other components so that 'the company' works as one.

The actual structure of organisations differs widely, depending on the industry and the particular company, as well as the company's mission, size, technology needs and other factors. Most employees work within an organisational structure they did not create. In order to work well within that organisation and that structure, employees must understand the organisational structure, how the organisation functions, where the authority lies, what the tasks are, and how the work is accomplished.

The Organisation Chart

The organisation chart is a blueprint of the company's structure, a map showing all the components or departments of the organisation. Through a series of connecting lines, the chart positions all components to show the relationship of every department in the company, the chain of command and where employees fit into the firm's operations.

An organisation chart may be simple or complex, depending on the size of the corporation. Solid lines show the direct chain of command or the lines of authority in the company, that is, the reporting relationships or line positions. Dotted lines show staff or advisory positions, not line positions. Both will be addressed later in this chapter.

Specialisation and Departmentalisation within an Organisation.

The organisation of any business answers two basic questions: who will perform each of the functions needed? How will the employees who perform these functions be grouped together?

Specialisation

Specialisation (also called *division of labour*) describes the use of individuals, with specialised skills to perform specialised tasks. For instance, a person who owns his/her own business and works alone must perform all tasks. As the business grows, each new person may become responsible for one specialised area. The first person hired may be a sales representatives; the next person, a production supervisor; then an accountant; an advertising manager, and so on. Each additional employee takes over a specialisation.

Departmentalisation

Departmentalisation describes the grouping together of jobs into manageable work units or departments. This is usually based on function, geography, product or service, customer, process, matrix or a mixture/combination of these.

When employee groupings are based on functions, all positions that are related to the same functional activity are brought together in one department. For example, everyone who handles accounting and bookkeeping, including related clerical positions, might be grouped into the accounting department. Other functions are finance, production, marketing and human resource management.

Some firms are divided not by function but by geography. The regional units may be large (continent or country) or small (a town bank). Within a region, the unit may be organised by function, but the region itself represents a geographical unit of the parent organisation.

A firm may establish departments based on their *products or service.* For example, a clothing manufacturer might have separate men's and women's divisions. The women's division might have its own departments for formal, casual, athletic and other products, as will the men's division.

In some firms, departments are organised by *customer.* A telephone company, for example, may have a separate department for residential customers and another for business customers. Service organisations such as banks and travel agencies often separate business clients from individual clients. In such cases, the product or service itself might be the same for all customers, but the separate departments allow the firm to target its marketing, advertising and other functions more effectively.

Departmentalisation by *process* is most common in manufacturing companies, where divisions may be machining, assembly, painting and furnishing.

A *matrix organisation* is an organisation form pioneered by the US National

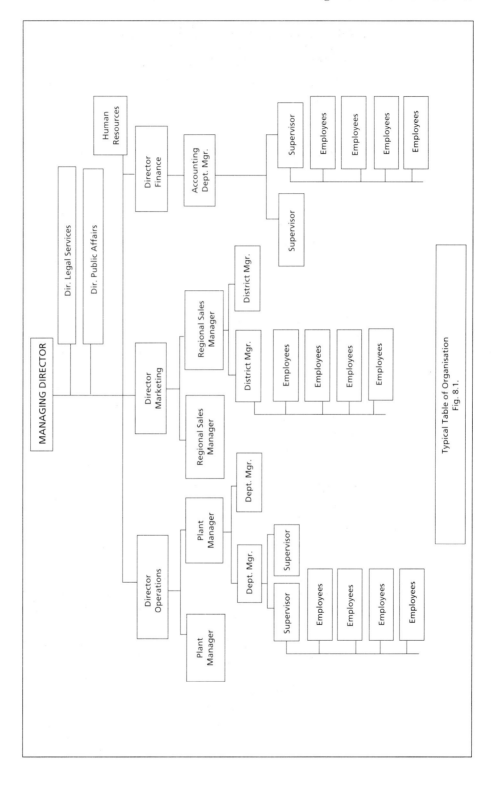

Typical Table of Organisation
Fig. 8.1.

Aeronautical and Space Administration (NASA), consisting of a matrix in which people are brought together from different functional departments as a task force for a specific project. The assigned people have two distinct reporting lines, one to the task-force leader and the other to their supervisors. One disadvantage of this sharing of command is that, according to Fayol's classical management organisation theory an employee should have only one boss. Another is that the matrix is temporary; it is dissolved when its task is completed.

Companies, especially large firms, need not follow one type of organisational form from top to bottom. Instead, they *mix and combine* forms. A company might organise its top level by function, the next level by geographic region and the lowest level by product.

Line and Staff Management

The management structure of an organisation consists of two types of management: line and staff management.

Line Management

Line management represents that part of the chain of command that has direct responsibility for achieving the goals of the organisation. Line managers have direct authority and responsibility for producing and selling the goods or services produced by the company.

Staff Management

Staff management supplies advice, support and expertise to line management but staff managers have no direct authority or responsibility for producing and selling goods and services. Staff managers, advise they do not order. Lawyers, accountants, and human resource personnel are some examples of staff positions.

Small organisations can function without staff positions. But as size and complexity increase, the need for staff functions also increases.

Centralised versus Decentralised Structures

Organisational structures can be described as centralised or decentralised. *Centralised* describes organisations in which most of the decision making authority is retained by upper-level management working out of a central location. *Decentralised* describes organisations in which much of the decision-making authority is delegated – that is, assigned – to lower management. Multinational organisations and firms, in which major divisions are separated by geographic units, often have decentralised decision-making.

Small businesses start with authority centralised, often in one individual. But as the business grows and the number of decisions increases, the firm may move toward greater decentralisation.

The Role of Delegation

Delegation plays a key role in understanding the concepts of centralisation and decentralisation. To delegate means 'to assign to someone'. Delegation is the assignment of a task by a manager to a subordinate. Successful delegation requires managers to balance responsibility, authority and accountability.

Responsibility

Responsibility originates at the time an individual accepts a task. Once that individual accepts an assignment, he/she has an obligation, a responsibility, to accomplish or perform the assigned task.

Accountability

Accountability, the acceptance of credit for success or blame for failure, accompanies responsibility. The lowest organisational level that has sufficient ability and information to carry out a task competently is accountable for that task. For example, if the Chief Executive complains that the grass needs cutting adjacent to the main entrance, the person employed to tend the grass (i.e., the one who has the competence to know how and when to cut grass, and has been given the time and equipment to carry out the grass cutting) will be blamed for not doing the job. This person is accountable. However, if the problem is one of not caring for the whole of the grounds, which are generally run down and unattractive because unskilled staff and unreliable equipment are used, then the manager responsible for employing groundsmen and providing equipment is accountable.

Authority

Authority is the power to make decisions, to give commands or orders, and to control the resources necessary to accomplish the assigned task.

The Need for Balance

If a manager delegates to an employee the task of checking time cards, for example, and the employee accepts that task, the employee becomes responsible for completing that task. However, to complete that task effectively, the employee must have the authority to complete the task, that is, whatever power is needed to accomplish that task. At this stage the employee has both the responsibility and the necessary authority to be held accountable for accomplishing the task assigned. In all cases, however, the ultimate responsibility always remains with the manager.

Span of Management and Organisational Height

The span of management (also called *span of control*) is the number of people that one manager is responsible for supervising. A wide span exists when there are a large number of subordinates reporting to one manager. A narrow span exists when a manager has only a few subordinates.

Organisational height refers to the number of levels of management in a firm. Organisational height is described as tall or flat, references that are more understandable if you picture an organisation chart. A tall organisation has many levels of management (the chart would also be 'tall'). The opposite of a tall organisation is a flat one, which only has a few levels of management (its chart would look 'flat').

A good example of a tall organisation is the British Army. Consider privates as workers and all the corporals, sergeants, lieutenants, captains, majors, colonels and generals as managers or supervisors.

Law firms, even very large law firms, have comparatively few partners supervising the associates and are therefore very 'flat' organisations.

The wider the span of an organisation's management, the more likely it is to be 'flat'. Tall organisations are costly as more managers are required, and the speed at which information flows both upward and downward is reduced. Flat organisations fit more closely the description 'lean and mean'.

The design of organisational structures is a dynamic process influenced by changes in an organisation's size, product, market and competition. That structure has an impact on employees' job performance and job satisfaction is rooted in Herzberg's 'Two Factor' theory of motivation.

Herzberg's Motivation-Hygiene Theory

Frederick Herzberg's theory holds that the degree of satisfaction and the degree of dissatisfaction felt by workers, as a result of performing a job, are two different variables and are determined by two different elements. Herzberg calls the dissatisfaction factors *hygiene factors,* and the satisfaction factors *motivation factors.* (See Table 8.1).

Hygiene factors are sometimes called *dissatifiers*. Work conditions, pay and company policy must be present to an acceptable degree in order for employees not to be dissatisfed with their jobs. Improving these factors, although reducing dissatisfaction, will not lead employees to work harder. As for salary, an across-the-board or cost-of-living raise would be a hygiene factor, whereas merit raise (an individual bonus based on the achievement or over-achievement of an accepted goal) would be a motivation factor.

Motivation factors must be present to an acceptable degree for an employee to be satisfied, and if increased, they will lead employees to work harder. They are sometimes called *satisfiers*. The greater the chance for promotion, for example, the more likely it is that people will work harder.

TABLE 8.1 Herzberg's factors

Hygiene Factors (dissatisfaction)	Motivation Factors (satisfaction)
Company Policies	Responsibility
Salary	Recognition
Supervision	Achievement
Social Interaction	Growth
Working Conditions	Challenge

Herzberg's theory is utilised when designing the jobs that employees perform - i.e., how tasks are combined as job enlargement or job enrichment. In job enlargement, the employee is given more things to do within the same job. Job enrichment provides the worker with more tasks to do and greater control of how they are done. By blending more planning and decision-making into jobs, employees' sense of responsibility, motivation and opportunities for growth are increased.

The Organisation within the Organisation

Every business has its formal organisation – the organisation established by the management as outlined on an organisation chart. Within every business there is also an informal organisation – groupings of people based on interactions and friendships; a network unrelated to the relationship shown on the company's organisation chart. Employees, acting on their own needs, establish the organisation within the organisation.

The rapid pace of change in business has led companies to rely more heavily on informal organisation. The informal relationships that develop in an organisation not only help satisfy social needs of employees but also assist in getting things done. While the formal structure has defined channels that delay information gathering and decision-making, the informal network can cut through the formal obstacles and contribute to the information gathering and decision-making processes.

SUMMARY

The problem about the organisation of a business is the conflict between the need for change and the need for stability. The design of the organisation should reflect its needs to reach objectives as effectively and efficiently as possible. On the other hand, there is a human need for knowing 'where you are' within an organisation. Management is often reluctant to make significant organisational changes too quickly due to feelings of insecurity within the department and possible work incompetence. The design of the organisation, and any subsequent changes to this design, require the most careful planning and involvement of all concerned if business objectives are to be achieved.

SELECTED READING

Buckley, Martin. 1994. *The Structure of Business.* Pitman.
Maitland, Ian. 1993. *The Business Organisation.* Blackwells.
Whitehead, Geoffrey. 1989. *Organisation and Administration for Business.* Hutchinson.
Clark, Peter & Stainton, Neil. 1993. *Innovation in Technology and Organisation.* Routledge.

Part 4

Managing People and Production

<table>
<tr><td>9</td></tr>
</table>

Human Resources Management

A firm's human resources are all of its employees. Human resource management (HRM) was once called personnel management. The newer term reflects the most recent attitudes toward employees as resources, not just personnel.

Human resource management involves every aspect of dealing with employees as a resource: planning, staffing (recruiting and hiring), training and development, performance appraisal and compensation.

Planning

Just as a business must plan for its financial and equipment needs, it must also plan for its personnel needs, a process often called *manpower planning*. The first step of HRM planning is to forecast future human resource demand; the second step is to forecast future human resource supply. Together, forecasts of supply and demand inform management of potential problems and therefore allow management to prepare for, and possibly avoid, future shortages in the labour supply.

Forecasting Human Resources Demand

A company will forecast its human resource demand based on its strategic plans for new business ventures, new products, expansion or contraction of existing product lines, and economic trends. To forecast demand accurately requires information on job analysis, job description and job specifications.

A job analysis is a detailed study of the tasks to be performed, and the skills required by the individual to accomplish the work. The job description and job specification are developed from this analysis.

Job description details all key tasks and responsibilities of each position, as well as the relationship of one job to another.

Job specifications address the knowledge, skills, education and experience required to perform a job. With this information, HRM can forecast how many people will be needed for what jobs and what the qualifications are for each position.

Forecasting Human Resources Supply

A company will forecast human resource supply by considering: (i) its present work force and (ii) any future changes or expected movement that may occur within its work force. Many firms conduct a human resource audit on a regular basis and use the information gathered to establish a human resource information system, which is essentially an inventory of people, their skills, education and training. The supply forecast begins with this inventory of present number of employees and their skills. Then it takes into account normal attrition, that is, all the usual reasons why employees leave (e.g., to take another job, to relocate to other areas, to retire). Finally, the company determines whether it will need additional or fewer employees in the future.

If the company's strategic planning calls for downsizing (a future decrease in the number of employees), the smaller future supply after attrition may be sufficient, depending on the skills of the remaining staff. If the strategic plan estimates organisational growth, new people will have to be found and hired to staff the new positions, and to replace those lost through normal attrition.

Matching Supply and Demand of Human Resources

Once forecasts for both supply and demand have been completed, HRM planners can establish a course of action to match supply and demand. They consider not only the number of people but the skills needed.

If the forecast shows that the demand will be greater than the supply, the HRM managers will develop a plan for recruiting and selecting new employees. Timing is important: it is not efficient to hire workers before they are needed.

If the forecast shows that the supply will be greater than the demand, HRM managers will develop a plan to reduce the work force. The most humane course is to allow a reduction through normal attrition, but attrition is a slow process. The company will not replace employees who leave, allowing the work force to eventually shrink to the point where supply equals demand. To hasten the process, a firm may offer early retirement to workers near retirement age, giving them additional benefits in return for leaving. Together, these methods may bring supply and demand into alignment; when they do not, the company will release surplus workers (i.e., make them redundant).

Staffing the Company

Staffing involves all aspects of supplying the organisation with the human resources it needs. Staffing, therefore, involves three activities: recruiting, selection and acquisition, and orientation.

Recruiting

Recruiting is the process of finding and attracting sufficiently qualified job applicants for the available jobs. Failure to attract sufficient applicants limits the choice. On the other hand, attracting too many applicants makes the evaluation process cumbersome and difficult.

Many firms adopt the policy of promoting from within the company, a basic internal recruiting strategy. The purpose of this policy is to motivate employees and retain quality personnel.

External recruiting attempts to find and attract qualified applicants from outside the company, for example, through newspaper advertisements, employment agencies or on college campuses. Although it is more expensive, external recruiting, by definition, brings to the company people with new opinions, ideas, perspectives and skills.

Selection

Selection is the process of gathering information about applicants, and using that information to choose the most appropriate applicant. The object of selection is also to eliminate inappropriate candidates.

The proper applicant is the one whose qualifications are most appropriate for the job, not necessarily the applicant with the most qualifications. The information is drawn from application forms, CVs, references, interviews and company-administered skill and aptitude tests (nondiscriminatory tests that are valid predictors of performances).

The principle of job-relatedness states that all human resource decisions, policies and programmes should be based on job requirements. Indeed, the objectives of HRM selection policies are always to match applicants' qualifications with job requirements and to develop employees' skills to meet those requirements. For example, an airline's decision to hire only female flight attendants violates the principle of job-relatedness because being female is not essential to performing that work. On the other hand, a clothing designer's policy to hire only women to model dresses is in keeping with the principle of job-relatedness.

Contract of Employment

Not later than 13 weeks after the beginning of an employee's period of employment with an organisation, the employer must give the employee a written statement containing details of the job. This must include job title, benefits, pay scale, working hours, pension scheme, methods of ending contract of employment, and disciplinary and appeal procedures. In addition to these written-down terms, there are also implied terms, especially with regard to the employee's duty of care to employer, other employees and support for management. The Employment Protection Act, 1978, covers the rights of employees.

Hiring and Induction

Hiring is the process that takes place after a selection has been made and the job has been offered and accepted. Induction is the process of acquainting new employees with the company's policies and procedures and with the personnel with whom the new employees will be working.

Training and Development

HRM's responsibility does not end with hiring new personnel and providing them with an orientation. HRM is also responsible for training and development, providing employees with the skills they need to perform effectively on the job and to grow.

Training Programmes

There are many ways in which employees can develop their skill(s). These include seminars and workshops of all kinds, available for example, from the company's training department, taken at a local college or sponsored by a major supplier. Programmes may be designed for new employees, for managers only, for sales people and so on. They may be aimed at developing specific skills, at correcting problems, at expanding broad business knowledge or at offering opportunities for promotion.

Training may be offered on or off the job. As the name suggests, on the job training is offered at work. The trainee learns by working under a supervisor or the supervisor of an experienced employee. Off the job training may take place in a classroom, at the work location or at some location away from the work site.

Management Development

Management development is a specialised form of training, designed to improve the skills and talents of present managers or to prepare potential managers. Management development programmes build conceptual, analytical and problem-solving skills, rather than the technical skills of training programmes. Some programmes are offered by in-house personnel, by other managers or by training specialists. Such programmes are tailored to the needs of that particular organisation. Other programmes are conducted at management training centres, university campuses, hotels, conference centres, suppliers' offices, trade associations and other locations.

Evaluating the Effectiveness of Training and Development

Training and management development programmes are expensive. In order to be cost effective, they must improve the performance of the company. The most common test of effectiveness is to measure how well people perform both before and after training. For example, if the goal of a safety training programme is to decrease the number of accidents in a factory, then the number of accidents per day, week or month would be measured and compared both before and after employees completed the safety training programme.

Performance Appraisal

Performance appraisal is a formal programme comparing employees' actual performance with expected performance. Performance appraisal is an effort to see how well employees are doing their jobs, and to evaluate their contribution to the organisation. It is used in making decisions about the training, promotion, compensation and termination of employees.

Ideally, this annual process begins with both the supervisor and the employee establishing and agreeing to clear, reasonable, measurable goals for the year to come. Then, during the year, the supervisor and the employee meet to discuss the progress made towards achieving each goal and any reason why the goals should be changed (e.g., a change in priorities set by the company or by the supervisor).

A less objective method is to judge or rate the employee. Using a scale, the supervisor rates the employee on qualities such as safety habits, output, initiative and punctuality.

Whatever appraisal method is used, the supervisor, should always discuss the results with the employee, explaining the basis of the evaluation, praising or rewarding good evaluations, and specifying how the employee can improve. During the discussion, the supervisor must be sure to offer the employee the opportunity for any rebuttal. Well-defined and well-implemented appraisal procedures can improve productivity, employee morale and protect a company from lawsuits alleging discrimination or unfair treatment.

Separation

Separation describes both voluntary and involuntary departure of a person from an organisation. There are various types of separations or conditions under which employees leave an organisation.

Resignation

Resignation is voluntary. An employee resigns to take a position with another company, to relocate to another part of the country, or to pursue another career interest. For management, resignations are generally the easiest type of separation to oversee.

Retirement

Retirement, either voluntary or mandatory, can be planned for in advance since age establishes the date of retirement. An employee may elect voluntary retirement after a certain number of years of service or attaining a specified age. Early retirement is sometimes offered to employees as a method of reducing the work force. Some companies establish an age threshold at which retirement is required.

Layoff

A layoff is a temporary involuntary separation made with the expectation of recall at a later date.

Redundancy

Redundancy is a permanent separation that results from a company reorganisation which reduces the number of positions, or from a retrenchment in the work force on account of poor business. Payments (redundancy payments) are due to the ex-employee according to the rules set out in the Contract of Employment (see above).

Termination

Terminating or firing an employee is a permanent, involuntary separation. The reasons for dismissal must be business-related and should be documented. Managers should keep careful records of past performance reviews, formal warnings to the employee, breaches of work rules or policy and poor performance. Clear procedures must be followed before an employee is dismissed. These procedures would have been stated in the Contract of Employment (see above). Failure to follow these procedures may result in the ex-employee obtaining a judgement of 'unfair dismissal' against the employer. Although it is unlikely that the dismissed employee will be reinstated, substantial damages can be awarded.

Compensation

Compensation is the monetary payment employees receive in return for their labour. It is not to be confused with compensation for being dismissed or made redundant!

Forms of Compensation

Workers are compensated in various ways:

- **Wages**: compensation based on the number of hours worked or units produced.
- **Salary:** the compensation paid in return for doing a job, regardless of time worked or output.

- **Commissions:** payments based on a percentage of sales revenues.
- **Bonuses:** extra rewards; compensation in addition to wages, salary or commissions. Bonuses may be distributed to all employees or only to those who are eligible for special rewards for having exceeded specific goals.
- **Profit sharing:** the distribution of a percentage of a firm's profits among its employees.

Measuring Wages

Labour is a major cost of business. An effective compensation system, therefore, is important not only to control costs but to attract and retain employees. Most firms establish careful policies and strategies for establishing compensation levels.

Wage level compares the wages paid in one firm to the level paid by comparable firms. Most firms attempt to set levels at, or near, the average of prevailing wage rates within an industry or geographic area, or both.

Wage Structure refers to the relative pay level for all the positions within a firm. Businesspeople agree that the office manager should earn more than the caretaker, but how much more? Job evaluations help determine the relative worth of each job within a company.

Individual wages must be determined within the wage structure for a particular firm. Each position usually has a range of compensation. For example, for secretaries, the hourly rate may range from £2.50 to £12.00 in one company, depending on skill, experience, seniority and performance.

The Equal Pay Act of 1970 requires that workers doing the same job should receive the same pay. *Comparable worth* specifically addresses the disparity between men's and women's earnings. Comparable worth seeks equal pay for jobs requiring about the same level of education, training and skills as well as for jobs that are of equal value to the company.

As more and more women enter the work force, comparable worth becomes more and more of an issue. The Sex Discrimination Act of 1975 (updated in 1986 to include manufacturing industries) together with the Equal Pay Act (amended in 1984 to allow for a more scientific rather than emotional measurement of work undertaken by both sexes) has gone a long way to eliminating lower pay for females in many industries.

Employee Benefits

Employee benefits, though nonmonetary, are still a form of compensation. In fact, benefits may account for as much as one-third to one-half of a company's compensation budget. Benefits are given in addition to wages or salary. Some benefits, for example, workers' compensation, unemployment insurance and Social Security are mandated by law. Vacation time, sick leave and holidays are also employer-paid benefits.

Health, dental or life insurance and pension plans may be funded by the employer fully, or the cost may be partially paid by the employee. Some companies also offer private use of company cars, free creche facilities, recreational facilities or subsidised lunchrooms. As the range of benefits has grown, so have benefit costs and concern over those costs.

One new approach offered in the US, is the cafeteria approach. Under this plan, the employee is allocated a certain lump sum for benefits; the employee is then free to choose how that sum will be allocated by selecting the benefits he or she wants from a 'cafeteria' selection. This approach is designed to increase employee satisfaction and motivation as well as limit costs.

The Impact of Government Legislation on HRM

Government legislation has had a very significant impact on HRM practices in the UK, and continuing EC legislation will soon add more changes although the UK government has so far refused to accept some major issues such as the Social Chapter.

In addition to the Equal Pay and Sex Discrimination Acts noted above, the UK government has also introduced a Race Relations Act (1976) which makes it unlawful to discriminate against anyone by treating them less fairly on racial grounds. A Code of Practice has been produced by the Commission for Racial Equality.

SUMMARY

People are the most important resource in a successful business. Human resource management plays a vital role in an organisation's success. How managers recruit and select applicants, and how they train and develop employees determines the managerial talent at all levels of the organisation.

SELECTED READING

Handy, Charles. 1995. *Gods of Management: Changing Work and Organisation.* Arrow.
Brewster, Chris & Hagewisch, Ariane. 1994. *Policy and Practice in European Human Resource Management.* Routledge.
Slade, Elizabeth. 1995. *Tolley's Employment Handbook.* Tolley.
Honeyball, Simon. 1988. *A Guide to the Employment Act.* Butterworth.

Labour-Management Relations

Labour-Management relations (*industrial relations*) are concerned with the maintenance and improvement of communications between employer and employees. From the employer's viewpoint, industrial relations is about the right to manage as is deemed fit. From the employee's viewpoint, industrial relations is about securing the best possible living standards. Good industrial relations strikes the best balance between these often conflicting objectives.

Trade Unions

In the UK, a trade union is defined by the Trades Union and Labour Relations Act, 1974, as an organisation whose principal purpose is the regulation of relations between members and their employers. Members pay a subscription to fund the activities of the union which employs a number of full-time officials. In order to be fully recognised, unions must have no other income than that which it obtains from its members. In order to continue a full range of services to its members, many unions have merged with others in similar areas in order to be more efficient. Unions have to submit accounts to an independent body each year in order to maintain their independent status. There are basically four different types of unions in the UK:

- **Craft Unions:** these are restricted to those who hold the necessary craft qualifications for membership. These qualifications could be obtained by apprenticeship or other recognised training programmes. The Amalgamated Engineering Union is a craft union, with over 750,000 members, who work in a large variety of industries.
- **General Unions:** these require no formal qualifications for membership. Members may be skilled or unskilled. The Transport and General Workers Union is the largest union in the UK with over one million members.
- **Industrial Unions:** these restrict membership to those working in a specific industry, such as coal mining. Members may come from a range of operational levels, from unskilled workers through to managers. Some are more 'white collar' than others. For example, the CPSA (Civil and Public Service Association) represents employees in the public sector.

● **Staff unions:** these have members who are 'white collar' workers. Typical examples are teachers and nurses.

Current Role of Unions

Between 1970 and 1990 there has been a marked change in union activity in the UK reflecting the changing employment environment. This new environment is due to new types of jobs and working practices, the growing number of women in work, the growth in part-time employment, the growth of the service sector with the corresponding decline in the manufacturing sector, and the growing affluence of employees generally.

Trade Union Recognition

There is no law which states that a union has to be recognised by an employer to represent the rights of all or certain employees. Such recognition is voluntary, but is usually done by employers who wish to have a good industrial relations environment. The trade union can only act within the limits agreed by the employer and union members.

The Role of Shop Stewards

Shop stewards are elected by members of a union, whereby one of their number represents their interests to the employer and communicates with full-time officials of the union. Shop stewards report back to members on the progress in disputes; they also recruit new members and collect union fees.

Government and Industrial Relations

Changes in union activity in the UK have also been accelerated by a Conservative government which has strongly opposed militant union activity by introducing a number of employment acts. These acts have imposed rules on employers, unions and their methods of negotiation.

Employment Act, 1980

In the Employment Act of 1980 secondary picketing (picketing by union members not in dispute with their employer) is not allowed. Closed shop practices are also banned unless supported by 80 per cent of the workforce.

Employment Act, 1982

This Act enabled trade unions to be fined if they acted illegally. It also stopped union-only labour contracts or closed shop agreements.

Employment Act, 1988

This Act strengthened the rights of union members who disagreed with union actions. Secret ballots are needed to elect union officers and to instigate strike action.

Employment Act, 1990

This Act made unions responsible for unofficial action taken by their members. In addition, individuals could not be refused a job if they were not already members of a trade union.

Trade Union Act, 1984

This Act strengthened union democracy by insisting that all recognised unions have a secret ballot every ten years if they held funds to support political activity, and every five years to re-elect full-time executives.

Union and Management Negotiations

The methods and procedures used by unions and management to negotiate contracts are many. Once a union is recognised, a negotiating committee will be appointed to begin collective bargaining.

Collective Bargaining

Collective bargaining is the process of negotiating a contract between labour and management. The union is represented by the negotiating committee, which includes a representative from the national union office. The management team is made up of people from the company's industrial relations, personnel and legal departments.

The union usually presents its demands first, and then management answers with a counter proposal. After a number of 'give and take' meetings, a first contract is developed. If both sides cannot reach an agreement, the union may bring one of its 'weapons' into play. On the other hand, agreement may be close and both sides refer to their respective backers, the union membership and the employers, for ratification of the agreement. If this happens, a formal contract is drawn up and signed.

Contract Issues

Many different issues are negotiated by labour and management, thus becoming part of the labour contract. These issues will vary from company to company, or from time to time, but certain issues are almost always present – money, working hours and job security.

Forms of Union Action

There are several 'weapons' that unions can use as part of their bargaining force. The most extreme weapon unions have in their arsenal is the *strike*. A strike combines a withdrawal of labour and the picketing of the employer's premises. Primary picketing is legal and is carried out to achieve three objectives:

1 The employer is faced with operating a factory or other workplace with little or no output while still having to pay a significant amount of fixed costs (such as rent) whether the factory is producing or not.
2 The pickets try to draw media attention to their activity and raise support from the public at large.
3 The pickets want to prevent, by peaceful and non-aggressive argument, the entry of suppliers' vehicles and also any other non-striking or substitute labour from gaining entrance to the workplace.

Another union 'weapon' is the *slowdown*. During a slowdown, workers deliberately take time over their work, thus increasing the costs of production per unit of output produced.

Work to rule is another 'weapon' used by unions. Workers stick rigidly to the rule book relating to their particular job, when common practice has allowed a safe alternative. For example, railway systems have very detailed rules which, if carried out to the letter, would involve extremely high costs and much loss of time. Common practice may allow short cuts which are seen to be as effective and not reduce safety levels.

In some industries, it is common to work overtime as a normal activity, whereas the contract of employment does not contain required overtime working. A *ban on overtime* can significantly reduce the working capacity of an organisation, and more staff would need to be employed at a higher cost than the overtime premium payments.

Another union 'weapon' is the *withdrawal of goodwill*. Employees stop acting in cooperation with management – for example, in participating with the security rules of the business.

Although not often officially supported by the union, labour can stop work (unofficial strike), occupy a factory by a 'sit in', and 'black' or boycott goods from certain suppliers.

Management 'Weapons'

Management also has 'weapons' that can be used. These can take the form of substitute labour, locking out all employees, maintaining ultra-strict discipline according to the rules, demotions, mass suspensions and the removal of equipment.

Mediation and Arbitration

Management and labour will use those 'weapons' in an industrial dispute which they feel will best promote their cause and achieve their objectives. In most disputes a compromise agreement is often obtained and both parties are to some extent satisfied that they have reached a satisfactory agreement. However, in many large disputes, the entrenched positions are difficult to eliminate and the services of a mediator and/or arbitrator is required. A *mediator* acts as a communicator between parties, whereas an *arbitrator* determines the compromise solution to the problem which is binding on both parties. Arbitrators can only function if both parties agree to accept the consequent solution. In 1974, the UK government set up an independent body, ACAS, to improve industrial relations

The Advisory, Conciliation and Arbitration Service (ACAS)

ACAS was set up in 1974 as an independent service funded by the government. ACAS is managed by a council of nine members: three from the Confederation of British Industries (CBI) representing the employers; three from the Trades Union Council, representing labour; and three independent members.

ACAS only gets involved in an industrial dispute if invited by both parties. ACAS is sometimes asked to come up with a solution binding on both parties (the arbitration role), whilst at other times it is asked to help with communication problems which might exist (the conciliation role).

Although ACAS gets most of its publicity from 'firefighting' major industrial disputes, a greater part of its role is in individual grievances and also advisory work with unions and employers groups. The latter often involves surveys, projects and working parties on subjects such as pay schemes and training.

SUMMARY

Businesses can only be operated efficiently with the full cooperation of owners, managers and operations. Every employee is a stakeholder in the business and by implication an essential member of a team. Poor management leads to aggressive unionisation of the workforce and no winners. The biggest managament problem in the 1990s is change and its implications regarding skills needed and number of operators. Changes in workforce must be forecast and planned, and involve all stakeholders and their representative bodies. Failure to inform those concerned will lead to discontent and the rise of defensive and expensive solutions. Managers of business must be skilled in negotiations and accepted procedures.

SELECTED READING

Drake, Charles. 1985. *The Trade Union Acts – with Commentary.* Sweet & Maxwell.
Blyton, Peter & Turnbull, Peter. 1994. *Dynamics of Employee Relations.* Macmillan.
Ewing, Keith. 1991. *The Right to Strike.* Clarendon Press.
Fowler, Alan. 1990. *Negotiation: Skills and Strategies.* Institute of Personnel Management.

11 Producing Goods and Services

An Overview of the Production of Goods and Services

When one party gives something of value to another in return for a product or a service, an exchange takes place. Millions of such exchanges occur everyday whenever customers pay money ('something of value') for goods such as clothing, milk and tyres, and whenever they pay money for services (e.g., accounting, medical or legal services).

In all cases, the exchange should satisfy both the buyer and the seller, and this satisfaction is measured in terms of *utility*, the power of that product or service to satisfy a human need. In this sense, the customer does not purchase a product or a service but a utility.

There are four types of utility: utility of form, utility of place, utility of time and utility of possession. Production creates utility of form by processing inputs into finished products, whether those finished products are tangible goods, intangible goods or services. Thus, utility of form will be addressed in this chapter on the production of goods and services. The other kinds of utility are created by marketing and will be examined in Chapter 12.

Producing Goods

Producing goods depends on production and operations management (POM) which is the systematic direction and control of the process that brings together the resources of raw materials, equipment and labour, and transforms those resources into finished goods. Production is the transformation process, and operations are the systems used to create goods in the production process.

Production Processes

Production processes can be classified in three ways: transformation, analytic versus synthetic, and product flow.

Transformation

There are three processes that manufacturers use to transform raw materials into finished goods.

- **Chemical transformation:** this alters raw materials chemically. For example, petroleum is a raw material that can be transformed into plastics, gasoline and other products.
- **Fabrication:** this mechanically alters the form and/or shape of the raw materials. Steel wire, for example, is transformed into nails or staples. Lumber can be turned on a lathe and transformed into chair arms or stool legs.
- **Assembly:** this involves putting together components into either a final product or a component product, that is, a product that will become part of a more complex product. For example, fabricated lumber, arms and other parts are assembled into chairs. Electronic components are assembled along with other parts into computers.

Analytic versus Synthetic

A second way to classify production processes is by the method in which resources are used to transform materials into finished goods.

- **Analytic processes:** these break down basic resources into components. For instance, a flour mill breaks down a raw material, wheat, into a new product, flour.
- **Synthetic processes:** these combine a number of raw materials to produce a finished product. A bakery, for instance, transforms flour, eggs, shortening and sugar into a cake.

Product flow

The third classification is based on how the plant, or production facility, is arranged, and how the product moves through that plant.

- **Continuous process:** this describes any method where the flow of transformation from resources to finished product is smooth, straight, uninterrupted and features long production runs. A manufacturer of chocolate bars uses the same process continuously to produce a steady product of consistent form, flavour and quality.
- **Intermittent or batch process:** the flow in a batch process is best described as 'stop and go', with short production runs. A printing plant, for instance, shuts down presses between product runs as it sets up the paper and inks needed for the next job. While the manufacturing process (in this example, the printing process) is the same - the finished product differs from print run to print run.

Types of Production

By following a series of steps or processes, production transforms resources into a form people need or want. Just as there are several types of production processes, there are several types of production.

Production Line and Assembly Line

In a *production line*, material is moved past teams or individual workers. Each worker or group of workers performs one specific step in the progression. If only assembly operations are performed, the line is known as an *assembly line*. For example, brake pads may be produced from raw materials on a production line. But in a car manufacturing plant, the finished brake pads are just one of the components on an assembly line that turns out finished cars.

Automation

Mechanisation, the substitution of machines for human labour, led to *automation*. In automated production, mechanical operations are performed with little or no human involvement. Automation was born during the Industrial Revolution, when machine-spinning replaced hand-spinning of textiles.

Although it has a high initial cost, automation reduces the cost of producing each unit (unit cost) and ensures uniform high quality. A bakery may automate the measuring and mixing of ingredients along with baking, for example.

Robotic and Computerised Production

Robots are machines that perform some of the mechanical functions of humans. *Robotics*, the use of robots in production processes, substitutes mechanical energy for human energy and is now common in many manufacturing processes. Robots perform a single task, such as welding with great accuracy, and without the boredom or fatigue that human workers feel. Robots that can be adapted or directed by computers to perform several tasks are called *flexible robots*.

Computer-Aided Design (CAD)

Computer-aided design allows a designer to rely on the powers of computer technology to produce technical drawings, sketches and various other kinds of product specifications. Aided by CAD, the designer can even check for design or engineering weaknesses.

Computer-Aided Manufacturing (CAM)

Computer-aided manufacturing uses the computer to analyse product design. The computer helps determine the steps necessary for producing the product, as well as preparing and controlling the equipment used in making it.

Productivity

Productivity is the measure of the relationship between (i) the total amount of goods and services being produced and (ii) the resources needed to produce them. The inputs, the equipment, the materials, the planning and the cost of labour all contribute to productivity as reflected in the value of the end product.

The major benefit of automation and mechanisation has been increased productivity. However, where the higher cost of labour puts domestic products at a disadvantage in world markets, companies must be more technically innovative in order to compete better.

Operations

Operations refer to the systems used to create goods: site selection, plant layout, purchasing, routing, scheduling, quality, inventory and others all discussed below.

Production Facility Planning

Once a decision to produce is made, management must decide where and how the production is to be carried out. Management must also decide where to locate the production facility and what the specific layout of the facility should be.

Site selection is the process of determining where the production facility is to be located. Some of the factors to be considered are location of the market; availability of suppliers, utilities and labour; cost of land and development; government grants; local business rates; and transportation. The site-selection process weighs up the advantages and disadvantages of various sites.

Layout is the overall arrangement at the facility, the order in which machines, equipment, work stations, aisles, storage areas and supply areas are arranged. The major patterns are:

- **Process layout:** this groups similar types of equipment or materials used in the process. A metal fabricating plant will generally group its presses, lathes and welding equipment in separate locations.
- **Product layout:** this follows an arrangement based on the successive production steps, from beginning to end, for a particular product. The car assembly line is a typical example of product layout.
- **Fixed-position layout:** this places the product in a fixed or stationary position in the plant; workers and equipment are brought to the product as work progresses. The fixed-position layout is common in the aircraft and construction industry because of the large size of the product.

Operations Planning and Scheduling

The better a system is designed, the easier it will be to operate. However, no system runs by itself.

A production system (operation) that always turns out the same product at the same rate needs little ongoing planning and scheduling operations. A system that turns out a variety of products at different rates requires more ongoing planning and scheduling operations.

The function of operations planning is to determine the types and amounts of resources needed to produce specified goods, and to plan for the purchasing, routing, scheduling and dispatching of these resources. Resources include people, money, material and equipment.

Purchasing

Purchasing involves decisions concerning not only how much raw material or components to buy but also where, when and at what price. Suppliers must be considered on the basis of price, quality, reliability and delivery. The quantity ordered depends on the rate the material is used, when it will be needed and the time needed to deliver it to the production facility once the order is placed.

Routing

Routing determines the sequence in which all phases of production must be completed to produce the goods and, therefore, the path the materials must take through the plant. A plant producing frozen peas must take peas in, remove them from the pods, cook them, divide them into portions and then freeze them.

Scheduling

Scheduling refers to the process of determining when an activity will take place and how long it will take to complete. Two commonly used scheduling techniques employ Gantt charts and program evaluation and review technique (PERT) charts.

Named for Henry Gantt, who developed the technique in the early 1900s, the *Gantt chart* is a graphic scheduling device in bar-graph format. A Gantt chart shows progress graphically, indicating what has been done, what is to be accomplished and whether the time schedule is being met. Gantt charts can be used both as a planning and as a control tool. They are useful for repetitive projects or products that are made up of relatively few activities.

	Dept.	Week 1	Week 2	Week 3	Week 4
Cut Tops	1		▨		
Cut & Shape Legs	2	▨			
Build Drawers	3	▨	▨		
Assemble	4		▨	▨	
Paint	5				▨

Figure 11.1 Gantt Chart for Company Manufacturing Desk
Since drawer construction is the longest process it must start earliest. Cutting and shaping the legs can begin half a week later followed by cutting tops, so that assembly can begin the middle of the second week as a supply of all needed parts becomes available. Painting will not begin until assembly is completed.

PERT charts is another commonly used technique to aid scheduling. Suppose two activities B and C can be undertaken simultaneously. Activity B requires three days to complete and activity C requires four days to complete. Both must be completed before production can move to activity D. If activity B is delayed, there is one day slack time available before activity C is completed. If, however, activity C is delayed, then the completion schedule is jeopardised. Keeping activity C on schedule is critical to maintaining the overall production schedule. The path of activities, whose schedules must be maintained to avoid such delays, is called the *critical path*. The planning method designed around these activities is the critical path method (CPM) and is a commonly used technique for scheduling complicated production processes.

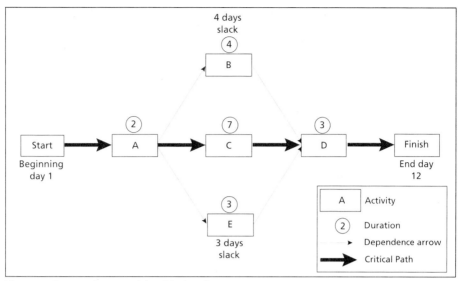

Figure 11.2 Pert Diagram with Critical Path

Dispatching

Dispatching – the issuing of detailed work orders – is based on the planning, scheduling and routing decisions made to complete the production of goods. Dispatching takes the plans that have been made and makes them operational.

Materials - Requirements Planning (MRP)

Materials-requirements planning is a computer-based system that ensures the availability of needed parts and materials at the right time, at the right place. By comparing customer orders, product specifications and inventory of raw materials and parts, MRP can help determine what should be ordered, when it should be ordered, and which deliveries should be accelerated or delayed. MRP's major benefit is that it avoids downtime – time when production is suspended because parts or materials are not available.

Controlling

Controlling, as indicated in Chapter 7, is closely related to planning. The control function enables production and operations managers to ensure that production proceeds as planned. Two key control areas in production and operations management are quality and inventory.

Quality Control

Quality control is the process of ensuring that final quality meets the planned requirements.

The *control function* must allow for adjustments and corrections, at the right time. If, for instance, quality-control inspectors are placed at the end of the assembly line, all they can do is weed out products that fail to meet quality standards; they cannot adjust or correct problems. On the other hand, when purchasing departments ensure that parts purchased from suppliers are indeed high-quality parts, they have contributed strongly to quality control early in the process. The failure of many firms to compete in world markets has been blamed in part on inferior quality, including poor delivery. Inferior quality in turn can then be blamed in part on ineffective quality control.

Statistical quality control is of two types: process quality and acceptance quality – both of which are based on probability sampling . A relatively small process sample is taken to minimise the risk that an ongoing good process has not deteriorated into a poor process. An acceptance sample is taken to minimise the risk that a quantity delivered or produced (a batch) does not contain more than an agreed percentage of defectives.

Developed in Japan, *quality circles* are small groups of workers who meet regularly to discuss and help solve problems related to quality. The group, usually fewer than 20 employees from the same work site or task area, focus on operational problems. The problems addressed can either be assigned by management or generated by the group. Solutions are presented to management, which in turn analyses and accepts, rejects or modifies the recommendations. Different names for quality circles exist such as Error Cause Removal Teams or Quality Improvement Teams.

Inventory or Stock Control

Inventories tie up cash, and high inventories tie up a great deal of cash. Keeping inventories of inputs at the lowest levels necessary to meet customer demand reduces the amount of money invested in inventory, and frees that cash for other uses. At the same time, it reduces inventory-related costs, such as inventory handling and storage. Materials-requirements planning (MRP), described earlier, is one way managers control inventory.

Another method is *Just in Time* (JIT). This reduces inventories to a minimum by arranging for materials to be delivered to the production facility 'just in time' to be used in the manufacturing of a product. This method requires precise and complex coordination using MRP. JIT inventory control is widely used throughout the car industry and is being adopted in other industries.

In order to compete successfully in world markets in the future, businesses must increase productivity, the measure of efficiency that compares how much is produced with the resources used to produce it. In the battle to achieve lower production costs and higher productivity and quality, management is turning to more sophisticated methods of planning and control, as well as to greater use of mechanisation, automation and computerisation.

Producing Services

The service segment of the UK economy has always been important. It has been growing in recent years and currently accounts for nearly half of the UK's GNP. In many ways, the production of services and the production of goods are similar, but they differ in a number of important ways.

First of all, goods are produced, services are performed. Furthermore, all services are intangible. Inputs for services are not materials but people with needs or with possessions that need care. Outputs are not finished products but people whose needs have been met or whose possessions have been cared for. These differences, and others, will become clear in the following discussion.

For goods, the focus of the production process is on the goods produced. For services, the goal of the production process is to create services rather than goods, and the focus of the production process is on the transformation process and the outcome.

Service Production Processes

Production and operations management (POM) for services is concerned with the same categories as for goods - namely, transformation, analytic versus synthetic and product flow - but the elements in each category vary.

Transformations are much more varied in producing services. Input for a service might be sick or injured people, the transformation process might be medical care; and the output, healthy people. Among the great variety of other services available are those provided by lawyers, consultants, entertainers and educators. Three transformation processes in producing services are:

● **Assembly:** the assembly process involves putting together various components in an effort to service people's needs. A supermarket assembles meat, vegetables and groceries to satisfy customers' need for food.
● **Transportation:** the transportation process includes moving goods (e.g., from the factory) and warehousing goods until sold. The transportation process includes other forms of shipping, as well as moving people by airline, bus or other means of transportation.
● **Clerical:** the clerical process transforms information. The clerical transformation of data makes up a large segment of the service economy, including all the many services performed in data-processing and word-processing functions.

While few services can be characterised as *analytic*, many employ the *synthetic* process. The synthetic process entails combining a number of raw materials to produce a service. For example, McDonald's combines rolls, meat, lettuce and sauce into a hamburger and thereby produces a service - feeding a hungry customer.

The *flow of services* tends to be intermittent rather than continuous. For example, a barber does not cut hair on a continuous basis. The service, a haircut, is delivered one at a time as customers arrive.

Types of Service Production

Service production tends to be labour intensive, requiring more labour than goods production. But service production is not so capital-intensive, requiring less capital expenditure for plant and equipment. Exceptions are hotels and airlines, for example, which do require considerable capital. Service production does not lend itself to assembly-line or production-line organisation:

- **Mechanisation:** the substitution of machines for human labour is also found in the production of services. A car wash, for example, replaces hand work in washing and waxing a car with a mechanised process.
- **Automation:** as we have already seen, mechanisation led to automation. For example, one-hour film developing services have automated most of the processes as a way of speeding up and standardising their service. Bank ATMs (automated teller machines) or 'cash machines' are also examples of the automation of services.
- **Computerisation:** computers contribute greatly to many of the transformation processes. Financial planners, brokers, catalogue stores and travel agents rely heavily on the use of computers. Interior decorators and contractors use computer-assisted design (CAD), and many beauty shops utilise computer imaging to show how a new hairstyle will look.

Characteristics of Services

Unlike goods, services such as legal services or car repairs are intangible. There are other differences found in the special aspect of services.

A service cannot be stored or inventoried. It cannot be produced in advance. If it is not used when available, it is wasted. An empty theatre seat or any empty airline seat is a sale lost forever. In other words, a service is perishable.

Many services are highly customised. There are differences not only between one service and another, but within a single kind of service. For example, a haircut is unique, it is different from all other haircuts.

Services cannot be separated from the provider. Services are produced and consumed at the same time. The customer of a service has the ability to affect the transformation process to a degree that customers of goods essentially cannot. A potential customer for a good can only choose not to purchase the good if it is not suitable, but a customer of a service can complain, make suggestions, requests or otherwise affect (or customise) the process. The degree of customer involvement depends upon whether the service is part of a high or low-contact service.

High-contact services include the customer as part of the service. The customer who purchases a manicure must go to the beauty shop to receive the service, and a passenger who purchases rail transportation must board the train. Both these examples illustrate high contact with the customer. High-contact services tend to reduce the extent to which a service can be standardised. Fast-food restaurants move toward greater efficiency through standardisation by offering only a limited menu. For low-contact services, such as television repair, the customer is not as closely involved with, or does not become part of, the service.

Planning Service Operations

The planning and scheduling of service operations present some of the same problems as planning for products, but offer several additional challenges unique to services.

Site location is a critical decision in any high-contact service. Because of the extra-close involvement with customers, the location must be convenient for the customers. In a low-contact service, proximity to suppliers or cost and availability of space may be more important than accessibility to, or the convenience of, the customer. In a high-contact service there is often a proximity of competitive services to assist potential customers. For example, estate agents in large towns are often sited close to each other.

For low-contact services, the *layout* of the facility should be designed to best accommodate the production of the service. The layout for high-contact services is designed around the customer's physical and psychological needs and expectations. Depending on the service involved, décor, waiting rooms, dressing rooms and washrooms are an important aspect of layout planning.

Scheduling Service Operations

Scheduling operations involve scheduling the workers, the work and in certain operations, the customer.

Scheduling High-Contact and Low-Contact Services

For high-contact services, the customer must be accommodated. A high contact customer expects service on the spot. In a low-contact service, such as watch repair or dry-cleaning, the customer expects the service to be completed by a certain time, but is not concerned with specifically when the service is actually performed. In both low and high-contact services, it is sometimes possible to employ part-time workers in periods of peak demand. As in producing goods, Gantt and PERT charts can help with scheduling services.

Queuing Theory

A queue is a waiting line. Queuing theory applies to organising and controlling waiting time in lines to lessen customer waiting time and balance personnel cost. For example, a bank could open ten counters and have a very short waiting line, perhaps none, but the cost would be very high. Queuing theory helps determine how many clerks are needed to keep the line at an acceptable reasonable length for customer satisfaction.

Appointment Scheduling

Appointment scheduling is an effective method in certain situations. In a doctor's surgery, for example, patients are often scheduled so as to allow minimum waiting time for the patients, and maximum flexibility for the doctor and staff. Without scheduling appointments, the waiting room might be full at one period and empty at another, leaving the staff waiting idly for patients at times and being over busy at others.

Fixed Scheduling

Airlines or buses prepare detailed advance, fixed schedules of their service so enabling customers to accommodate their needs according to the provider's schedule.

Routing

Routing is closely connected with layout. In producing goods, material is moved through the process. In producing services, the customer is often moved through the process. For example, customers are routed through a cafeteria line, or through the check-in baggage, seat assignment and boarding procedures on an airline. Routing in a cafeteria should ensure: that clean trays are available at the beginning of the line before the customer gets there; that food is available; and that the tables are cleared as soon as possible, ideally, so that customers find tables when they finish paying.

Controlling Services Production

Both the quality and the quantity must be closely controlled in the production of services. In addition, prompt service and delivery dates are important if customers are to be satisfied.

Quality control in service operations, especially in high-contact services, is strongly dependent on the quality of the people who come into contact with the customer. Good human relations skills and the ability to work with people are of prime importance. Managers must hire the right type of workers and then motivate them highly.

Because services are intangible and cannot be inventoried, *quantity control* is a function-controlling demand. For greatest efficiency and cost effectiveness, demand must be balanced with the people and the facilities available. Quantity control techniques include maintaining fixed schedules, as airlines do, using an appointment system and delaying delivery in the case of low-contact services. Another technique is to provide incentives for moving demand to off-peak periods – for example, by offering off-peak fares in transportation, special prices for delivering coal supplies during the summer and theatre seat discounts during weekdays.

SUMMARY

Goods and services can only be profitably supplied if they meet the agreed quality needs of the customer, and are produced as efficiently as the most efficient producer in the marketplace. The need for constant improvement requires business managers to constantly re-examine the methods of production, and to predict competitors' operations. Not only must the supply of products and services be planned, but they must be controlled to ensure conformance to the plan. Ideally, the total involvement of each employee in ensuring customer satisfaction is the goal of all business organisations.

SELECTED READING

Deming, Edwards. 1986. *Out of Crisis.* MIT.

Part 5

Marketing Management

---

12 | The Marketing Concept

An Overview of Marketing

Marketing is often defined as 'the process of planning and executing the conception, pricing, distribution, and promotion of ideas, goods and services to create exchanges that satisfy individual and organisational objectives'.

Product decisions include package design, branding and development of new products. Pricing deals with setting profitable and justified prices. Product and pricing are discussed in Chapter 13. Distribution, the physical distribution and selection of marketing channels, is discussed in Chapter 14. Promotion - personal selling, advertising and sales promotion – is discussed in Chapter 15.

The Concept of Utility

An exchange must have *utility*, the power of a good or service to satisfy a human need. In this sense, the customer does not purchase a product, but a utility.

Production gives form utility by converting inputs into finished products, forms the buyer wants to have. There are three kinds of utility created by marketing:

- **Place utility:** this satisfies a need by making a product available at a location or place where a customer wishes to purchase it. When a customer visits a shoe shop at a neighbourhood shopping area, she wants the shoes she travelled for available at that store, not at the store in the centre of town.
- **Time utility:** this satisfies a need by making the product available when the customer wants it. If a customer wants a special-order product within a certain

time, for example, in three weeks, the order needs to be available within three weeks not four.
- **Possession utility:** this satisfies a need by transferring the title or ownership of the product to the customer.

Marketing Functions

The marketing function involves exchange, physical distribution and facilitating. These are further broken down into eight major functions, all of which are essential if the marketing process is to be successful.

The Exchange Functions

The exchange functions are any transactions in which two or more parties trade or swap something of value.

- **Buying:** this involves understanding what and why customers buy.
- **Selling:** this is the transfer of title from seller to customer, and is the heart of marketing and creates possession utility.

Physical Distribution Functions

Physical distribution functions make it possible for the customer to buy the product and involve the flow of goods from producers to customers.

- **Transportation:** this is the movement of goods from the place of production to the place of purchase, and provides place utility.
- **Storage:** this supplies time utility by supplying a place to store goods until the final sale can be made, ensuring that the product is available when customers want it.

Facilitation Functions

Facilitation functions help, or facilitate, all the other functions.

- **Financing:** financing helps at all stages of marketing by advancing credit to wholesalers and retailers, and by supporting purchases by credit customers.
- **Standardising and grading:** Standardising and grading set uniform specifications for products or services, so that size and quality can be compared and facilitation of production, transportation, storage and sales can occur.
- **Risk-taking**: Risk-taking enters marketing in various ways. Risk situations include new-product introductions, potential losses from bad debts (accounts receivable), and obsolescence of product and theft.
- **Gathering market information:** gathering market information through market research is necessary for implementing all marketing decisions.

The Development of Marketing Orientation

From the Industrial Revolution to the early 1900s, business had a production orientation. Consumer demand grew at a rate that outpaced supply, enabling manufacturers to sell virtually all they could produce. Therefore, manufacturers' primary orientation was to improve the efficiency and capacity of production.

In the 1920s, supply began to overtake demand. Producers now found they had to sell goods to consumers whose basic demands were already satisfied. With production soundly in place, companies developed a sales orientation to ensure that their products were purchased over their competitors'. Business spent large amounts of money on advertising and sales.

By the 1950s, businesses began to realise that their sale depended on satisfying customers' wants. Advertising and sales efforts were not enough. Businesses developed a customer orientation or marketing orientation, focusing on customer needs and wants, and developing goods and services to meet them.

Markets and Market Segmentation

Few companies try to sell their products to everyone. Instead, companies pick out one or more groups within the overall population. Each group represents a market.

Markets

A market is a group of individuals, organisations, or both that have needs for a given product, and have the ability, willingness and authority to purchase that product. Markets can be described as *consumer* and *industrial*.

The *consumer market* consists of people who buy products for their personal use or consumption, and not to make a profit. Firms whose products are sold to the final user are engaged in consumer marketing.

The *industrial market* includes organisations that buy products for use in day-to-day operations or in the production of other products to sell for profit. Within the industrial market there are:

- **Producers market:** this market buys products specifically for manufacturing other products. For example, a pencil manufacturer buys wood for use in the production of pencils.
- **Governmental market:** this market, national and local governments, buys goods and services for internal operations or to provide citizens with road, water and other services. For example, a road department might buy reflective markers (cats'-eyes) for use on roads, or the national government might purchase parts for military aircraft.
- **Institutional market:** this market includes churches, schools, hospitals, clubs and other institutions. Customers in the institutional market have different needs, and selling to the institutional market requires a different approach. For example, selling books to a school is different from selling books to an individual consumer in a one-on-one transaction.

● **Reseller market:** this market consists of intermediaries, such as wholesalers and retailers, who buy finished products and sell them for profit.

Market Segmentation

Marketers further break down the overall market into target markets. A target market is any group of people who have similar wants and needs and may be expected to show interest in the same products. Categorising markets according to common customer traits is called *market segmentation*. By definition, the people in a market segment share common traits or behaviours that influence their buying decisions.

Industrial Segment

The segmentation of the industrial market is centred around the product; there is little likelihood that steel will be sold to a shoe manufacturer. Industrial markets are often concentrated geographically. For many industrial products or raw materials, the number of customers is limited.

It is also possible to target by industry. A bottle manufacturer can segment its market into drug manufacturing, food or cosmetics industries.

Consumer Segment

The consumer market can be segmented several ways:

● **Geographic areas:** where people live often affects buying decisions. Urban residents have less need for four-wheel drive vehicles than people in rural areas do. By using postal codes, business marketers can segment a specific neighbourhood with particular group characteristics such as income level.
● **Product use:** one way to segment a market is to examine product use, how consumers will use the product. A shoe manufacturer will view the markets for athletic, casual and dress shoes as separate markets. Truck dealers can segment the markets for pickup trucks, articulated vehicles or vans by the end use of the vehicles.
● **Psychographics:** information on motives, attitudes, activities, interests and opinions of consumers helps segment the market. Psychographics, which describes the researching and gathering of such information, informs marketers that, for example, members of environmental organisations may be more likely to purchase more hiking equipment than members of museum associations.

Products

Marketing views the wide range of products by dividing them into two broad groups: consumer products and industrial products.

Consumer Products

Consumer products are goods or services produced for sale to individuals and families for personal consumption. Consumer products are either convenience goods, shopping goods or speciality goods.

Convenience goods, products such as milk, chocolate, soap and newspapers, are purchased frequently and with little shopping effort. Convenience goods are available at many outlets. Buyers pick up these products at the nearest store, without wasting much energy and time shopping or comparing available brands. The seller's main marketing tool is location. Although the price may be higher at a convenience store than, say, at a grocery store, the unit price of convenience goods is generally low, as is the profit margin (the difference between the product's cost and its selling price). Stores use mass advertising rather than sales techniques to promote the fact that they carry convenience goods.

Shopping goods are products that consumers actively shop for, comparing prices, values, features, quality and styles, before finally making a purchase decision. Shopping goods include refrigerators, television sets, men's suits and bicycles as well as nonconvenience items such as groceries and meat. They are sold in different kinds of stores. They are often marketed both by national advertising, on the part of the manufacturer, and by local advertising, on the part of the retailer. In many cases, especially with appliances and clothing, the efforts of salespeople come into play. Profit margins tend to be moderate (except for groceries) in order to cover the costs of promotion and personal selling. Margins on groceries tend to be lower with high volumes making up for low margins.

Shoppers make extra efforts to find and purchase *specialty goods:* expensive items that are not purchased frequently, such as fine crystal, jewellery, cars and clothing with high brand recognition and loyalty. Specialty goods are stocked by few stores (or dealers, in the case of cars) and are promoted on the basis of quality, image or unique characteristics. Selling is on a personal level, and profit margins are high.

Industrial Products

Industrial products are sold to private business firms or public agencies for use in the production of their goods or services. Industrial products include iron ore and other raw materials, chemicals, tools, textiles and hardware. Advertising is generally limited to trade journals.

Industrial products are sold by sales representatives calling on the buyers personally. In industrial firms, purchases are frequently made by teams or committees.

The Marketing Concept

The marketing concept stresses the need for the entire organisation to achieve customer satisfaction while achieving the organisation's goals. All functional areas - product development, production, finance and marketing - have a role in achieving customer satisfaction. The marketing concept starts with market research.

Market Research

Market research is the systematic gathering, recording and analysing of data concerning a particular marketing problem.

Research helps to determine the needs of the ultimate user, how well these needs are being met by products on the market, and how products might be improved. After the problem is identified and the research planned, the factual information can be gathered in a variety of ways, including telephone and mail surveys, personal interviews and observation.

Marketers must interpret and analyse the factual information to determine the choices available and to establish a marketing strategy. The total marketing strategy must design and produce a product that will satisfy all customer needs. To achieve this goal, the marketing strategy must address four elements of the marketing concept, commonly call the *four Ps*: price, product, promotion and place.

The Marketing Mix

As already noted, a target market is any group of people who have similar wants and needs, and may be expected to show interest in the same products. In order to sell effectively a product to its target market, marketing must consider the four Ps discussed below.

Product

The product must satisfy the final user's needs. Satisfying consumers may require changing the product frequently (as in the fashion industry), improving existing products to meet competition, introducing completely new products or maintaining existing products that have strong consumer loyalty.

Price

The product must be priced at a level that will be acceptable to buyers and still yield an acceptable profit. A higher price may increase the unit profit but limit the number of sales. A lower price may raise sales volume. In some cases, a higher price may give shoppers the impression of higher quality and may, therefore, raise sales.

Place

The product must be placed (distributed) so that it is available where and when it is needed. Distribution also concerns choosing sales outlets and transporting the product from the producer to either the outlet or the customer. Convenience items require wide distribution. Specialty items have fewer, more carefully selected outlets. Mail-order items are sent directly from inventory to the consumer and require efficient means of distribution.

Promotion

The product must be promoted so that consumers will be aware that it is available to satisfy particular needs. Promotion includes advertising, personal selling, sales promotion, public relations and publicity. Car manufacturers rely on national press and television advertising to get customers into the showroom, after which personal selling makes the actual sale. Less expensive products often rely on packaging to accomplish the sale, or on sales promotions such as coupons, samples, trading stamps or rebates.

Public relations spreads goodwill about the company and its products or services, by sponsoring television programmes or sports events. Public relations also includes information provided to the public in a planned fashion. Publicity, which is free communication to the public, can help a firm's public relations programme if the publicity delivers a positive message. Bad publicity, on the other hand, can hurt a firm's image.

Evaluating the 'Mix'

Having set objectives and established a strategy to meet these objectives, the firm must again return to market research for feedback to evaluate the effectiveness of their efforts. Feedback is intended to provide answers to some of the following questions:

● Is the product addressing customer wants and needs?
● Is it priced competitively but profitably?
● How effective is the distribution?
● Is the promotion effective?

Based on the evaluation of feedback, management will modify any of the elements in the marketing mix to improve performance.

Consumer and Industrial Buying

Each consumer's buying decision is influenced by economic, demographic, psychological and social factors, and the marketing strategy must consider all those factors if it is to be effective.

Economic Factors

Purchasing power is created by income, but not all income is available for spending. There are national and local taxes which have to be paid. Part of the net balance is used to pay for necessities such as rent, food and clothing. The income remaining is 'discretionary' in that there is some choice in spending it on cars, holidays and education, for example. Knowing the level of discretionary income is particularly important to marketers. Allowance must also be made for the income available but not yet earned, and income available by using credit cards and bank loans.

Demographic Factors

Demographic information offers data such as age, income, gender, ethnic background, race, religion, marital status, social class, education and size of family. Using this information, marketers can target products or advertising to appeal to very specific groups of consumers. For instance, consumers in the 18 to 25-year-old range; married couples with a combined income of over £25,000; or pensioners with university degrees who live in the South-East of England. Demographic studies show which groups are growing, where there are large numbers of people whose primary language is other than English, along with other helpful information.

Psychological Factors

Psychological factors, such as attitude or personality enter into the customer's buying decision. A decision may be rational or emotional, or it may be a combination of both.

Rational motives are reasons for buying a product based on a logical evaluation of product attributes such as cost, quality and usefulness.

Emotional motives, the subjective reasons for purchasing a product or a particular kind of product, include imitation of others and aesthetics. Buying coffee ice cream because of its taste or a car because of its 'sporty' looks are emotional reasons for making purchases.

Social factors enter into a consumer's decision to buy, for example, a deodorant to suppress body odours. Actions by a consumer's social class, subculture or a fashion leader can serve as a motive for making a purchase decision.

Industrial buying is based on a more limited group of factors, such as cost, reliability, uniformity of product, delivery time and service. In that sense, industrial buying is more rational than consumer buying.

SUMMARY

Marketing is the means for finding out what the customer requires and ensuring that the customer constantly buys your product or service. A competitive environment ensures that no business, except the rare monopoly, can become complacent about its selling operations. International trading and the emergence of many more industrialised countries has put pressure on existing producers who respond by anticipating customer needs and establishing trust within existing supplier–customer relationships. Strong links between an existing supplier and customer can 'lock out' a new competitive supplier, sometimes making the 'cost of change' to a new supplier too expensive.

SELECTED READING

Anderson, Alan & Dobson, Thelma. 1994. *Effective Marketing*. Blackwell.

13 Products and Pricing Strategies

The Product

The last chapter introduced the marketing concept and addressed various aspects of marketing goods and services, that is, of marketing products. This chapter will focus more closely on products and on the pricing strategies used to market products effectively.

To begin with, what is a *product*? Products are goods or services that satisfy buyers' needs and demands. Products are, therefore, the focal point of business. Goods are tangible objects and devices (such as food, vacuum cleaners and toothpaste) and services are deeds, acts and performances (such as transporting materials, entertaining people and banking). A product can be stored, a service cannot.

Product Line

A group of products is known as a *product line*. Companies may start with a single product or just a few products, and then over a period of time, develop additional products to expand their product lines and increase their revenues and profitability. The new products may be very similar to the company's 'original' products. For example, General Motors offers a wide range of vehicles for different uses at differing prices, but all its products are vehicles and vehicle parts. On the other hand, the new products may be outside the company's original product line. For example, Proctor and Gamble expanded its original product line (soaps) to include a number of new product lines (including food, paper goods and baby products). To succeed in any industry, companies must be innovative and develop new products that meet consumers' needs, or at the very least, keep up with product advances in their industry.

Profit Differentiation

Product differentiation is the process of developing and promoting differences between one company's product and all the other similar products that are available. The object is to create a specific demand for the firm's product by developing a special product image. For example, Bernard Matthews has effectively differentiated between its turkeys and all other turkeys available in the marketplace, therefore creating consumer demand for its products over all others. Another example can be seen when companies try to develop 'designer' labels in an effort to promote product differentiation.

Product Mix

A company's product mix identifies all the products that the firm offers. The breadth of the mix is measured by the number of product lines it contains, and the depth of the mix is measured by the number of individual items in each product line.

Because customers' preferences and attitudes change, and because competitors develop and offer new products or change existing ones, a company's product mix does not usually remain unchanged for long. Instead, a company will alter its product mix by adapting an existing product, developing new products or dropping existing products from its product line.

Product Life Cycle

A product's life cycle measures its longevity in the marketplace and describes its existence in terms of the four key stages of a product's life, namely, the product's introduction, growth, maturity and decline.

Some products seem to retain their popularity and remain profitable forever. For example, Mars chocolate bars have been successfully marketed for many years. At the other end of the spectrum are fad items, products that complete their life cycle quickly, 'living' perhaps only a few months from introduction to decline. For example, hula hoops and tubular hoops that were popular for a very short period in the 1960s, enjoyed a very short life cycle.

Introductory Stage

During a product's introductory stage, consumer awareness and acceptance of the product is understandably low. As the company actively promotes and distributes the product, sales rise gradually, but the initial profit is low because development and marketing costs are high when a new product is introduced. During the introductory stage, all marketing decisions are critical to the product's success. The company must be very careful to set the price appropriately, choose distribution channels wisely, promote the product vigorously and so on. Throughout the introductory stage, the company must be alert to any adjustments that may be needed to help establish the new product, for example, price adjustments and the addition of new distribution channels.

Growth Stage

In the growth stage, sales increase more rapidly as consumers become more and more aware of, and familiar with, the product. With increased sales come increased profits, thanks in part to greater production volume and lower manufacturing costs. However, in the early part of the growth stage, other firms are likely to enter the market with new competitive products, thus causing prices and profits to drop for the original producer. To meet the needs of the growing market and to beat the competition, the original producer may alter the product: introduce new colours, models, sizes or flavours; or promote it in a way that builds brand loyalty.

Maturity Stage

The product's maturity stage begins while sales are still increasing, but at this stage, the rate of increase is slower. Because the product is established and mature, it will sell on its own needing minimal promotion. As a result, profitability increases.

Later in its maturity stage, the product's sales will peak and then begin to decline. Profits, too, decline throughout the maturity stage and price competition increases. In order to bolster sales, manufacturers increase promotion of the product and offer dealers incentives and various assistance to help support mature products.

Decline Stage

In its decline stage, a product's sales volume and profits decrease more rapidly. The number of firms offering competitive products also declines, leaving only 'specialists' remaining in the marketplace. Now, production and marketing costs are the key elements that determine the product's profitability. New products, new technology or the switching of consumers to competing brands may well lead the firm to drop the product from its line entirely.

Extending the Life Cycle

In a product's decline stage, marketers attempt to extend the product's life cycle and maximise short-term profits, for example, by developing new uses for the product, by attracting new users and by making inexpensive alterations in packaging, labelling or pricing. Sometimes, a product's life cycle may be extended by a temporary renewed interest in the product (as for a certain style of clothing).

New-Product Development

Marketing experts closely follow the life cycle of the products they are responsible for. Perhaps the best defence against the loss of revenues and profits resulting from ageing and declining products, is *new-product development*: the replacement of mature products with new products that have solid potential growth.

The new product may be an adaptation of an existing product, an imitation of an existing competitor's product, or a truly innovative new product. In any case, developing and introducing new products can be risky, time consuming and expensive. The evolution of new-product development follows six steps:

1. Generate Ideas

Where do ideas for new products come from? Many companies have research and development departments for the specific purpose of searching for new products.

But ideas for new products may come from anywhere, such as marketing managers, engineers, customers, competitors, consultants or any other source.

2. Screen the Ideas

Screening is the process of evaluating ideas to determine whether the company should indeed implement ideas that are generated. Not all ideas are good. Even ideas that are profitable may not be appropriate to a particular organisation for some reason. For example, developing the new ideas may be too costly for one company but not for another; or the new product may require an additional sales force for one company but not for another.

3. Prepare a Business Analysis

When the preliminary screening determines that a new product is worth pursuing, the company then prepares a business analysis. A business analysis evaluates and quantifies the product's potential by: estimating sales; positioning the product among competitors (if any) in the marketplace; calculating costs and determining profitability; identifying the resources needed; and comparing the cost and evaluating the fit of the new product in the product line as well as the firm's overall long-term objective. Will the new product seriously damage sales of an existing, profitable product?

4. Develop the Product

When the business analysis is positive and promising, the company then proceeds to develop the product. The first questions to be answered concern technical and economical issues, and are intended to test whether it is feasible to make the product. What will production costs be? Will unit costs be low enough to justify a reasonable selling price? When questions such as these are answered, the company uses the data to evaluate product development yet again. If it decides to continue, the next step is usually to develop a working model, or prototype, of the product.

5. Test the Market

Before the company begins full-scale production, it proceeds with a limited production (based on the prototype) and test-markets the product. Typically, in test-marketing, the firm introduces the product in a specially selected area; an area chosen specifically because it is representative of the entire market in terms of consumers' habits, lifestyle and economic level. From the data produced by test-marketing, the company can determine how the larger total market might react to the product, packaging and pricing.

Test-marketing has many advantages; for example, it permits the company to experiment with pricing, advertising and packaging. However, the costs of test-marketing products can be high. As an alternative, therefore, companies will sometimes organise focus groups and consumer panels to elicit information from potential consumers about the product, packaging and pricing.

6. Commercialise the Product

The results of test-marketing allow the company to refine further and fine-tune the product, packaging and pricing, and finally to commercialise the product. Commercialisation is the introduction of the product into the market mainstream. Usually, companies introduce products not nationally but gradually, selecting geographical areas carefully and then expanding from one area to an adjacent area, step-by-step, until the product reaches full commercialisation.

This deliberate step by step approach allows the company to plan more precisely for full-scale manufacturing and national marketing, and to prepare budgets accurately. In other words, this deliberate step by step process helps avoid product failure and ensure success. However, it cannot guarantee success. The business world has many examples of products that were very carefully researched and developed but failed nonetheless. Two of the more famous stories concern the Ford Edsel, a disastrous new car launch from the mid-1950s, and Coca-Cola's 'Classic' story (the attempt to change the taste of Coke failed, forcing the company to return to the original flavour with the new name ('Classic Coke').

Branding and Brands

Deciding on a name for a product is an important part of product development. Before we discuss brands and branding, note the distinctions in the following terms:

- A *brand* is a name, term or symbol that identifies one seller's products and distinguishes them from competitors' products.
- A *brand name* is the part of a brand that can be spoken. The brand name may include letters, numbers, words or pronounceable syllables (such as Proctor and Gamble or Rover).
- A *brand mark* is a symbol or design that is part of a brand (such as the Ford car badge or the BT 'herald').
- A *trademark* is a brand registered with the Patent and Trademark Office, protected from use by anyone except the trademark owner. The distinctive shape of the Coca-Cola bottle is protected by a trademark.

A brand name should be distinctive, easy to say and easy to remember so that customers continue to buy that brand. Furthermore, because brands and marks are assets, companies must carefully protect brands from misuse and unauthorised use, which can destroy the success of a brand and completely lose brand status for a product.

Once a brand becomes commonly used as a generic name, not a brand name, it loses its brand status. For example, cellophane, nylon and band-aids have lost their brand status. One way companies protect brands is to make sure that a brand name is always followed by the generic name of the product, as in a Xerox copy, a Xerox photocopier and so on.

Types of Brands

Many products have brand names and these are often classified according to who owns them.

- **Manufacturer (or producer) brands:** also called national brands, these are brands owned by the manufacturer. Most appliances, packaged foods, all cars and clothing lines (such as Levi's) are examples of manufacturer brands. Establishing a brand name on a national level is expensive, but the rewards are great. For consumers, nationally known manufacturer brands represent consistently reliable quality and widespread availability. Consumers are confident that a box of Shredded Wheat cereal will have a consistent quality wherever it is sold.
- **Licensed brands:** these are brands that the owners have licensed to some other manufacturer, permitting that manufacturer to use its brand on another product. For example, Walt Disney Company licenses other manufacturers to market products, such as watches or pyjamas, with the Mickey Mouse brand that the Walt Disney Company owns.
- **Store (or private) brands:** these are brands owned by an individual retailer or wholesaler (e.g., St Michael owned by Marks and Spencer). Most major grocery chains have private brands for their food products.
- **Generic brands:** these are products with no brand name at all. Their plain packages merely identify the type of product - A4 pads, peanuts, washing powder. Some consumers are attracted by the lower price of generic brands, while others question their quality and consistency (although most are produced by the same manufacturers of name brands).

Brand Loyalty

Companies spend large amounts of money to achieve brand loyalty to create a following of regular buyers of their products. Consumer confidence and satisfaction are the major elements in the success of a brand, and companies work hard to earn this.

The first step in establishing brand loyalty is to develop *brand recognition*, that is, to educate consumers to identify one particular brand and to convince them that it consistently represents high quality. The tools for achieving brand recognition are advertising and promotion.

Once consumers recognise a particular brand, marketers next try to persuade them to exercise a *brand preference* when they make a purchase; a preference for their particular company's brand, of course.

The ultimate goal of brand loyalty is the final stage, *brand insistence*, which is very difficult to achieve. At this stage consumers will not accept substitutes; if the product is not available in one store, they will seek the product in another store. Convenience or shopping products seldom achieve brand insistence, although speciality items often do.

To maintain brand loyalty, the company must continue to offer a product that has a consistently high quality, is priced fairly and represents competitive value.

The company must also support the same marketing efforts that established brand loyalty.

Branding Strategies

Any producer or retail store can brand its products. A producer may market products under its own brands, private brands, or both. Likewise, a store may choose to carry only its own brand, producer brands, or both. Producers and stores that choose to brand products may do so in one of two ways;

- **Individual branding:** this is a strategy in which a firm uses a different brand for each of its products. Proctor and Gamble uses a different brand name for Fairy, Zest, Camay and each of its many other soap products. The advantage of individual branding is that a problem with one brand will not affect the others.
- **Family branding:** this is a strategy in which a firm uses the same brand name for most, or all of its products. For example, General Electric, Xerox and Sony all use family branding the items in their product mix. One advantage of family branding is that new products have a head start since the brand name is already known. Promoting one product also helps promote all products in the product line. On the other hand, customer dissatisfaction is also shared by all products made by the company.

Packaging and Labelling

Packaging describes all aspects of the physical appearance of the product, including its container and wrappings. The package serves several useful purposes. First, the package provides a holder or container for the product. Second, it protects the product from damage or tampering. Third, the visual effect of the package (its shape, colour and printing) helps distinguish the product and influences purchasing decisions.

Frozen food is now commonly packaged in cardboard (instead of aluminium) to make the foods easier to cook in microwave ovens. Furthermore, frozen foods are packaged in various sizes in an effort to target sales to specific markets (such as single portions for single-person households, and giant economy size for large families).

Labelling provides information on a product and/or its package. The Trade Descriptions Act of 1968 requires listing the product name, package size, contents and the name and address of the manufacturer on all product labels. Additional information on product claims, directions for use, safety precautions, ingredients and fibre content is also required under the Consumer Protection Act of 1987, and also under the Sale of Goods Act 1979.

Warranties

A warranty is a statement by a seller that a product meets certain standards of performance:

- **Express warranty:** a written explanation of the responsibilities of the producer in the event that the product is found to be defective or otherwise unsatisfactory.
- **Full warranty:** the producer's or seller's guarantee to repair or replace a defective product within a reasonable time at no cost to the customer.
- **Limited warranty:** restricts the producer's or seller's offer in specific ways, for example, to certain problems or parts.

Warranties can be effective in selling products. Mitsubishi, for example, successfully uses its three-year, unlimited mileage warranty to motivate consumers to buy its products. To avoid the problems caused by unclear or confusing language, the Unfair Contract Terms Act of 1977 requires warranties to meet certain minimum standards.

Pricing

Clearly, pricing is a very important aspect of business success. A product's price is the amount of money a seller will accept in exchange for that product at a given time, under given circumstances. No matter how well a product is designed, if it is priced too high consumers will not buy it; and if it is priced too low, it will earn little or no profit.

Price functions as an allocator. Producers make goods and services for consumers who they believe are able and willing to buy those goods and services. Price allocates these goods and services among those consumers. Price allocates financial resources (sales revenue) among producers according to how well their products satisfy customer's needs. Price also helps customers to allocate their own financial resources among various products available, thus satisfying their needs and wants.

To put pricing in perspective, let us briefly review supply and demand. In Chapter 1, we defined supply as the amount of output of a product that producers are willing and able to make available to the market, at a given price and at a given time. We defined demand as the willingness of purchasers to buy specific quantities of a product, at a given price and at a given time. The point where supply and demand meet represents equilibrium – the supply at a given price equals the demand at that price.

In theory, equilibrium does not take into consideration whether the producer will make a profit at that price. In theory, in a system of pure competition no producer controls the price of its product. All producers must accept the equilibrium price. If they charge a higher price, they will lose sales; if they charge a lower price, they will lose sales revenue.

In the real world, however, a producer tries to control pricing by creating *perceived value* among consumers. Through product differentiation and advertising, for example, a producer attempts to persuade consumers that its products are better and have an additional value for some reason. If the producer is successful, consumers will perceive that a product has a value greater than its actual value, and the producer can then charge a higher price for that product.

Pricing Objectives

A company may have a variety of pricing objectives in setting the price of each product. While making a profit is the primary concern, it is not the only consideration or objective.

Profit-Making Objectives

In an effort to maximise profit, a firm will charge the highest price it believes it can charge without causing sales volume to fall. If it sets prices too low, the firm will sell more units but may lose money or miss the opportunity to make additional profit on the units sold. If it sets prices too high, the firm may make a greater profit on each unit, but it will sell fewer units and lose money. Because it is impossible to calculate in advance what the maximum profit might be, some firms target a return on investment as their profit goal.

Market Share Objectives

A firm's market share describes its percentage of total industry sales. When introducing a new product, a company will often deliberately set a low price, accepting lower profits in the short term in order to encourage consumers to try the new product. For an established product, a company may set a lower price to protect or to increase its market share. The assumption is that higher market share will help establish brand loyalty, hurt competitors and pay off in the long run. An increased market share allows economies of scale that lead, among other things, to lower unit costs.

Loss-Containment and Survival Objectives

In an effort to survive an especially difficult problem or a particularly traumatic situation, a company may feel forced to accept a severe short term pricing policy and lower its prices drastically in an effort to attract customers, contain losses or remain in the market. Facing such a situation in 1989, Continental Airlines offered a $49 fare on nonstop flights to attract passengers, increase income and cover its fixed costs.

Social and Ethical Concerns

The first company to develop a cure for AIDS would be in a position to charge any price, whilst demand for the product would still be extremely high regardless. However, only the very rich would be able to afford the high price tag.

For certain products, a company's pricing policy should address social and ethical concerns. In the case for the cure for AIDS, most companies would probably adopt a pricing strategy that provides a 'reasonable' return. To do otherwise would be unacceptable and probably raise a public outcry.

Company Image

A firm's pricing policy reflects the company image, how that firm is viewed by the public, and manufacturers try to establish pricing policies that will enhance their public image.

Perfume manufacturers often adopt a pricing policy that sets a high price on their products in an effort to enhance the perception of glamour and exclusivity, a perception that a lower price tends to erase.

Pricing Methods

Once a firm has established its pricing objectives, it must select a strategy and pricing method to reach its goals. The market will ultimately determine the selling price of the product. Pricing methodology is often more art than science.

Cost-based Pricing

Pricing may be cost-based – that is, established by the cost of producing one unit of the product.

Determining Total Costs.

Cost-based pricing is based on covering variable costs and some fixed costs. *Variable costs*, mostly material and labour, are those costs that change or vary as more goods or services are produced. For example, in printing magazines, the cost of paper is a variable expense. If the paper cost per magazine is 35p, then the cost of paper for printing 4,000 magazines will be twice as high as the cost of paper for printing 2,000 magazines. Yet the cost of the paper per magazine remains the same - 35p per unit.

Fixed costs include rent, insurance and management salaries. These costs remain constant ('fixed'); they are unaffected by the number of units produced. The magazine's rent does not change whether it prints and sells 2,000 or 4,000 copies a week. The rent is a fixed cost.

In cost-based pricing, the seller uses variable and fixed costs to determine the *total cost* of each unit.

Determining Mark-up and Profit Margin

The seller determines the amount of profit or mark-up desired, and adds this mark-up to the total cost. Together, the total cost plus the mark-up equals the *selling price*.

Mark-up is expressed as a percentage of the total cost or a percentage of the retail price. The difference between the total cost and the selling price is known as the *profit margin*. For a manufacturer, 'cost' means production cost and 'selling price' is the wholesale price (that is, the manufacturer's selling price). For a retailer, 'cost' means the wholesale price it pays for a product and 'selling price' means the retail or list price at which it sells the product.

For example, let us look at an item with a unit cost of £100, a mark-up of £20 and a selling price of £120. What is the mark-up percentage? The mark-up percentage can be based on the unit cost or it can be based on the product's selling price:

$$\text{Mark-up percentage on Cost} = \frac{\text{Mark-up}}{\text{Cost}} = \frac{£20}{£100} = 20\%$$

$$\text{Mark-up percentage on Selling Price} = \frac{\text{Mark-up}}{\text{Selling Price}} = \frac{£20}{£120} = 16.6\%$$

Calculating the breakeven point

The *breakeven point* is the number of units that must be sold at a given price, to cover both fixed and variable costs - that is, the number of units that must be sold to recover expenses without making a profit. The calculations involved are part of what is known as a *breakeven analysis.*

To complete this analysis, the firm must know its fixed costs and its variable costs. Then, using demand estimates and other market data in conjunction with this analysis the firm can establish the price for a product.

Let us look at the breakeven analysis for a firm that has fixed costs of £40,000 and variable costs of £60 per unit for a product selling at £120.

$$\text{Breakeven point (units)} = \frac{\text{Total fixed costs}}{\text{Selling price - Variable costs}} = \text{x units}$$

$$\text{BEP (units)} = \frac{£40,000}{£120 - £60} = \frac{£40,000}{£60} = 667 \text{ units}$$

With this breakeven analysis, the firm can evaluate other prices:

Selling price	Breakeven quantity
£100	1000
£110	800
£120	667
£140	500

In this way, the firm can establish its official price based on realistic costs.

Competition-based Pricing

Companies often use their competitors' pricing as a guide in establishing their own prices. Competition-based pricing is most effective when competing products are very similar or when price is the main differentiation between products. Competition-based pricing is popular among retailers because it requires little analysis and is not likely to start a costly price war.

Pricing Strategies

Sellers must consider many factors in choosing a pricing method and setting a basic price, for example, markets, goals, product differentiation and the life cycle stage of each product. All these factors contribute to the seller's pricing strategy. The specific strategy applied to a product varies, of course, depending on whether the product is new or is an existing product.

New-Product Strategies

When introducing new products to the market, companies consider two contrasting options:

- **Price skimming:** this is the strategy of charging a high price for a product during the introductory stage of its life cycle. The seller assumes the buyer is willing to pay the high price for some reason, for example, because of the novelty, prestige or status associated with owning this new product. When the novelty wears off and competition increases, the company drops the price. Skimming is a strategy that helps the seller recover high development costs, but if it is successful, it creates a lucrative market that may attract competitors.
- **Penetration pricing:** this takes an opposite approach to skimming. In applying the strategy of penetration pricing, the company sets a low price, anticipating that it will quickly garner a large market share for the product, achieve economies of scale and reduce unit costs. Penetration pricing is often used by new companies because this strategy allows the firm to sell as many units as possible early in the product life cycle, discourage competition and quickly establish a name for the company. However, penetration pricing is less flexible than skimming; it is easier to lower prices than it is to raise them.

Pricing Existing Products

In pricing existing products, a firm can adopt one of three obvious strategies:

- **Above the market:** companies pricing products above the market imply that their higher price means higher quality. Rolex watches are priced above the market.
- **Below the market:** pricing below competitors' prices can effectively build market share if the quality of the product is acceptable. For example, Budget offers rental cars below the price of Hertz.
- **At the market:** pricing at the market is often most successful for products that differ little from one firm to another. Steel, processed foods and petrol often use market pricing. In such instances, companies compete through advertising or personal selling rather than price.

Pricing Tactics

For both new and existing products, marketers must choose pricing tactics that will implement their strategy for reaching their pricing objectives. A number of tactics can be utilised.

Psychological Pricing

Retailers who use psychological pricing believe that consumers react somewhat emotionally. For example, consumers will respond to odd pricing such as £9.99 or £49.95 more favourably than to £10 or £50. Adherents believe that customers focus on the whole pound number and round down. This tactic is not limited to low-price items. Car manufacturers will price a car at £9,950 rather than £10,000.

Threshold Pricing

A related tactic is threshold pricing, which assumes that customers have a maximum price, a threshold, in mind and that they will not exceed it. At one time, when Cadbury felt the threshold price for a chocolate bar was 20p, it chose to reduce the size of the bar rather than exceed the threshold price.

Price Lining

Following the strategy of price lining, retailers offer goods at a limited number of key prices that reflect definite price breaks. For example, a store may sell three lines of men's socks, one at £2.50, one at £3.50 and a third at £5.00, thus eliminating minor price differences whilst at the same time simplifying selection and checkout. A fast food store or a cinema refreshment counter will offer small, medium and large size soft drinks at three set prices, regardless of the flavour or the brand selected.

Multiple-unit Pricing

Multiple unit pricing, commonly used by supermarkets, sets a single price for two or more units such as two cans for 99p, rather than 50p a can. To encourage multiple purchases, retailers will package merchandise in multiple units. Packaging items in multiple units and selling them as a single unit is likely to increase sales.

Prestige Pricing

Prestige pricing assumes that consumers will consider a higher price as evidence of higher quality. In an effort to keep prices at specific levels and avoid discounting, some manufacturers label their products with a suggested retail price. To prohibit retailers from remarking and discounting merchandise, some manufacturers sell only to retailers who agree to uphold the suggested retail price for their products.

Discount Pricing

Discount pricing offers a price reduction as an incentive to purchase a product. Retail stores often remark the suggested retail price to emphasise that the product is offered at a discount. Some common discounts are:

- **Cash discounts:** to receive a cash discount, the customer must make payment in cash.
- **Seasonal discounts:** these are offered in the off-season, that is, during a season other than the expected season for purchasing the product or service. Buying garden equipment in winter, ski equipment in summer, trips to Spain in the winter, or coal in July all represent opportunities for seasonal discounts.
- **Trade discounts:** these are price reductions offered only to intermediaries and agents - wholesalers, distributors and other people 'in the trade'. A manufacturer, for example, may offer an appliance retailer a 40 per cent trade discount on a microwave oven with a list price of £100. The net price (price after discount) to the appliance dealer is £60. (The role of intermediaries will be covered more fully in the next chapter.)

● **Quantity discounts:** similar to trade discounts, quantity discounts offer price reductions to buyers who purchase in large quantities. Retail examples include case prices for soft drinks, motor oil and wine, all lower per unit than if bought separately. Similarly, other products may be less expensive when purchased by the dozen. Selling products in quantity often reduces packaging and other costs of the product, allowing those savings to be passed on to the buyer.

SUMMARY

All products have a life cycle over which they grow, mature, decline and eventually die. Cycles can last for weeks or decades, often requiring different marketing strategies at different parts of the product life cycle. These strategies often involve pricing strategies, although there are very few businesses in existence which can successfully price a product at cost, plus a margin for profit. Such businesses, if they do exist, either underprice and make less profits than they should, or overprice and make little or no sales. Frequently, pricing strategies are planned for a group of products or services, where the profits from one product tend to support the smaller profits from another. Thus, as these products proceed through their life cycle so the support changes.

SELECTED READING

Lewis, Gregory. 1992. *Pricing for Profit.* Kogan Page.
Wright, Christopher. 1989. *Product Liability.* Blackstone Press.
Holt, Knut. 1988. *Product Innovation Management.* Butterworth.

<table>
<tr><td style="border:1px solid; width:120px; text-align:center; font-size:2em;">14</td><td style="font-size:2em;">Placement / Distribution
Strategy</td></tr>
</table>

Every product begins with the producer and ends with the consumer, which is either an individual or an industrial consumer. The route that the product travels from beginning to end is called the *channel of distribution* or the *marketing channel*. The marketing channel is made up of a sequence of marketing organisations that link producers with consumers. These organisations are called *intermediaries* or *agents*.

Major Marketing Channels

The channels of distribution for consumer products and industrial products are different, and within each category the patterns of distribution are also different. The four most common channels for consumer products and the two most common channels for industrial products are listed in Table 14.1.

TABLE 14.1

Consumer Channels

Producer →	→	→	→	Consumer
Producer →	→	→	Retailer →	Consumer
Producer →	→	Wholesaler →	Retailer →	Consumer
Producer →	Agent →	Wholesaler →	Retailer →	Consumer

Industrial Channels

Producer →	→	→	Industrial User
Producer →	Agent / Intermediary →		Industrial User

Consumer Channels

● **Producer to consumer:** the route from producer to consumer is a direct channel; it has no intermediaries. Most services travel the direct channel, from service provider to consumer. But most consumer goods arrive at their destinations through intermediaries; few goods travel the direct channel. Exceptions among consumer goods are producers such as Avon and

Tupperware which sell directly to the consumer to maintain close ties and to save intermediary costs.

● **Producer to retailer to consumer:** producer to retailer to consumer has one intermediary along the route, a retailer, who buys from the producer and sells to individual consumers. This channel of distribution is commonly used by retailers who buy large quantities and retailers who deal in bulky products such as furniture and other products that are costly to handle. This channel is equally popular for products that must reach the consumer quickly, either because they are perishable or quickly outdated (e.g., fashions).

● **Producer to wholesaler to retailer to consumer:** this is known as the *traditional channel*. Producers generally prefer dealing with wholesalers when the number of retailers is too cumbersome. In such cases, the wholesaler is a welcome intermediary, selling products to retailers or perhaps to other smaller wholesalers.

● **Producer to agent to wholesaler to retailer to consumer:** this pathway is common for inexpensive products that reach millions of consumers (e.g., coffee). The agent or distributor may handle many different products from many different producers.

Industrial Channels

● **Producer to industrial user:** this is a direct channel. The manufacturer uses its own sales force to sell directly to the industrial user. Manufacturers of heavy equipment such as mainframe computers often use the direct channel.

● **Producer to agent/intermediary to industrial user:** this channel uses the services of an agent/intermediary, who may be a wholesaler or an independent distributor representing the producer on a commission basis. Industrial companies distributing consumable supplies, small tools, accessories, or standardised parts often favour this channel of distribution.

Vertical Marketing Systems (VMSs)

Vertical channel integration results when two or more members of a channel are joined under a single management. The resulting channel is known as a vertical marketing system (VMS). Examples of VMSs are a large discount chain that buys directly from a manufacturer and warehouses its own stock, thereby doing away with the need for a wholesaler (e.g., an oil company that owns its wells, refineries, terminals and service stations).

There are three types of VMSs:

● **Administered VMS:** in an administered VMS, one of the channel members dominates the other members, usually because of its great size. For example, Proctor and Gamble, one of the country's largest consumer products manufacturers, dominates the intermediaries that carry P&G products.

● **Contractual VMS:** under a contractual VMS, the rights and obligations of channel members are defined by contracts or other legal measures.

● **Corporate VMS:** in a corporate VMS, production and distribution are joined by common ownership. A grocery chain that manufacturers its own line of canned food is an example of a corporate VMS.

Market Coverage

To decide which distribution channel is best, producers must consider many factors, such as the nature of the product, production capability, consumer buying patterns and marketing resources. For example, the nature of some products may limit market coverage to certain areas. If the producer's marketing resources are limited, the company may decide to use regional rather than national promotion. If production capacity is so limited that it curtails sales potential, the producer may opt for exclusive rather than widespread distribution. In any case, producers must evaluate such factors in order to develop the appropriate market coverage.

Intensive Distribution

Intensive distribution describes the efforts of a manufacturer to achieve the widest possible availability for a product. Manufacturers of chocolate, soft drinks, cigarettes and other convenience items will sell to any and all intermediaries or retailers willing to stock and sell the product.

Exclusive Distribution

Exclusive distribution uses only a single retail outlet in any one geographic area. Depending upon the merchandise, the area may be a neighbourhood, a city, a suburb or a larger area. Exclusive distribution is generally limited to prestigious and/or expensive products such as fine china, Rolex watches or BMW cars. However, while the distributor may have exclusive rights for an area, there may be no limit on the number of retailers who can carry the product.

Selective Distribution

Selective distribution lies midway between intensive and exclusive distribution. Here the manufacturer limits distribution to a selected portion or percentage of the available outlets in each geographic area. For example, clothing, major appliances and furniture manufacturers selectively distribute their products. Franchisers such as McDonald's and KFC are selective in choosing franchise locations to avoid competing within their franchise families.

Marketing Intermediaries

Marketing intermediaries are often the target of criticism from the press, consumers and other marketers, who claim that intermediaries are generally inefficient and costly, while simply adding unnecessarily to the price that consumers ultimately pay for products. Undeniably, however, intermediaries perform an important service. If they were eliminated, the functions they perform would then be performed by others, possibly raising, instead of lowering, costs.

Consider for example, the added expense Nestlés would incur if it dealt individually with every outlet that carries its chocolate bars. Nestlés would then ship to hundreds of thousands of accounts instead of to a relatively few distributors. Its shipping and billing costs, for example, would increase as it hired additional people to handle the greater volume of smaller shipments and the increased number of customer accounts.

Wholesalers

Wholesalers provide a number of services to retailers and to manufacturers.

Wholesalers' Services to Retailers

Wholesalers buy large quantities from manufacturers, stock the items in one location, then sell and deliver smaller quantities to retailers. Wholesalers stock a variety of goods that the retailer would otherwise have to order from many producers rather than from one wholesaler. By maintaining inventories, wholesalers make products available to retailers on demand, with less waiting time and with greater economy than if the retailer had to order directly from the producer. In addition to stocking goods, wholesalers also supply several other services that are of value to retailers.

In an effort to help retailers sell merchandise to consumers, wholesalers may supply (often free, or perhaps at cost) *promotion assistance*, for example, window and counter displays.

Wholesalers also provide retailers with valuable *market information* concerning consumer demand, supply conditions and new products. In the process of dealing with producers and retailers, wholesalers naturally gather useful information which they gladly relay to retailers in the normal course of business.

Wholesalers' prompt and frequent deliveries enable retailers to maintain lower inventories than would otherwise be possible and at the same time service their customers effectively. Thanks to this indirect form of *financial aid*, retailers need not tie up useful capital in large inventories. Many wholesalers provide generous credit terms, even extending loans in some industries.

Wholesalers' Services to Manufacturers

Manufacturers (even large, innovative, successful manufacturers) benefit from the services provided by wholesalers.

Wholesalers provide the manufacturer with an *instant sales force*, at a great saving. Imagine, for example, how Campbell Soups or Proctor and Gamble might function without wholesalers. The size of, and therefore the expense of, maintaining a sales force capable of calling on the thousands of retail establishments that carry Campbell Soups or Proctor and Gamble products would be enormous without wholesalers.

By stocking goods for resale, wholesalers *reduce inventory costs* for manufacturers. Manufacturers' expenses are reduced for materials, storage and other costs of maintaining a large inventory of finished goods.

When wholesalers extend credit to retailers, wholesalers assume the credit risk, thereby *reducing credit risks* for manufacturers.

Just as wholesalers provide retailers with an information network, they also provide manufacturers with the same kinds of valuable *market information* – consumer demand, buying trends and so on.

Types of Wholesalers

There are three key types of wholesalers:

● Merchant wholesalers.
● Commission merchants, agents and brokers.
● Manufacturers' branch offices and sales offices.

The largest group is merchant wholesalers, which makes up more than half of all wholesalers.

Merchant Wholesalers

Merchant wholesalers are intermediaries who purchase goods in large quantities and resell them to retail and industrial users in smaller quantities. They take title to the goods and store them in their warehouses until the goods are sold. Merchant wholesalers maintain their own sales forces and function as independent businesses. Their range includes: general merchandise wholesalers, who carry a wide range of different products; limited-line wholesalers, who carry only a few related lines; and specialty line wholesalers, who carry a select group of products within a single line, such as gourmet foods. Merchant wholesalers may provide full services or limited services to retailers.

● **Full service wholesalers:** these perform the entire range of wholesaler functions listed previously (i.e., selling, warehousing, delivery, financing and promotion).
● **Limited service wholesalers:** as the name implies, these offer customers selected wholesaler functions. Limited service wholesalers take title to the goods and warehouse them, but they have smaller sales forces. They are less likely to supply market information, credit or promotion services.

Commission Merchants, Agents and Brokers

Commission merchants, agents and brokers also offer wholesaler services.

● **Commission merchants:** these represent the manufacturers and are paid preset fees by manufacturers based on sales. Unlike merchant wholesalers, commission merchants do not take title to the goods they sell. Instead, they arrange for delivery of merchandise from the manufacturer to retailer.

- **Agents:** sometimes called *sales agents*, these represent one or more manufacturers within a specific territory. Agents work on a commission basis. They solicit orders but do not arrange for delivery. The manufacturer ships the merchandise and bills the customer directly.
- **Brokers:** these specialise in a particular commodity and represent either a buyer or a seller. They do not take title to the merchandise, but instead receive a fee or commission (generally from the seller) for bringing the buyer and seller together, just as estate agents do.

Manufacturers' Branch Offices and Sales Offices

Manufacturers may own and operate wholesaling operations of two kinds:

- **Branch offices:** these are merchant wholesale firms owned by the manufacturer. Branch offices perform all the merchant wholesale functions. Because they are owned by the producer, branch offices stock only goods manufactured by their own firms.
- **Sales offices:** these are also owned by the manufacturer; but unlike branch offices, sales offices act as agents, selling not only their company's products but often other products that complement their company's product line. For example, a sales office for a tyre manufacturer may also carry car batteries and alternative car accessories manufactured by other companies.

Retailers

In the chain of distribution, retailers service the end customer – the consumer. Retailers vary in size, from small family operations, to giants like Debenhams and Dixons stores. Although individually owned stores account for 85 percent of all retail stores in the UK, they account for only slightly more than half of total retail sales. Retailers also vary in the services they offer and the merchandise they carry, as well as in their marketing approaches. Retailers can be classified as in store or nonstore retailers.

In Store Retailers

In store retailers maintain permanent locations where merchandise is regularly on display and available for purchase.

Department Stores

Department stores carry a wide range of merchandise, from fashion items to kitchen appliances and furniture. Department stores are service oriented, offering delivery service, sales help, credit and liberal return policies to customers. Together, department stores, including all their branches in shopping malls or in the suburbs, account for the bulk of total store sales.

Specialty Stores

Specialty stores usually sell only one type of merchandise, for example, sporting goods and equipment. Specialty stores are designed to meet the needs of a particular market segment. Many are small, individually owned operations, whilst most of the larger specialty stores are part of a chain.

Chain Stores

Chain stores are groups of stores owned by one individual or one company. Waterstones, Dillons and similar booksellers are examples of well-known chain stores. Their competitiveness lies in their ability to respond to trends more quickly than the large department stores.

Discount Stores

Discount stores are self-service, general merchandise outlets offering products, including brand names, at lower prices. Discount stores have inexpensive decors, open for long hours and offer limited services to reduce their expenses.

Catalogue Showrooms

Catalogue showrooms feature a wide assortment of merchandise, samples of which are displayed in the showroom. Merchandise is delivered from a warehouse attached to the showroom. Catalogue stores such as Argos are able to offer discount prices by lowering their operating expenses. They employ fewer sales personnel, omit delivery expenses (customers pick up merchandise at the store), have lower display costs and control shoplifting effectively.

Warehouse Stores

Warehouse stores are minimal service outlets that carry large inventories of foods, home furnishings, building supplies and so on. They are generally found in low rent areas. In a warehouse store, merchandise may sit in packing cases on pallets, and customers may even be expected to supply their own paper bags or boxes to carry their purchases home.

Convenience Stores

Convenience stores, as the name implies, offer customers a number of specific conveniences in return for which they charge higher prices compared to supermarkets. However, customers are willing to pay the higher price for the 'conveniences', which include store location (convenience stores are nearby, serving the needs of a neighbourhood), product variety (they are small but carry a limited variety of products) and store hours (they are open very long hours like Smiths Convenience Stores in Norwich, which open 20 hours a day, 365 days a year).

Supermarkets

Supermarkets such as Tesco and Sainsburys are the major sellers of food products in the UK. In addition to these national giants, independent smaller supermarket chains service regional areas. Supermarkets operate on the basis of high volume and low margins. Competition is on the basis of price. In addition to canned, fresh, process and frozen foods, they stock items such as paper goods, cleaning products and toiletries.

Scrambled Merchandising

Scrambled merchandising, a recent development, describes the odd mix of unrelated merchandise that a modern grocery store may offer in addition to traditional foods – for example, motor oil, cosmetics, books and magazines and housewares. Such stores may offer brand name, generic and unadvertised products.

Hypermarkets

Hypermarkets are an outgrowth of the trend toward scrambled merchandising. Developed in Europe, hypermarkets are large scale outlets that combine features of both supermarkets and discount stores and offer, for example, everything from cabbage to clothes dryers under one roof.

Nonstore Retailers

Nonstore retailers do not maintain conventional store facilities to which customers travel. Instead of customers travelling to stores, these retailers travel to their customers by television, telephone, door-to-door selling, mail order, home parties and vending machines.

Door-to-Door Retailers

Door-to-door retailers are sellers' representatives who sell directly to consumers in consumers' homes or offices. As part of the selling process, the representative may demonstrate the product, and may also deliver the product at the point of sale or after the sale. Domestic household products are frequently sold on this basis (e.g., Kleen-Ezee).

Mail Order Retailing

Mail order retailing is a rapidly growing segment of the retail market. Most households receive catalogues of various kinds offering merchandise by mail order. The range of merchandise is virtually unlimited. Clothes, foods, furnishings, stationery, jewelry, appliances, books and magazines, tools, computers and computer supplies, are all available through mail order.

Each mail order catalogue contains an order form, which the customer completes and returns to the firm. To facilitate ordering, UK merchandisers such as Littlewoods and Lands End now provide toll-free telephone numbers for ordering merchandise, which customers charge to their credit cards.

Party Retailers

Some manufacturers, notably Tupperware, maintain a network of part-time representatives who market the manufacturers merchandise in customers' homes at parties. The representative schedules a party with a customer at the customer's home. The customer then invites friends, relatives, neighbours or co-workers to the party where the sales representative demonstrates the merchandise and takes orders. As a reward for hosting the party, the customer earns a commission based on sales and receives free merchandise.

Vending Machines

Vending machines dispense many convenience goods such as chocolate bars, cigarettes and beverages. Around-the-clock automatic teller machines are considered vending machines. Placed in convenient locations, vending machines require no sales personnel. On the other hand, they do require servicing, repair and maintenance due to vandalism and normal wear and tear, thus adding to the expense of operating vending machines.

Television Marketing

Everyone who watches television with any regularity is very familiar with commercials and advertisements, of varying lengths, that attempt to persuade viewers to buy a product or service. Some commercials try to elicit an immediate response, offering toll–free numbers to order magazines, recordings and other products. These commercials are part of television marketing; a long and well established means of reaching consumers.

With the advent of cable television in the UK and all the additional channels available through cable, television selling is no longer limited to commercials. Television now broadcasts home-shopping channels devoted exclusively to selling merchandise, which is displayed on screen while a salesperson describes the merchandise in great detail and urges viewers to call the toll-free telephone number and place an order. A new dimension has been added to the marketing mix.

Shopping Centres

Built by private developers, shopping centres are self-contained retail centres that offer a variety of stores serving diverse consumer needs. The shopping centre management tries to assemble a coordinated mix of stores that will generate consumer traffic. In an effort to attract shoppers, these centres provide adequate parking and pleasant surroundings.

Neighbourhood Shopping Arcades/Areas

Along many major roads are neighbourhood shopping areas which consist of convenience and specialty stores such as chemists, fast food outlets and grocery stores. The key to success for these arcades/areas is the convenience it provides to consumers in the immediate surrounding area; the neighbourhoods that lie within a few minutes' driving time of the arcade/area.

Community Shopping Centres

In addition to specialty and convenience stores, community shopping centres may offer one or two medium-sized department stores. Because they offer more stores with a larger assortment of products and specialty items, community shopping centres draw shoppers from a wider area than neighbourhood arcades. Here too, the shopping centre management tries to achieve a balance in the mix of stores and products, and will often stage special events such as art shows and handicraft fairs to increase customer traffic.

Regional Shopping Centres

In addition to branches of large department stores, regional shopping centres may feature numerous specialty stores, restaurants, multi screen cinema complexes, national chain stores and a range of franchise operations. Located on major traffic arteries, regional shoppping centres compete effectively with, and frequently outdo, the downtown shopping areas. The Gateshead Metro Centre in the UK is one of the largest shopping centres in Europe, and competes with local large city shopping centres in Newcastle, primarily on the basis of its huge car parking facilities. Marketing and advertising for regional shopping centres is well coordinated and many special events are held to attract consumers.

Sunday Markets

Sunday markets take place on large 'out of town' areas where car parking must be easy and adjacent. Sunday markets started in order to avoid, possibly illegally, the Sunday trading laws in England. Although these laws have been repealed, Sunday markets still continue to thrive because of the large variety of trading stalls, low prices and entertainment or 'leisure' value.

Physical Distribution

Physical distribution includes all the orderly and economic activities required to move goods from the producer to the ultimate consumer. It combines the functions of inventory control that is warehousing, order processing, materials handling and transportation. Marketers have integrated all these functions in an effort to achieve greater efficiency, and to get the right merchandise to the right place at right time and at the right cost.

Inventory Control

Holding costs describes all the expenses incurred in buying and storing inventory. Keeping inventory at the right level keeps holding costs at a minimum and avoids stockout costs (the sales losses that result when merchandise is unavailable and out of stock). Inventory control is the art and science of balancing holding costs against stockout costs. Understandably, the computer is now an invaluable tool in all aspects of managing inventory, including order processing, warehousing and materials handling.

Order Processing

Order processing includes all activities involved in receiving and filling customers' orders, as well as procedures for shipping, billing and granting credit. Delivery time is a function of order processing. Whether the order is for a sofa to be delivered to an individual or for precision parts to be delivered to a manufacturer, prompt and certain delivery is important because: (i) it gives the seller a competitive advantage in the marketplace and, (ii) it reduces the costs of maintaining large inventories. The shorter the delivery time from the supplier, the smaller the inventory that must be maintained.

Warehousing

Warehousing combines several operations: not only the receiving, sorting, storing and holdings of goods, but also the assembling and shipping of goods when needed. All these operations are linked by order processing. There are different types of warehouses:

- **Private warehouses:** a company may have its own private warehouse or it may rent space in a general warehouse. One obvious benefit of owning a private warehouse is that the company can design and operate it to meet its specific needs. But the costs of operating a warehouse are high, and only certain firms can justify the expense.
- **General warehouses:** general warehouses supply various warehousing services and charge clients accordingly. Most general warehouses are large facilities located on the outskirts of metropolitan areas, accessible to rail and road transportation.
- **Distribution centres:** unlike warehouses, distribution centres are in-and-out operations. Their purpose is not to store goods for indefinite periods but to receive bulk shipments and reship or distribute the goods, usually quickly and in smaller quantities. For example, when a large retail chain like B&Q receives a shipment of 5,000 power saws from a manufacturer, the shipment is delivered to a B&Q distribution centre, where small quantities of the saws are reshipped to Sears outlets nationwide.

Materials Handling

Materials handling (the physical handling of goods in warehousing as well as transporting) is an important element in distribution costs. Properly designed, materials handling procedures can increase usable warehouse capacity, reduce breakage and spoilage, and save time.

One goal of materials handling is to reduce the number of times a product is handled by using techniques such as *unit loading*. Unit loading combines smaller items and packages into single standardised loads that can be efficiently handled by trucks or forklifts. Containerisation, a variation of unit loading on a grand scale, combines sizable numbers of individual items or unit loads, packs them in large containers or trailers, and handles and ships the container as a single unit.

Transportation

Transportation involves all aspects of shipping products through the channels of distribution to the ultimate consumers.

Carriers

Firms supplying transportation services are called *carriers*. There are different types of carriers, including:

- **Common carriers:** these are companies whose service is available to all shippers. Railways, airlines and most long-distance trucking firms are common carriers.
- **Contract carriers:** these do not serve the general public: they are available for hire only by commercial shippers.
- **Private carriers:** these are owned and operated by a shipper for its own business use.
- **Package carriers:** these provide delivery services for many retail stores, mail order firms, businesses of all kinds and individuals. The oldest package carrier in the UK is the Royal Mail which offers a variety of services. Many private carriers compete with the Royal Mail in delivering packages (e.g., TNT, DHL, and Group 4). All of which offer overnight delivery throughout the country and in many cases, overseas. In addition to these national services, many small, specialised package delivery services operate in metropolitan areas.
- **The role of freight forwarders:** shippers can hire agents called *freight forwarders* to pick up the merchandise from the shipper and assume responsibility for delivery. The forwarder selects the carrier, frequently combining small shipments into one large load for which the carrier charges a lower rate.

Means of Transportation

There are several means of transportation, each with its own advantages and disadvantages.

- **Railways:** all railways in the UK are common carriers, except for a few operated by coal mining companies. Railway freight volume has decreased in recent years, but railways still transport a greater volume than any other type of carrier, principally because railways are the least expensive form of transportation for many products. Railways are routinely used for transporting heavy equipment, raw materials, commodities, foodstuffs and timber. Rail transportation also offers a 'piggyback' service: loaded truck trailers are put on a special railway car and transported by rail to a depot near their destination, where they are off loaded to complete the rest of the journey by truck.
- **Trucks:** these are more expensive than railways, their primary competition, but trucks offer several advantages, including door-to-door service, flexible scheduling, greater convenience and added accessibility to rural or suburban areas not serviced by rail.
- **Airfreight:** because airfreight is the most expensive carrier, air transportation is often restricted to high value, lightweight, perishable and rush delivery goods. Jumbo jets now enable airlines to carry bulk or containerised cargo. All certified airlines are common carriers. Charter lines and some freight lines are contract carriers.
- **Ships:** cargo ships and barges are the least expensive, but the slowest form, of

transportation. As a result, water transportation is used for nonperishable bulk goods such as ore, grain, oil and petroleum products, as well as for many kinds of international cargo.

- **Pipelines:** a highly specialised form of transportation, pipelines are used primarily for moving petroleum and natural gas. Pipelines are completely automated and are unaffected by weather, allowing the product to move slowly, constantly and dependably.
- **Telecommunications:** for many service companies, the product is information, which can be transported by means of telecommunications: computer networks, modems and facsimile machines.
- **Couriers:** these provide messenger services for delivering small packages and important documents quickly and safely.

Choosing a Carrier

Factors to consider when choosing a carrier include the merchandise's size, weight and type; the distance involved; the firm's overall distribution system; the speed required; the flexibility of the carrier; and of course costs. When goods are in transit or in storage, they incur carrying costs for inventory, insurance and so on. Japanese manufacturers have developed a 'just in time' (JIT) inventory system, which ensures a continuous flow of materials from suppliers and thereby minimises the amount of goods held in inventory. JIT inventory systems require fast, reliable transportation.

SUMMARY

Getting the goods or services to the customer at the right time and place are essential components of any marketing plan. Quality of product is often coupled with quality of delivery promise. Transportation methods are changing as a result of technological advances, and suppliers must be aware of all developments in air freight, transcontinental railways, and even electronic methods (such as the Internet) for getting goods and services to the customer. In addition, changes in social behaviour, such as leisure shopping, also require constant attention.

SELECTED READING

Cooper, James. 1988. *Logistics and Distribution Planning.* Kogan Page.
Cox, Roger & Brittain, Paul. 1993. *Retail Management.* Pitman.
O'Brien, L. G. 1991. *Retailing, Shopping, Society, Space.* David Fulton.

Promotional Strategy

Promotion includes all techniques designed to induce customers to buy products. Promotion may communicate, inform, influence or remind people in the markets, which the organisation serves, about the organisation and/or its products. The promotional mix describes the particular combination of methods that each firm uses in its promotional campaign to reach its target market(s).

Promotion Methods

There are four basic methods of promotion:

- **Advertising:** this is a paid message communicated through a mass medium to a wide general audience by an identified sponsor.
- **Personal selling:** this includes personal communication aimed at informing one or more prospective purchasers and persuading them to buy a firm's products.
- **Sales promotion:** this describes all activities or materials that directly influence customers or salespeople. Where advertising uses media such as newspapers and television, sales promotion uses displays, demonstrations, samples, coupons and other selling efforts.
- **Publicity:** this is a nonpersonal message delivered through mass media, free of charge, usually in a news story. The marketer cannot control the content of the publicity. Company-influenced publicity is known as *public relations*.

These four areas of promotion are discussed in detail later in this chapter.

Promotional Objectives

The broad, basic objective of promotion is to create sales, which in turn generates profits. But promotion performs several additional functions: it communicates information, positions products and controls sales volume.

Communicating Information

Consumers cannot buy a product unless they have been informed that the product exists. The information communicated to consumers may take many different forms. The information may be direct, as in an announcement concerning a product's availability, or it may be indirect, as in a flyer, brochure or article on technological advances. The information may be targeted to a specific group or to several groups. It may be communicated in print media (through letters, flyers, brochures, newspapers, magazines or billboards), in broadcast media (radio, television), by telephone or by computer.

Positioning Products

Companies position products by establishing a clearly identifiable image, including identifying that image of the product in consumers' minds. Before a company can position a product, the company must identify which segments of the market are potential purchasers and which other products it will compete against.

Controlling Sales Volume

Companies that experience seasonal sales patterns can often effectively promote their products during slow periods in an effort to increase sales during those periods, and to stabilise sales volume throughout the year. For some seasonal products, such as lawnmowers, promotional efforts are designed to maximise sales volumes at certain times of the year.

Promotional Strategies

Once a firm has established its promotional objectives, it must develop a promotional strategy to achieve them. The company may use a push strategy, a pull strategy or a combination of both.

Push Strategy

The idea behind a *push strategy* is to drive or push the company's product through wholesalers and retailers, who will then persuade customers to buy the product. The product is presented to the potential customer, as opposed to the customer's demanding the product - hence the term 'push'. The push strategy stresses personal selling (on the part of wholesalers and retailers) over advertising (on the part of the manufacturer), and is widely used by marketers of higher-priced goods and industrial equipment.

Pull Strategy

A pull strategy emphasises mass advertising to move goods into consumers' hands. This strategy is designed to create a demand on the part of the consumers and 'pull' them into retail outlets to purchase the product. Marketers of lower-priced convenience goods rely on the pull strategy to market their products.

Advertising

As listed previously, the four methods of promotion are advertising, personal selling, sales promotion and publicity. Advertising is a paid, nonpersonal message delivered through a mass medium. Advertising has great flexibility; it can be aimed with great effect to reach a very broad general audience, or targeted to reach a narrower, carefully chosen niche group. Advertising also provides flexibility in delivering various kinds of messages.

Types of Advertising by Purpose

Advertising can be categorised according to its purpose and its message as selective, institutional, primary demand and advocacy advertising.

Selective Advertising

Selective (or brand) advertising promotes specific brands of products and services. This is the most widely used form of advertising, accounting for the major portion of advertising budgets. There are different types of selective advertising.

- **Immediate response advertising:** selective advertising for the purpose of persuading consumers to make purchases within a short time is called immediate response advertising. Most local advertising is for this purpose.
- **Reminder advertising:** selective advertising aimed at keeping a firm's name before the public is called reminder advertising.
- **Comparative advertising:** selective advertising that compares specific characteristics of two or more identified brands is called comparative advertising.

Institutional Advertising

Institutional advertising is designed to enhance a firm's image or reputation, to build goodwill rather than sell merchandise. For example, British Airways uses the phrase 'The World's Favourite Airline' in all its institutional advertising in an effort to enhance its public image.

Primary Demand Advertising

Primary demand advertising is designed to increase consumer demand for all brands of a good or service. Trade and industry groups, such as the Potato Marketing Board, use primary demand advertising to build consumer demand for potatoes (Britain's buried treasure) without mentioning any brand names or company names.

Advocacy Advertising

Advocacy advertising attempts to influence individuals' or organisations' attitudes and opinions. Companies and trade associations such as the National Union of Teachers use advocacy advertising to encourage public support for, or public opposition to, specific legislation.

Types of Advertising by Message

The message underlying product advertising often depends on that particular product's life cycle stage. The message can be described as informative, persuasive or reminder.

Informative Advertising

The goal of informative advertising, used primarily in the introductory stage of a product's life cycle, is to make potential customers aware of both the new product and the company. Informative advertising can help establish a primary demand for a product.

Persuasive Advertising

During the growth stage of a product's life cycle, when the product is already established, persuasive advertising is used to influence consumers to buy the company's product as opposed to competitors' products. During the maturity stage of a product's life cycle, persuasive advertising can help maintain the level of sales.

Reminder Advertising

Reminder advertising reinforces brand loyalty and keeps the product's names before the consumer during the later part of the maturity stage and all of the decline stage of the life cycle.

Advertising Media

An advertising medium is the specific communication vehicle used to carry the firm's message to potential consumers. The main media are newspapers, television, direct mail, radio, magazines and billboards. Newspapers receive the largest share of advertising revenue closely followed by television. Direct mail advertising is the fastest growing medium. Each medium has its own advantages and disadvantages.

Newspapers

Newspapers are the most widely used advertising medium. Almost every market is covered by at least one daily newspaper. Newspapers offer flexible, rapid coverage and they are read by many people. However, papers are discarded after they are read, few offer colour print, and reproduction quality is poor. Also, newspaper messages are difficult to target to specific audiences.

Television

Television allows advertisers to combine colour, sound and motion and to create effective dramatic presentations. Television has many advantages. Networks can provide advertisers with very detailed information on viewer demographics, allowing advertisers to choose carefully the most appropriate programme for the advertiser's particular message. National advertisers are able to reach huge numbers of people using national or regional networks, whilst local advertisers can buy time on a local station.

Television also has some disadvantages. The cost of television advertising is very high. Because there are many commercials - running 10, 15, 30 or 60 seconds each - viewers may not pay close attention to the commercials, or they may ignore them altogether (by leaving the room, using the mute button on the remote control, using the time to talk with someone and so on). Once the commercial has been broadcast, it is gone. The increasing popularity of recording programmes for watching at a more convenient time allows the viewer to cut out advertising messages.

Direct Mail

Direct mail includes letters, flyers and cards sent directly to consumers' homes or their places of business. Generally, flyers attempt to pull the customer to the store, while letters push for an immediate direct order. Direct mail allows advertisers to select target audiences fairly precisely, and it can be easily personalised.

It is true that much of direct mail is considered junk and thrown away, but what is read is taken seriously. When used skilfully, direct mail is cost effective and successful. Thus, recognising its effectiveness, many businesses are allocating a growing proportion of their advertising budgets to direct mail.

Radio

Radio advertising is restricted in the UK to local stations and to one or two specialist networks which allow advertising, such as Classic Radio. However, there is increasing pressure to allow more radio advertising which is significantly cheaper than TV advertising. One major drawback is the fact that many listeners use radio as 'background', paying little attention to the advertisements.

Magazines

Magazines offer the ability to select and reach specific consumer targets because there are magazines for every interest imaginable. Artwork reproduction is excellent in all major magazines, and there is plenty of space for product information. Some magazines publish different regional editions, giving advertisers more flexibility in selecting target markets. Magazines have a long life, and because they tend to be passed on, they are read by more than one person. One disadvantage of magazine advertising is that advertisements must be submitted well in advance of the publication date, and an advertisement's location is not guaranteed.

Billboards

Billboards and other outdoor advertising are relatively inexpensive and offer high repeat exposure. However, targeting is nearly impossible, giving advertisers no control over who sees the advertisement.

Other Media
Advertisers, always innovative, have used various other media to communicate their messages, including telephoning, skywriting, electronic scoreboards at sports stadiums, airships, balloons, bus shelters, *Yellow Pages* directories, shopping bags and displays on supermarket shopping trolleys. Indeed, even product packaging is a form of advertising.

Planning the Advertising Campaign
An advertising campaign is a detailed strategy organised in stages. The stages may vary somewhat, but they should include the following basic steps:

- **Identify and analyse the target:** identifying the target precisely is crucial to the success of the campaign. To pinpoint the target, advertisers must first analyse: the geographic distribution of consumers; demographic information such as age, sex, income and level of education completed; and consumers' attitudes both toward the product and toward competing products.
- **Define the advertising objectives:** the advertising goals must be stated precisely and in measurable terms, including the time span, the sales-increase goals (expressed in either £ revenue or market share) and the specific information to be conveyed.
- **Create the advertising platform:** the advertising platform includes the key selling points or features that are to be incorporated into the advertising campaign.
- **Determine the advertising appropriation:** the advertising appropriation is the total amount of money budgeted for advertising in a given period. Appropriations may be based on a percentage of existing sales, projected sales or competitors' spending on advertising.
- **Develop the media plan:** a media plan specifies exactly which media will be used, which ads will be featured, and when the advertisements will appear. A typical goal might be to reach the most people in the target audience for each pound spent or to make the strongest impact in the selected target market.
- **Create the advertising message:** the product's features, the characteristics of the target audience, the object of the campaign and the choice of media, all help determine the content and the form of the advertisement message, including the copy and the artwork used to illustrate the message. For radio and television, the message will also include sound.
- **Evaluate the effectiveness of the advertising:** the success of a campaign should be measured both during and after the campaign. Feedback permits adjustments during the campaign and provides valuable information to guide future campaigns.

Advertising Agencies

An advertising agency is a professional business organisation equipped to undertake all phases of the preparation, development and execution of advertising campaigns for its clients. Among the services that agencies provide are identifying and analysing target audiences, writing copy, preparing artwork, creating and preparing commercials, casting talent, media buying, budgeting campaigns and identifying spokespersons.

The agency bills the client for all production services and media expenses, then adds the agency's commission on total billings. Although large companies and companies that advertise a great deal have their own in-house advertising departments, they still use independent agencies to handle their advertising campaigns.

Regulation of Advertising

Advertising claims for products and services are sometimes exaggerated, deceptive or blatantly stretched beyond what can be proven. Advertisers must keep within the law (in the UK, the Trades Description Act) and must not make claims which are false. In the UK, the Advertising Standards Authority (ASA) is responsible for maintaining standards of advertising and responds to complaints from the public. A separate authority, the Independent Broadcasting Authority, supervises the standards of advertising on independent TV and radio. In general, voluntary agreements are effective within industries such as the British Code of Advertising Practice supported by most media except TV.

Personal Selling

Personal selling describes all individual communications intended to inform consumers about, and persuade them to buy, the company's products or services. Of all promotional methods, personal selling is the most adaptable, but is also the most expensive. Thus, personal selling is used more often to sell higher-priced items.

Personal selling can take one of two forms: selling products to other businesses, which includes many multimillion-dollar sales (e.g., heavy equipment), and retail sales, which involves selling consumer products to individual buyers.

Basic Tasks in Personal Selling

Personal selling is made up of three basic tasks; order processing, creative selling and missionary selling.

Order Processing

Order processing describes sales that require little persuasion but in depth service, including handling all steps from order placement to delivery, as well as any follow up that may be necessary. The salesperson's main responsibility is servicing the account and ensuring customer satisfaction. In some cases, the salesperson is a route salesperson, someone who calls on customers regularly (daily, weekly, monthly): For example, route salespeople for bread companies and milk companies call on retail stores daily, checking each store's supply of merchandise and restocking shelves immediately from inventory carried on their delivery trucks.

Creative Selling

Creative selling requires salespeople to apply a variety of techniques to persuade customers to buy a product, often because the benefits are not readily apparent to customers, or because the price is high. Car sales, sales of new brands or new products require creative selling. Creative selling is more complicated than other forms of selling. The steps in creative selling are described below:

- **Prospecting and qualifying:** prospecting is the process of finding and identifying potential customers (called *prospects*, short for prospective or likely customers). Salespeople find the names of prospects in a number of ways, for example, from company records, customers, friends, business associates and lists. The salespeople must then qualify each prospect – that is, he/she must evaluate potential customers to determine whether each has the authority to buy and the ability to pay. Each potential customer that passes this initial screening is a qualified prospect.
- **Making the approach:** the approach describes the first few minutes a salesperson spends with the qualified prospect. In personal selling, these first few minutes are crucial, because during this short time the salesperson makes that important first impression, which affects the salesperson's credibility and rapport with the customer.
- **Presenting and demonstrating:** the presentation is the salesperson's delivery of the promotional message; his or her full explanation of the product, its features, its uses and its benefits to the prospect. If possible, during the initial conversation with the customer, the salesperson tries to discover the customer's needs so that he or she can then tailor the presentation to that particular customer's needs. When appropriate, the salesperson should demonstrate the product.
- **Answering objections:** no matter what the product or its price, prospects will usually have some objections – that is, prospects will question the need for the product or show uncertainty about buying it. The reasons for objections may not always be clear, but objections often show that the buyer is interested. An experienced salesperson reads objections to learn the customer's feelings and attitudes, and to determine which selling points to reinforce with each customer. Strong objections, of course, show that the customer is not interested.
- **Closing the sale:** the closing is the most critical part of the personal selling process. This is the point when the salesperson asks the prospect to buy the product. Professionals use a wide range of techniques to close sales. For example, some salespeople 'assume the sale' and begin their close by completing an order form or asking indirect questions such as 'which delivery date is best for you?' or 'would you like to start with a small order?'

- **Following up the sale:** follow up activities after the sale include processing the order quickly, delivering the order on time, providing instructions on the care and use of the product and, if necessary, providing maintenance and repairs. Good follow up helps establish customer loyalty and is an important source of market research information.
- **The special role of telemarketing:** telemarketing is a specialised form of personal selling, namely, using the telephone for any or all steps in the selling process, from the approach to the close. The use of telemarketing has been growing steadily because it provides a cheaper alternative to face-to-face personal selling. Telemarketing may be used instead of outside salespeople, or it may be used in conjunction with outside salespeople, for example, for prospecting or for scheduling sales calls.

Missionary Selling

The objective of missionary selling is to promote the company's long-term image, rather than make a quick sale. Sales representatives for drug companies, for example, promote their products by calling on doctors, who in turn will then prescribe the company's pharmaceuticals to their patients. But the actual sale is made in the pharmacy.

Sales Promotion

Sales promotion, an important part of the promotion mix, includes all the related activities that companies sponsor in an effort to persuade customers to make purchases. Sales promotion can take a variety of forms, including coupons, point of purchase displays, trade shows and purchasing incentives (free samples, trading stamps and premiums).

Coupons

Coupons are certificates that entitle the bearer to a saving off a product's regular price. Coupons appear in newspapers and magazines, are sent through direct mail and are enclosed with packages of products to encourage repeat purchases. Coupons are often effective, both in attracting new customers and in inducing present users to buy more of the product.

Point of Purchase Displays

Point of purchase displays are designed to catch customers' attention at specific, prominent locations, for instance, at the ends of aisles or near the checkout counter at supermarkets.

Trade Shows

Trade shows – exhibits sponsored by industries and associations – allow companies to display and demonstrate their products to customers who have a special interest in a specific product. For example, computer software shows, furniture shows and gift merchandise trade shows attract buyers who are already interested in a given type of product.

Purchasing Incentives

Free samples, trading stamps and premiums are all used as purchasing incentives. Free samples also allow the customer to try the product without cost or risk; they may be given out by local retailers or sent directly to the consumer. Trading stamps are offered as a bonus for patronising certain stores. Premiums are gifts given to consumers in return for buying a specific product. Air Miles is a very popular incentive for a variety of purchases such as petrol.

Publicity and Public Relations
Publicity

Publicity refers to all unpaid messages about a company, its products or its personnel that appear in magazines and newspapers, or are broadcast on radio and television. Note the distinction between advertising, which is paid for, and publicity, which is free.

All media are eager to print or broadcast news that will be of interest to readers, listeners or viewers, and business organisations are equally eager to provide the media with publicity releases, for example, bulletins specially written and designed to satisfy media needs for news. Because publicity releases follow the format of newspaper stories or columns, they are easier for the media to use 'as is', with few or no changes. At the same time, their news format makes publicity releases appear objective and therefore more believable than company-paid advertising. For marketers, therefore, publicity is a form of free advertising. In the hands of expert publicists, publicity can be used to show the company at its best advantage or to downplay a negative image.

Because it is free for the company, the firm has less control over the media's use, or non use, of news releases. For many different reasons, the media do not use all the releases they receive from various organisations.

Public Relations

Public relations defines company-influenced publicity; publicity that the firm pays for and therefore controls. The goal of public relations is to establish a positive image and sense of goodwill between the company, its customers and the general public. To achieve this goal, companies contribute to art exhibitions, sponsor soccer and tennis tournaments, provide financial support for charitable and community organisations and so on.

SUMMARY

As this chapter shows, promotional strategy is part of the greater marketing picture. Marketing is involved in all decisions related to determining a product's characteristics, price, production quantities, sales and service.

SELECTED READING

Carnegie, Dale. 1981. *How to Win Friends and Influence People.* Simon & Schuster.
Jefkins, Frank. 1992. *Advertising Made Simple.* Butterworth-Heinemann.
Northmore, David. 1993. *How to Get Publicity for Free.* Bloomsbury.
Haywood, Roger. 1992. *All About Public Relations.* McGraw Hill.
Lancaster, Geoffrey. 1994. *Selling and Sales Management.* Pitman.

Part 6

Management Tools

<table><tr><td>16</td><td></td></tr></table>

Accounting and Financial Statements

Accounting is a management tool used in the control function of management. More specifically, accounting is the systematic collecting, analysing, classifying, recording, summarising, reporting and interpreting of business transactions. Book-keeping is routine record-keeping, a necessary part of accounting and producing financial information.

The Role of Accounting in Business

In the accounting process, the input is raw data and the output is financial statements. Financial statements are essential for management because they provide information needed to make every business decision. *Managerial accounting* is concerned with providing information to be used within the firm. *Financial accounting* is concerned with reporting to outside users such as stockholders, potential investors, the government or lenders.

The Role of Accountants

The accountant is concerned with all aspects of a company's financial operations. The accountant is involved with the start up of a company and the raising of funds, the control and profit reporting operations of a company, and also with those unfortunate companies which are liquidated. In the UK, although anyone may 'keep the books' of a company and update records on sales, purchases and cash records, an independent chartered or certified accountant is required to prepare the business accounts of a limited company each year, according to the provisions of the Companies Act 1985. The process of verifying the accuracy of these accounts is called *auditing*. Large companies will employ their own quali-fied accountants who prepare accounts for independent auditors.

In the UK, there are four main accounting institutions whose members are recog-nised as professionally qualified:

- **The Institute of Chartered Accountants:** there are three institutes, one for England and Wales; one for Scotland; and one for Ireland. Chartered accountants work in many different capacities. Many belong to independent professional organisations (such as Cooper & Lybrands) and act as independent auditors, although they are also accessible by the public. Others are employed by companies as part of the team of cost and management accountants. Chartered accountants are more often concerned with the legal issues than other accountants, and are very much involved with taxation, management buy-outs (MBOs), inheritance problems, liquidation of companies and raising finance (e.g., share issues).
- **The Chartered Association of Certified Accountants:** members of this association have the same statutory rights as chartered accountants to act as independent auditors, but the majority are employed by companies as part of the cost and management team.
- **The Chartered Institute of Management Accountants:** members of this institute are initially employed by companies for day-to-day financial recording and control. However, many members progress to become senior managers in such areas as operations and information systems, where their financial and wider business management skills prove very useful.
- **The Institute of Public Finance and Accountancy:** members of this institute provide accountants for government and nationalised industries which require more specialised training.

Other organisations represent the interests of people employed in the areas of financial recording such as the Association of Accounting Technicians, and the Institute of Chartered Secretaries and Administrators.

Users of Financial Information

The primary purpose of financial information is, of course, to inform people both within and outside the organisation. The primary users are managers. In addition to the company's managers, other users include government taxing agencies (Inland Revenue, the Customs and Excise), shareholders and potential investors, and suppliers and lenders.

Managers

Finances affect every company decision. Managers need financial information concerning sales revenues, costs and debtors (accounts receivable) to make decisions about pricing, resource allocation, investment in plant or equipment, and a wide range of other decisions. Much of this information is proprietary, that is, restricted to use within the firm and therefore not disclosed to outsiders.

Government Departments

Government Departments, including the Internal Revenue and the Customs and Excise, require companies to substantiate their income for the purpose of confirming tax liabilities.

Government Regulatory Agencies

In the UK, the government requires all companies to register a set of audited accounts with the Companies House each year. Failure to do this within the time limit specified can result in the company being heavily fined.

Shareholders

By law in the UK, a company must supply shareholders with a summary of the firm's position and firms comply by providing an annual report. Shareholders analyse the information provided in the annual report to make a number of decisions about the firm – for example, investment decisions and voting decisions concerning company management. The interests of the shareholders are protected by the Stock Exchange, which has strict rules for those organisations which have shares traded on the public market.

Potential Shareholders

Potential shareholders use financial information to evaluate the present financial position of the company, to make decisions about the company's future potential to determine the likely return for their investments, evaluate the risks involved and so on.

Suppliers and Lenders

Before they extend credit or approve loans, suppliers and lenders require financial statements from the company. They use financial statements to determine whether a company is credit worthy.

The Accounting Process

The accounting process transforms raw financial data into useful reports. The process requires three distinct steps: capturing the data; processing the data; and communicating the results in the form of financial statements. The financial statements, in turn, provide information on sales revenues, costs, money payable (creditors), money receivable (debtors) and other financial data.

Central to understanding the accounting process are the accounting equation, double-entry book-keeping and accounting cycle.

The Accounting Equation

The accounting equation forms the basis for the accounting process:

$$Assets = Liabilities + Owners' equity$$

This equation shows the relationship of assets, liabilities and owners' equity.

Assets are things of value owned by the firm. They include tangible things such as cash, land, stock and equipment, and intangible things such as licences, patents and goodwill.

Liabilities are the firm's debts and obligations, which the business owes to others.

Owners' equity is the difference between assets and liabilities, that is, the amount that would remain for the firm's owners if the assets were used to pay off the liabilities.

Double-Entry Book-Keeping

Double-entry book-keeping describes a system in which each financial transaction is recorded as two separate accounting entries in order to maintain the balance of the accounting equation. A loan, for example, is entered as follows: The cash received is recorded as an asset, and the loan itself (that is, the outstanding debt) is recorded as a liability. Only by making both entries can the equation be kept in balance.

The Accounting Cycle

The typical accounting system uses five steps, collectively known as the *accounting cycle*, to transform raw business data into financial statements.

1. Analysing Source Documents

Basic accounting data originates from receipts, invoices, sales slips, order forms and other records or source documents of business transactions. Transactions must be analysed to identify how they are to be entered into accounting journals and ledgers.

2. Entering Transactions in the General Journal

Each transaction is first recorded in a general journal (a 'day' book) by date (i.e., in the order that transactions occur). Therefore, the journal offers a chronological list of all original transactions. It is a prime record.

3. Posting Transactions to the General Ledger

Entries in the general journal are made chronologically. These entries are then copied or posted to the general ledger not by date but according to categories or accounts.

The general ledger is a book of accounts containing separate pages or sections for each income account (such as sales) and for each expense account (such as telephone). Each item is entered twice. For example, if a product is sold for £100 cash, the sales account is credited (added to) with £100 and the cash account is debited (subtracted from) with £100. The words 'credit' and 'debit' are essentially accounting terms and must be used in this sense rather than the assumed general meaning.

4. Determining a Trial Balance

Since all entries in the general ledger are entered twice, the sum of all the debit entries must equal the sum of all the credit entries. A trial balance is the summary of the balances of all the general ledger accounts at the end of the accounting period. If the accounts balance, the accountant can prepare financial statements, the final step.

5. Preparing Financial Statements

The firm's financial statements are prepared from the information contained in the trial balance. Financial statements are organised and presented in a standardised format designed to make the information accessible to all interested parties. In the UK, financial statements comply with regulations and standards set by the Companies Act, and the various Statements of Standard Accounting Practice (SSAPs) issued jointly by the professional accounting institutions listed previously.

Financial Statements

Financial statements are periodic summarisations of a company's transactions. The most important financial statements are the balance sheet, the profit and loss account (or income statement), and statement of cash flows.

Balance Sheet

In the accounting equation, assets are listed on the left side of the equal sign, whilst liabilities and owners's equity are listed on the right side. Both sides must be equal, that is, they must balance. The balance sheet, as its name tells, shows a summary of all accounts and therefore shows the financial position of the firm on a specific date. (See Figure 16.1).

Assets

Assets are listed on the balance sheet according to their liquidity, the least liquid first. *Liquidity* measures the ease with which an asset can be converted to cash. Land and stocks are both assets, but stocks are more liquid because they can be sold much more quickly than land can be sold and converted to cash. Assets are described as current, fixed or intangible:

```
                         GOOLD CORPORATION Ltd
                    BALANCE SHEET - 31 December, 199-

Fixed Assets
  Intangible Assets
    Patents                                    12,000
    Goodwill                                   30,000        42,000
  Tangible Assets
    Delivery equipment          220,000
    Less depreciation            40,000       180,000
    Furniture etc.              124,000
    Less depreciation            30,000        94,000       274,000
    Total Fixed Assets                                                   316,000
Current Assets
  Stock and work in progress                   82,000
  Debtors                        80,000
  Less bad debts allowance        4,000        76,000
  Investments etc.                              84,000
  Prepaid expenses                               4,000
  Cash                                         118,000
      Total Current Assets                                 364,000
Creditors falling due within one year
  Bank loan & overdraft                         50,000
  Trade creditors                               70,000
  Sundry creditors                              20,000
      Total                                                140,000

Net Current Assets (Liabilities)                                        224,000
Total Assets less Current Liabilities                                   540,000
Creditors falling due after more than one year                          80,000

Net Assets                                                              460,000

Capital and Reserves
  Called up share capital                      300,000
  Reserves                                     160,000

Shareholders Funds                                                      460,000
```

Figure 16.1 The balance sheet

● **Current assets:** these are cash and other assets that can be quickly converted to cash, or assets that will be used in the 'current' year. Cash is the most liquid asset, followed by marketable securities, shares and bonds that can be readily sold. Next in order of liquidity is debtors (accounts receivable), money due to the firm within 30 to 90 days from customers, followed by any reserve allowance for doubtful accounts. Current stock of raw materials, goods in the course of manufacture (work in progress), and finished goods expected to be sold within the year are listed next, and finally, prepaid expenses (assets that have been paid for in advance but not yet used) such as the balance of any insurance premiums covering a future period.

● **Fixed assets:** these are assets that will be held or used longer than one year.

Typically, fixed assets include land, buildings and equipment. Because the value of many fixed assets decreases each year, this devaluation is accounted for through *depreciation*, a method of distributing the cost of fixed assets over a period of years. For each fixed asset, the amount depreciated is treated as an expense for that year and is subtracted from the value of that fixed asset.

● **Intangible assets:** not all assets are tangible. Intangible assets such as patents, copyrights, franchises, trademarks and goodwill have a financial value because they offer legal rights, advantages or privileges.

Liabilities

Liabilities are grouped into those which have to be settled or paid within one year (called *'creditors: amounts falling due within one year'*) and those which have to be repaid at a later date (*called 'creditors: amounts falling due after more than one year'*). Typical examples of the former are tax due and dividends authorised but not paid, bills and wages earned but not paid, and any bank overdraft. Examples of the latter are loans supplied by banks, mortgages on property, and other loans at known interest rates and repayment dates.

Note that if a 'long-term loan' is due to be repaid within one year, then it moves from one group of liabilities into theother.

Overdraft

Although bank overdrafts are often allowed to continue over very long periods, they are usually treated as short-term liabilities because the bank has the power to ask for immediate repayment if it feels that the loan is at risk.

Tax

In the UK, companies pay Corporation Tax which is based on the net profits as calculated by the Inland Revenue (IR). The IR has its own rules about allowable costs which can be used to calculate profit. Usually the agreed tax bill is due for settlement within nine months from the end of the business accounting year. Often the business year coincides with the government's fiscal year which   runs from 1 April to 31 March.

Owners' Equity

Owners equity can appear on the balance sheet in different ways, depending on the legal form of the business. If the business is a sole proprietorship owned, for example, by William Smith, owners' equity is listed as 'William Smith, Capital'. In a corporation, owners' equity is identified as 'shareholders equity'. 'Shareholders equity' contains two listings: 'share capital', which includes the amount of the shareholders' investment in terms of the face value of the share certificates issued; and 'reserves', which represents the increase in shareholders' equity that results from profitable operations that have been retained by the business, and sometimes the revaluation of fixed assets.

GOOLD CORPORATION

PROFIT AND LOSS ACCOUNT - For the year ending 31 December 199-

	£	£	£
Sales		930,000	
Less returns inwards	19,000		
Less quantity discounts	9,000	28,000	
Net sales			902,000
Cost of goods sold			
Opening stock		80,000	
Purchases	692,000		
Less purchase discount	22,000		
Less returns outwards	0		
Net purchases		670,000	
Cost of goods available for sale		750,000	
Less closing stock		82,000	
Cost of goods sold			668,000
Gross Profit on sales			234,000
Operating Expenses			
Selling expenses			
Sales salaries	60,000		
Advertising	12,000		
Sales promotion	5,000		
Depreciation - sales equip.	6,000		
Misc. selling costs	3,000		
Total Selling Expenses		86,000	
Admin. expenses			
Office salaries	37,000		
Rent	17,000		
Depreciation - office equip.	11,000		
Heat, Light & Power	5,000		
Insurance	2,000		
Misc. expenses	1,000		
Total Admin. Expenses		73,000	
Total Operating Expense			159,000
Net Operational Profit			75,000
Less finance charges			4,000
Net Profit before tax			71,000
Less corporation tax			10,650
Net Profit after tax			60,350

Figure 16.2 The profit and loss account

Profit and Loss Account

A profit and loss account (also called an income statement) is a summary of revenues and expenses for a certain period of time (usually for one year, but can be for any defined period). A profit and loss account covering the previous year must be included in a corporation's annual report. (See Figure 16.2).

Just as there is an equation for the balance sheet, there is one for the profit and loss account:

$$\text{Revenues} - \text{Expenses} = \text{Profit (or net loss)}$$

Revenues

Revenues (also called gross sales) are all receipts from customers' purchases; the money received for goods and services sold. Goods return, sales allowances and sales discounts are deducted from gross sales to yield net sales (the actual amount received).

Companies record their revenues (as well as their costs) on an accrual basis. An accrual basis records revenues and costs in the year in which the sale is made, whether or not payment is received or made in that year.

Revenues received from the company's main business have to be listed separately from other revenues. For example, rent paid to the company, interest received from banks, dividends received from securities, or even benefits from the use of a piece of surplus land as a public car park.

Expenses

Expenses fall into two general categories: (i) cost of goods sold and (ii) operating expenses.

(i) Cost of goods sold

Cost of goods sold is computed according to this formula:

$$\text{Cost of goods sold} = \text{Opening stock} + \text{Net purchases} - \text{Closing stock}$$

This is directly applicable to a trading business which purchases goods for resale. The net purchases are the costs of replenishing stocks.

For a manufacturing firm, the *net purchases* must include all the costs of manufacturing. Therfore, the cost of goods sold will contain:

- Raw materials stock consumed (the cost of timber, steel and other raw materials used to manufacture products).
- Work in progress stock consumed – that is, the cost of materials for all unfinished products now in some stage of the manufacturing process but not yet completed.
- Direct labour costs.
- Depreciation of manufacturing plant.
- Other production overheads such as supervision costs, consumables, power costs and maintenance costs.

A manufacturing business must include all the manufacturing costs which it could have avoided if it purchased the product from outside instead.

Stock is valued at the lower of cost or net realisable value. Net realisable value is often used by retail outlets where time and fashion can reduce some stocks to a nil valuation. Stock can be costed by any one of five methods:

1 The *identified item* method assigns an actual cost to each item, because the item can be associated with a specific invoice (or bill to pay). Hence the value

of stock remaining in the stores is simply the addition of all the associated invoice costs.

2 The *average cost* (AVCO) method assumes that the cost for each stock item is the same, and therefore assigns an average cost to each item. The average cost will change only when more stock of a different value is added to existing stock. The value of stock remaining in store is calculated on the basis of the last weighed average calculation.

3 The *first in, first out* (FIFO) method assigns the cost of the first item issued to the value of the first item placed into stock, even though all items (new and old) are indistinguishable. Stock remaining in the stores would be valued at latest prices.

4 The *last in, first out* (LIFO) method assigns the cost of the first item issued to the value of the last item received. Stock remaining in stores would tend to be valued at old prices. New prices are passed straight on to the customer, even though all stock items (new and old) are indistinguishable.

5 The *next in, first out* (NIFO) method assigns the cost of the next item or replacement to the cost of the first item sold. Thus, in times of increasing prices, the selling price would reflect the high cost of replacement.

For example, say a business had an existing stock of ten items of a material at a valuation of £1 each, and then purchased an additional ten items for £2 each. All items looked identical. Then assume that 15 items are drawn from stock. What is the value of the remaining stock?

● Under the AVCO system, the items are all valued at £1.50 each, the weighted mean. The items left in stock are worth £7.50.
● Under the FIFO system, the items left in stock are assumed to be the 'old ones', and are worth £5.
● Under the LIFO system, the items left in stock are assumed to be the new ones, and are worth £10.

Each system of valuation makes different assumptions. While all five systems are acceptable, each valuation system affects the balance sheet, income and taxes differently. Companies may choose from among these a method for their own internal reporting systems. However, the Inland Revenue does not accept FIFO or NIFO methods for calculating profit for tax calculation purposes since both tend to reduce profits (and taxes!) in times of increasing prices or inflation.

There are two major methods for calculating the *depreciation of fixed assets* over a time period, usually one year:

● **The reducing balance method** assumes that the depreciation of a fixed asset is a fixed percentage of the 'written down value' (WDV) each year. The WDV is the initial cost less the total depreciation over previous years. For example, if a percentage agreed is 10 per cent and the reduced balance of the asset (initial cost less accumulated depreciation over previous years) is £5,000, the depreciation charge will be £500. Consequently, the new WDV would be £4,500. At the end of the following year the depreciation would be 10 per cent of £4,500, or £450. Accountants use appropriate but different depreciation percentages for different categories of asset. For example, buildings may be depreciated at 5 per cent whereas office computers could be depreciated at 30 per cent.

● **The straight line method** assumes that depreciation is a constant charge each year over the life of the asset, assuming the life expectancy is known. The depreciation each year is the total loss in capital divided by the life expectancy. For example, if an asset costs £10,000 and is expected to be sold for £2,000 after five years use (the life expectancy within the business rather than the life expectancy of the asset), the depreciation each year is:

$$\text{Depreciation} = £10,000 - £2,000 = £8,000 \div 5 = £1,600 \text{ each year}$$

(ii) Operating expenses

Operating expenses includes all other costs beyond costs of goods sold. Two broad categories of operating expenses are selling expenses and general expenses.

Selling expenses include all costs related to the firm's marketing activities, for example, salaries of sales representatives, and advertising and promotion expenses.

General expenses, sometimes called *administrative expenses*, are general costs incurred in running a business, as opposed to costs specifically and directly associated with a particular item or service sold. General expenses include salaries of office workers, all the expense of operating an office (rent, the cost of office supplies, electricity, insurance and equipment) and other miscellaneous expenses (e.g., charitable donations and contributions).

Net Profit Before Tax

Net profit before tax is the profit earned, or the loss suffered, by a firm during the accounting period, before tax calculations are made.

Net Profit after taxes is derived by deducting tax. Since this figure appears at the end or bottom of the statement, net profit after taxes is sometimes referred to as 'the bottom line'.

Cash Flows Statement

In the UK, it is a requirement of the Accounting Standards Authority that all publicly owned businesses prepare a statement of cash flows (funds flow). This statement describes the company's cash receipts (money coming into the firm) and cash payments (money going out of the firm) for a specific period. It provides a detailed picture of the company's ability to generate and use cash.

The cash flows statement is only concerned with actual cash; while the profit and loss account also includes noncash items such as depreciation, allowances and discounts. (See Figure 16.3).

The cash flow statement summarises three areas in which cash is received and disbursed:

● **Operations:** this shows cash generated by and expended for the buying and

GOOLD CORPORATION Ltd		
CASH FLOW STATEMENT – Year ending 31 December 199–		
Cash flows from Operations	£	£
Net Profit		75,000
Adjustments:		
Depreciation	6,000	
Increase in Stock	(2,000)	
Decrease in Debtors	1,000	
Increase in Creditors	1,000	
Total adjustments		6,000
Net Cash provided by operations		81,000
Cash flows from Investments		
Payments for purchase of equipment	(15,000)	
Net Cash used in investing		(15,000)
Cash flows from Financing		
Long term loan received	10,000	
Net Cash provided by financing		10,000
Net increase in cash		76,000
Cash at start of year		42,000
Cash at end of year		118,000

Figure 16.3 Cash flow statement

selling of goods and services as part of the firm's main operating activities. Operations also include the effect of inventory changes, debtors (accounts receivable) and creditors (accounts payable) on cash flows.
- **Investing:** this reflects cash income from, and payments for, buying and selling securities, property or equipment.
- **Financing:** this includes cash flows from borrowing and issuing stock, as well as to repay loans and pay dividends.

Analysing Financial Statements

On the surface, the information offered in balance sheets and profit and loss accounts help answer a variety of questions about a firm's ability to do business, its profitability or its value as an investment. Just beneath the surface of these statements lies a wealth of information that can be easily uncovered by computing certain financial ratios.

Financial Ratios

A financial ratio shows the relationship between two elements of a balance sheet or profit and loss account. Financial ratios offer keen insights into a firm's present health and its future potential. Like soccer statistics, ratios are most useful in comparisons. For example, comparing the same ratio for the same company for several consecutive years may uncover a trend, a weakness or a strength in that company. Comparing a specific ratio for two companies in the same industry may show why Company A is stronger, or weaker, than Company B. The most common and most useful financial ratios are explained below.

Liquidity Ratios

Liquidity ratios indicate a firm's solvency and its ability to meet its short-term liabilities. Can it pay its bills? Liquidity ratios are especially meaningful to short-term lenders. The main liquidity ratios used are:

● **Working capital:** the difference between current assets and current liabilities:

Working capital = Current assets - Current liabilities
(current liabilities = creditors falling due within one year)

Working capital indicates how much liquidity would remain if a firm immediately paid off all its current liabilities.

● **Current ratio:** One of the most commonly used measures of liquidity is found by dividing current assets by current liabilities:

$$\text{Current ratio} = \frac{\text{Current assets}}{\text{Current liabilities}}$$

● **Acid test ratio:** also called the *quick ratio*, it is very similar to the current ratio. The acid test ratio is calculated by dividing quick assets by current liabilities:

$$\text{Acid test ratio} = \frac{\text{Quick assets}}{\text{Current liabilities}}$$

Quick assets are current assets less stocks and prepaid expenses, because these are not immediately liquid. Quick assets include cash and only those current assets that can be readily converted to cash (namely, marketable securities, accounts receivable and notes receivable).

Debtors Turnover

Debtors turnover is a measurement of how long debtors (customers who owe money on normal credit transactions) take to pay their bills. It would be nice if all debtors paid within 30 days, the time usually given on invoices. In real life, the time period is often much longer, and the smaller firm with little 'clout' is often at the mercy of the larger customer whose business is essential to the profitability of the small business. The longer the time to pay bills, the more likely the small business will become insolvent.

$$\text{Debtors turnover} = \frac{\text{Average outstanding debt x 52 weeks}}{\text{Annual credit sales}}$$

For example, if the average outstanding debt is £20,000 and the total credit sales for the year were £260,000, then:

$$\text{Debtors turnover} = \frac{£20,0000}{£260,000} \text{ x } 52 = 4 \text{ weeks}$$

Stock Turnover

Stock turnover is a measurement of the time between purchasing stocks and using them. The value of stock during this period represents 'dead money', money which could be used for other things. The shorter the stock turnover, the less cash tied up.

$$\text{Stock turnover} = \frac{\text{Average stock value x 52 weeks}}{\text{annual stock purchase}}$$

For example, if the average stock value is £40,000 and the total annual purchases are £260,000, then:

$$\text{Stock turnover} = \frac{£40,000 \text{ x } 52}{£260,000} = 8 \text{ weeks}$$

Gearing

Gearing is a ratio which shows the extent to which the firm's operations are financed through borrowing, as opposed to the shareholders' risk capital. Gearing is therefore of special interest to long-term lenders and investors.

$$\text{Gearing} = \frac{\text{Long-term loan}}{\text{Shareholders' equity}}$$

Long-term loan is represented by 'creditors falling due after more than one year', and the *shareholders equity* is the same as the net assets of the business (see Figure 16.1). Gearing can also be calculated as a ratio of long-term loan to fixed assets. It is always wise to seek the appropriate definition of the word 'gearing' in specific financial negotiations.

Most lenders would be wary of lending to a business which already has a gearing of 50 per cent or more (i.e., where its existing long term loans already total half as much as the money invested by the shareholders or owners of the business). In this case, the owners would need to seek additional funds from risk-taking investors or seek some form of guarantee from third parties such as the government. This happens with new, growing businesses where the government does offer a loan guarantee in return for higher interest charges.

Profitability Ratios

Profitability ratios indicate how effectively the firm's resources are being used.

● **Net profit margin:** this indicates how effectively the firm is transforming sales into profits:

$$\text{Net profit margin} = \frac{\text{Net profit after tax}}{\text{Net sales}}$$

● **Return on equity:** also called *return on investment*, this indicates how much profit is generated by each £ of equity:

$$\text{Return on equity} = \frac{\text{Net profit after tax}}{\text{Owners' equity}}$$

● **Earnings per share (EPS):** this is a widely used indicator of a corporation's success:

$$\text{Earnings per share} = \frac{\text{Net profit after tax}}{\text{Number of shares}}$$

Budgeting and Planning

Budgets

While financial statements capture a view of the past, budgets look forward to the future. Budgets are financial plans for a specific future-period, usually one year. Managers use budgets to guide them in their day-to-day operations and investors use budgets to evaluate future plans and future potential. The master budget includes several individual budgets that together, summarise planned financial activities.

Operating Budgets

An operating budget addresses a specific area of day-to-day business activities; that is, addresses a specific area of operations. Together, operating budgets of all operating divisions or groups make up an overall financial plan. An operating budget is typically developed for areas such as sales, production and operating expenses.

The *sales budget* projects sales income and sales expenses for all items listed in the profit and loss account (i.e., for all sales items that will generate income). The *production budget* and the *operating expenses budget* will pick up the sales estimates used in the sales budget. As a result, these budgets are interdependent. When combined, these budgets comprise the budgeted profit and loss account that gives the firm the 'total budget picture' for a given period. Like all budgets, if it is not satisfactory to management, it may need to be revised.

The *cash budget* is a plan that shows cash receipts and cash payments for a given period. The cash budget shows not only how much, but also when, cash is anticipated to be coming in and going out of the firm. Thus, the cash budget is an important tool for projecting borrowing needs. The cash budget is the last budget prepared.

Capital Expenditure Budgets

While operating budgets are concerned with the purchase of current assets, capital expenditure budgets detail a company's long-term plans for investment in plant and equipment. Capital expenditure budgets often involve large sums and reflect key management decisions.

The Budgeting Process

There are two main approaches to budgeting:

- **Traditional budgeting:** this approach uses as its base the previous year's budget. Managers modify the individual items to reflect increased costs, revised goals and so on, and they provide justifications for any new expenditures. As a result, traditional budgeting often overlooks outdated or wasteful programmes. There is little or no attempt to reconsider any item as to its appropriateness in the light of actual recorded performance.
- **Zero-based budgeting:** instead of using the preceding year's budget as a base, zero-base budgeting starts with no base, requiring managers to justify all expenses, in every budget, in every year. Zero-base budgeting often reduces unnecessary spending, but it requires additional time-consuming paperwork.

Planning

A company's plan is an outline of a its intended future actions needed to accomplish its goals.

Long-Range Plans

A long-range plan, commonly called a *Strategic* or *corporate plan*, covers actions over a two – five-year period, sometimes longer. Alternatively, a long-range plan may be made up of a series of one-year plans.

Short-Range Plans

A short-range plan covers one year or less and tends to be more specific than a long-range plan. As conditions change, the short-range plan will update, modify and adapt the long-range plan.

SUMMARY

All employees within a business have a need to know how well the business is doing in terms of profitability, especially since they are constantly being challenged to reduce costs. The scope of this need is dependent on the position of the employee within the organisation; the higher the position, the more detail required. If managers are charged with being profitable they have the right to know how the profits are being calculated, what trends are occurring, and what they can do to improve these profits in the short and long term. Modern businesses require an openness about accounts on a 'need to know' basis and an awareness that more and more employees 'need to know'.

SELECTED READING

Sizer, John. 1994. *An Insight Into Management Accounting.* Penguin.
Watts, B.K.R. 1994. *Business Finance.* M & E.
Johnson, William et al. 1988. *Baffled by Balance Sheets?* Kogan Page.
Glynn, John et al. 1994. *Accounting for Managers.* Chapman & Hall.

17 Management Information and Statistical Analysis

Data, Information and Information Management

In business, managers are paid to make decisions which are based on information. Whether the decision is complicated and critically important (whether to merge with another company) or simple and routine (which supplier to use for general office products), businesspeople need to evaluate information.

Information sources, which are many and diverse, offer 'hard' information and 'soft' information. 'Hard' information describes factual information such as actual sales figures from the past, government reports and surveys, actual production costs, actual expenses paid and so on. 'Soft' information describes nonfactual information such as opinions, feelings and beliefs. In any case, whatever the source, today's business managers have a wealth of information at their fingertips; such a massive amount of information, in fact, that today's company needs a management information system (MIS) (preferably computerised) to help collect, organise, analyse and distribute the overwhelming quantity of information available to its managers. Without its MIS, the data and the information available to a company is often useless.

The first step in understanding the role of information in general, and of the MIS in particular, in business management is to distinguish between information and data.

Data Versus Information

When managers complain that they receive too much 'information', they are often referring not to information but to data. *Data* are raw facts and figures, the raw materials of information, which usually have little or no meaning on their own. To be useful, data must be collected, sorted, organised and presented in a meaningful form, a form that managers can use to make decisions. Therefore, in this transformed state, data become information.

Kinds of Data

Data can be classified according to their source:

● **Internal data:** these are the data available from the company's records. For example, a company's financial statements and accounting records provide data on creditors and suppliers; its personnel files offer information on salaries and employee turnover; its invoices and sales reports contain data that can be valuable in establishing and understanding sales patterns.

● **External data:** these originate from sources outside the company. Newspapers, radio and TV keep managers informed of events and trends - data that could affect the company's business. Government agencies, such as the Central Statistical Office or the Office of Population Censuses and Surveys, can provide valuable data concerning current and projected unemployment, income and educational levels within market areas and so on. Customers, suppliers, bankers, even friends are sources of business data.

Data can also be classified as primary or secondary:

● **Primary data:** describes data gathered through original research on a specific problem or situation. A company may, for example, conduct a formal, thorough survey of its customers to find out customers' attitudes, preferences and opinions in an effort to collect primary data.

● **Secondary data:** originate not from the company but instead from other sources, for example, economic and industrial surveys. Thus, secondary data describe data that are already available. If the secondary data are inadequate, the company may decide to update the original source of the data.

Methods of Data Collection

There are three basic methods used to collect primary data:

● **Observation:** this is the process of watching and observing behaviour and performance. For example, to decide whether trucks should be redirected to other highways, the Department of Transport may monitor a particular stretch of road to observe how many large trucks use the road each day. A detergent manufacturer may set up video cameras in a supermarket to observe customers' selection process, such as how long customers look at different brands or how many different boxes they pick up before making their final selection.

● **Experimentation:** this is a process of controlled observation and testing, often conducted in a laboratory. A detergent manufacturer uses lab experiments to compare the ability of its detergent, against competitive products, to remove oil and grease stains, for example. Companies may also use experimentation to evaluate the effectiveness of training methods. The experiment may expose one group of employees, the control group, to only on-the-job training but the other group, the experimental group, to classroom training in addition to on-the-job training. After training is completed, the company then compares the job performance of both groups on identical tasks. In this way, the experiment can establish which training method was more effective.

● **Survey:** this method elicits opinions and attitudes and/or gathers facts from a specific group by means of questionnaires or telephone interviews. A manufacturer may easily be able to survey all of the 30 or 50 wholesalers it deals with, but in many cases it is impossible or impractical to survey all users. In most cases, therefore, researchers sample the total population. A *sample* is a small group that, ideally, is representative of the larger group. From this sample of the larger group, researchers can forecast or draw conclusions with some degree of accuracy. Television and newspaper election polls, for instance, sample voters and use the results of their sample to forecast the outcome of the election.

Management Information and the MIS

Data collection produces vast amounts of figures, statistics and other facts. But not all data, and as a result not all information, available to managers are useful, accurate or relevant.

The Need for Management Information

If managers are to make the 'right' decisions, they must have information that is timely, complete, concise, relevant and accurate:

● **Timely:** information, must be based on current or recent data.
● **Complete:** complete here does not mean exhaustive, rather that the information is sufficient for making this particular decision without guesswork.
● **Concise:** although information should be complete, it should be presented concisely in order to be more easily and quickly understood.
● **Relevant:** 'extra' information, data above and beyond the present needs for making the decision, detracts from the decision-making process and should be excluded.
● **Accurate:** the information should have no errors. Inaccurate information provides no foundation for making decisions.

Information that is timely, complete, concise, relevant and accurate gives managers a significant advantage in making decisions. Information that is vital to decision-making is called *management information*.

The MIS

To transform data into vital information and to use that information to the company's best advantage are responsibilities of the firm's management information system.

The Role of the MIS

The management information system (MIS) comprises all the tools and procedures that transform data into information that can be used for decision-making at all levels within an organisation. For example, the MIS helps track daily sales and provides reports comparing actual daily sales to: (i) actual daily sales in the same time period last year and (ii) estimated or budgeted daily sales for this current period. Managers can then compare this information with other reports that track, for example, the cost of goods sold. Together, these sales and cost reports help managers decide whether they should adjust their operations in any way. Without such MIS generated information, managers would indeed be working at a disadvantage.

Today, of course, computers are mandatory parts of any company's MIS. Computers facilitate the handling of financial, accounting, production, sales and cost data, all of which are vital to the effective operation of a modern business. The significant role that computers play in the MIS will be discussed in detail in the next chapter.

Functions of the MIS

The MIS has four main functions:

- **Collecting data:** one key MIS function is to collect data. Data, as already discussed, originate from a variety of sources, and computers make it possible to gather data in unique ways. For example, while bar code scanners allow checkers to total a customer's purchases, it can also track sales and goods in stock for the MIS.
- **Organising and storing data:** the MIS organises data efficiently to make data easily accessible, and stores data in databases. A database is an organised collection of data. A company usually has many databases, for example, a payroll database, an accounts payable database, an inventory database and a database of customers' names and addresses. Today even small companies can afford to computerise their databases. Computerised databases enable users to save, view, update, manipulate and print out the data stored.
- **Processing data into information:** once data have been collected, organised and stored, it can be processed to make the information useful to management. This can be printed out as it appears on the computer screen, or it can be manipulated in a variety of ways. For example, let us assume that a database lists the names and addresses of 1,500 retail stores. For each store it then lists: the last purchase, total £ purchases for the last 12 month period; amount currently owed and how long this amount is outstanding; and the sales representative's name or code number. Once this information has been stored in the database, the data can be sorted and manipulated to yield printed reports as shown in the following examples:

By store name in alphabetical order.
By date of purchase, either in chronological or in reverse-chronological order.
By quantity of last purchase.
By total annual purchases, either from greatest to least or vice versa.

By post code to show sales by geographic region.
By product-code numbers, showing sales for each product, and/or which stores purchased which products.
By amount owed, either from the largest amount to the smallest or vice versa.
By sales representative, showing the amount of sales for each sales representative and/or the products sold by each representative.

Furthermore, the data can be summarised in any of several ways, as well as calculated for, say, tax or commission purposes. All of this information can be derived from a single database.

● **Presenting data:** the data, however organised, must be presented in a meaningful and useful form. Information is most often presented in the form of reports and graphs, which can often be tailored to the specific needs of the people who receive the report.

Decision-Support Systems

MIS systems that are specifically designed to support complex decision-making are called *decision support systems*. Decision support systems are often intended for high-level decision-making and long-term planing, as opposed to daily or monthly operational processing or information needs. For example, managers use decision support systems in investment analysis, cash management and sales force deployment.

Statistical Analysis

Much of the information that management uses is statistical in nature, such as financial audits and cash flows, percentages and ratios, productivity levels, stock levels, averages and means, probabilities and risks, increases and decreases. To understand the meaning of the numerical data requires statistical analysis.

Statistics

Statistics are figures that summarise and represent factual data and are, therefore, especially meaningful. Statistics include the total quantity of goods sold in a particular period, the number of chocolate bars eaten in one year, a company's return on investment, a cricketer's batting average, and the infant mortality rate in the Europe. Many statistics are expressed as percentages, for instance, an inflation rate of 9.5 per cent and an unemployment rate of 6.2 per cent.

Probability

Probability attempts to measure the likelihood that an event will occur. For instance, in coin tossing the probability of landing on heads, as opposed to tails, is one in two, or 50 per cent. Given this probability, if a coin is tossed 100 times, it is expected to land on heads 50 times.

Probability has a significant impact on everyday business operations. In a given sales group, for example, suppose that out of every ten demonstrations given to qualified customers, sales representatives make four sales. Knowing this probability, the sales manager will be alerted to a possible problem when a sales representative suddenly makes, say, only one or two sales in ten demonstrations.

Sampling

Collecting and storing data can be expensive. Therefore, researchers often rely upon a representative sample. As already discussed, a sample is a small group that, ideally, is representative of the larger group (called the *population*). A random sample is a sample in which any person or item in the population has a known chance of being selected.

Displaying Statistical Information

Statistical information is often easier to communicate graphically rather than by lists of numbers. The types of diagrams most often used to display statistical data are frequency distribution tables, line graphs, bar charts, pie charts and pictographs.

Frequency Distributions

A frequency distribution is a table in which possible values for a variable are grouped into classes, and the number of times a value falls into each class is recorded. For example, Table 17.1 shows a frequency distribution of the weekly wages of 100 workers.

A table is a diagram that displays information in columns and rows. It is most often used to show the relationship between two or more related variables. (See Table 17.2).

TABLE 17.1 Frequency distribution table

Average Weekly Wage of 100 Workers	Frequency
250–275	7
276–300	12
301–325	20
326–350	46
351–375	10
376–400	4

Line graphs

A line graph shows a line connected by dots at various points plotted on a graph. Line graphs are very effective for showing changes in the value of a variable or trend over a period of time. (See Figure 17.1).

TABLE 17.2 An array table

Sales (Year)	Product X	Product Q
19X0	100	94
19X1	120	75
19X2	135	105
19X3	128	110

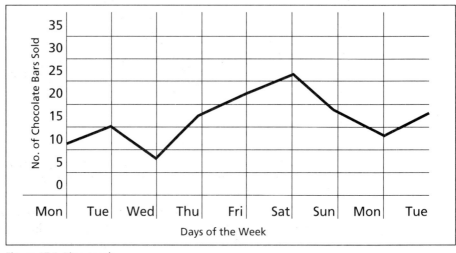

Figure 17.1 Line graph

Bar charts

A bar chart uses either horizontal or vertical bars to measure and compare several values, with the longest bar representing the greatest value. (See Figure 17.2).

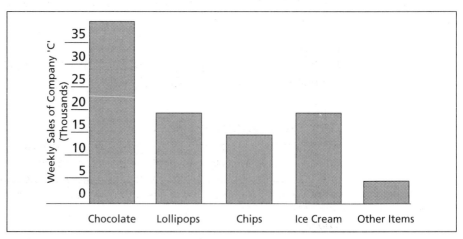

Figure 17.2 Bar chart

Pie charts

A pie chart is a circle that has been divided into sectors, each sector representing a different item. The whole pie represents 100 per cent of the value being measured, and each 'slice' represents the percentage of the whole for one particular item. If one sector represented 20 per cent of the data, the angle of the sector would equal 20 per cent of 360 degrees, or 72 degrees.

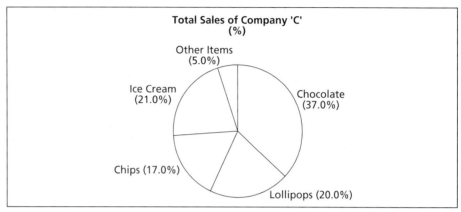

Figure 17.3 Pie chart

For example, a pie chart showing the distribution of a college's students by regional area might have one slice for each region of the country, the size of each slice depending on the distribution of students in that particular region. If the college has 20,000 students and one-quarter or 5,000 are from the northeast of England, then the northeast slice would take up one-quarter or 25 per cent of the pie. If 2,500 students are from the south, then a smaller sector representing 12.5 per cent would represent this group. Together, all slices would account for the total of 20,000 students (100 per cent).

Pie charts are particularly effective at underscoring the relative importance of items. (See Figure 17.3).

Pictographs

Similar to a bar chart, a pictograph uses symbols instead of bars to represent the information. (See Figure 17.4).

Analysing Statistical Data

An important starting point for analysing data is to determine some kind of centre point or some measure of central tendency. Measures of central tendency describe numbers that are most representative of the data. The three most common measures of central tendency are the mean, the median and the mode.

Mean

The mean, commonly called the *average* (but in fact one of many different types of averages) is the sum of all the items in a group divided by the number of items.

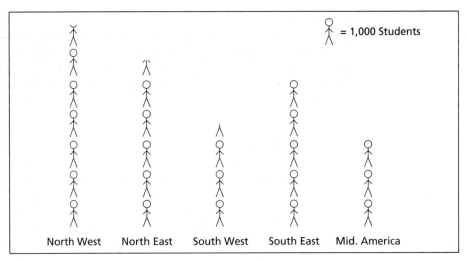

North West North East South West South East Mid. America

= 1,000 Students

Figure 17.4

Consider the data in Table 17.3. The total sales in a seven-day period were £1,463. To compute mean sales per day, divide £1,463 by 7 to get £209. The mean is the most reliable measure of central tendency when data are fairly evenly distributed.

TABLE 17.3

Day	Daily Sales
Monday	111
Tuesday	225
Wednesday	215
Thursday	170
Friday	270
Saturday	270
Sunday	202

Total:	1,463	
Mean:	209	
Median:	215	
Mode:	270	

Median

When all items in a group are arranged in order from the lowest to the highest, called an *array*, the median is the item in the middle. Thus, half the data will be lower than the median, the other half will be higher. When there are an odd number of items, the median works out perfectly – there will be only one midpoint. When there are an even number of data, the median is the mean of the two middle numbers.

The median is useful when data are not very evenly distributed, since its value is not affected by extremely high or extremely low values at the ends of the array. In Table 17.3, the median or midpoint is 215.

Mode

The mode describes the item or number that occurs most frequently in a group. In Table 17.3, the mode is 270, since it occurs twice. If no item occurs more than once, then there is no mode. Since the mode is the most frequent value, it is the value which is most likely to be found. The average family group comprises two adults and two children, the modal values.

Index Numbers

An index number is a percentage representing the degree of change between a base number (such as cost or price) in one period and the current number in the current period. The Retail Price Index (RPI), the best known index number, is used in economic forecasts in the UK. Published monthly by the Department of Trade and Industry, the RPI compares the current value with the base value of a 'basket' of goods and services purchased by the typical British household. The base value is the value of the same basket of goods and services in a specific base year.

Time-Series Analysis

Measurements fluctuate from one period of time to another, and managers must often explain such fluctuations. A time-series analysis, also known as a *trend analysis*, is a useful statistical technique for observing changes in data over time and basing forecasts on those observations.

Time-series analyses are used to forecast sales trends or utility costs. Changes are often explained in terms of three factors:

● **Seasonal variations**: these are predictable, repetitive changes closely tied to particular seasons of the year. In summer, for instance, ice cream sales increase; in winter, sales of hand gloves increase; and in the Christmas season, most retail stores enjoy higher than average sales.
● **Cyclical variations**: fluctuations that occur over a period of several years or more, and are linked to the business cycle, are referred to as cyclical variations. Cyclical variations result from changes in economic activity. For example, a change from economic prosperity and growth to recession and high unemployment.
● **Trend**: a consistent pattern of growth or decline in a particular industry or economy over a long period of time is known as a trend. An example of a secular trend is the steady growth in the number of microwave ovens purchased over the last ten years. Most time series analyses assume a linear, or straight line, trend pattern over the period of interest.

Correlation Analysis

Correlation analysis is a statistical technique that measures the relationship between two or more variables. *Variables* are the factors that change in a situation. Correlation analysis helps managers predict fluctuations in one variable when the levels of change in another variable are known. Variables in which the changes are already known or have been controlled are *independent variables.* Variables that change in response are *dependent variables.* For example, the independent variable (oven temperature) can be controlled to change the dependent variable (cooking time).

Correlations are identified as being either positive or negative. A *positive correlation* exists when an increase in one variable is linked with an increase in another variable. For example, if an increase in movie attendance is accompanied by an increase in popcorn sales, this shows a positive correlation between the two variables. Similarly, a decrease in movie attendance and a decrease in popcorn sales shows a positive correlation because both variables are changing in the same direction.

A *negative correlation* exists when an increase in one variable is accompanied by a decrease in a second variable, that is, when variables change in opposite directions. For example, the value of a car decreases as it gets older, showing a negative correlation between its value and its age.

SUMMARY

Businessmen need to understand and communicate data in order to process this data into information for making good decisions. Data often includes very large amounts of numbers and it is important to present them in a form which can be quickly assimilated. For example, a picture is worth a thousand words, whilst a graph or a pie chart is worth a thousand numbers. The use of a selected range of data instead of all the data, or the use of an average instead of all the numbers, involves a risk of error or misinterpretation. Understanding the risk and reducing it to acceptable levels is a key factor in decision making.

SELECTED READING

Surridge, Malcolm et al. 1993. *Finance, Information and Business.* Collins Educational.
Lawson, Michelle et al. 1995. *Maths and Statistics for Business.* Longman.
Whitehead, Paul. 1992. *Statistics for Business.* Pitman.
Lucey, T. 1995. *Management Information Systems.* DP Publications.
Robson, Wendy. 1994. *Strategic Management and Information Systems.* Pitman.

18 | Computers and Computer Systems

The computer has had perhaps the most significant impact on business in the twentieth century. A computer is an electronic machine that can accept and store data; execute a set of instructions (called programs); perform mathematical, logical and manipulative operations on data; and produce reports in a form that can be read either by people or by other machines. The chief advantage of a computer is the speed with which it can access and manipulate massive amounts of data.

Computers in the Business World

Most computers used for business purposes are digital computers, that is, computers that store and operate on data in the form of digits or numbers. Whether the data processed are letters, numbers or symbols, digital computers use the data only in numerical form. Analogue computers, on the other hand, use continuously varying signals, not digits. Analogue computers are particularly useful for very sensitive measuring devices, for instance in navigation. All computers discussed below are digital computers. As you will see, they are classified primarily according to their size and their speed of operation.

The Development of the Digital Computer
Early Machines
3000 BC: The Abacus
Computing devices began with the abacus, a simple calculating device that permits all the basic arithmetical processes by changing the position of beads or counters.

1642: Pascal's Arithmetic Machine
The French scientist-philosopher Blaise Pascal built the first digital adding machine, similar to the present-day desk calculator.

1890: Hollerith's Punched Card
Herman Hollerith developed punched cards for the purpose of counting and classifying data for the census.

1939–1944: Mark I
Aiken and IBM developed Mark I, the first fully automatic calculator, which could add, subtract, multiply and divide.

Computer Generations
From this point on, developments in computer technology are classified into generations, each marked by greatly increased computer speeds, more storage capabilities and a lower cost, compared to those of the previous generation.

1945–1958: Generation I
The first generation of computers is characterised by vacuum tube components for storage of numbers and computing operations. ENIAC was the first large all-electronic digital computer developed.

1958–1966: Generation II
In the second generation, tubes were replaced by transistors and magnetic core storage was introduced, thus increasing the speed of central processing units.

1958–1980s: Generation III
In the third generation, computers were faster and more reliable. They were characterised by the use of integrated circuits and increased miniaturisation. Well-known computers introduced in this period include the Apple II series of microcomputers, introduced in 1977, and the IBM PS series.

1980s–Present: Generation IV
Fourth generation computers use large-scale integrated (LSI) circuits and very large-scale integrated (VLSI) circuits, low-cost disk storage, and satellite computers that communicate with a central computer. Fourth generation computers are smaller, faster, more reliable and they use less energy.

Super-Computers
Supercomputers, the world's fastest computers, can perform many highly complex computations of large amounts of data with extreme rapidity, making them essential for mathematical problem-solving and for any computations requiring speed. Supercomputers are used mainly in engineering, mathematics and science.

Mainframe Computers

Mainframe computers are large, general-purpose systems that have the capacity to serve hundreds or thousands of users. Mainframes are in a central location, but users can access the system from individual terminals (keyboards at their individual terminals) that can be located anywhere. Mainframes were developed primarily for use in business, where their very fast processing speeds and very large data-storage capacities could be used to process, for example, a weekly payroll for several thousand employees. Universities use mainframes to process registration and enrolment.

Minicomputers

Minicomputers, computers of intermediate size and cost, are scaled-down versions of mainframe computers, handling fewer users and less information, usually with a slower processing speed. Minicomputers are usually used by small companies or departments within a larger company.

Microcomputers

Microcomputers, commonly known as *personal computers* or PCs, are smaller, general-purpose desktop computers that have rather limited storage capacities. The heart of a microcomputer is its central processing unit. In addition, a microcomputer has a monitor and keyboard, as well as one or more built-in disk drives. The disk drives read information stored on disk in electronic form, and they write information on to disks, thus allowing users to transfer data to and from the microcomputer. Common examples of microcomputers are the IBM Personal System/2 and the Apple Macintosh.

Portable Computers

The term *portable computer* covers a wide range of machines, from programmable calculators and electronic organisers to laptop computers, which are essentially smaller, lighter versions of microcomputers. Indeed, computer manufacturers are increasingly miniaturising equipment whilst at the same time increasing data storage capacity and speed of operation across the board on portable computers, microcomputers and minicomputers. As a result, today's laptop computer has the power of the microcomputer of just a few years ago; likewise, today's microcomputer has the power of older minicomputers.

Computer Hardware

Hardware refers to equipment and machinery, the components of a computer system. *Software* refers to the electronically stored commands or instructions that control and run the hardware. Computer hardware is varied. The main piece of equipment is the central processing unit; all other components are called *peripherals.* In the discussion below, peripherals are grouped into output devices and input devices.

The Central Processing Unit

The central processing unit (CPU) is the heart of the computer. The CPU contains the logic that directs and controls the operation of the machine. The CPU is that part of the computer that controls the computational part of the computer system.

Parts of the CPU.
The CPU has three main parts:

● The *control unit* is the component that manages and coordinates the operations of the computer.
● The *arithmetic logic unit* is the area of the CPU that carries out arithmetic computation.
● The *primary storage unit* is the area of primary memory for storing data and programs.

Chips
Chips, the electronic components that make computers possible, are tiny pieces of silicon that contain many minute electronic circuits. Chips empower the CPU to operate.

● **Microprocessor chips:** many computers today use a microprocessor or a microprocessing unit, which combines many of the functions of a CPU into just one chip. Microprocessors are often called 'computers on a chip'.
● **Memory chips:** memory chips are used for storing data within computers. Random-access memory (RAM) is used for primary memory. Information in RAM can be accessed randomly, that is, in any order. Read only memory (ROM) is generally used to store system programs that never change, including information that allows the computer to know what to do when it is turned on.

Secondary Storage

Most CPUs also have secondary storage devices, that hold data for future processing.

Floppy Disks
Floppy disks are magnetised disks ranging in size from 3.5–8 inches in diameter. The floppy disks are inserted into a disk drive that reads and writes data to and from the disk. Floppy disks may hold from 360,000 bytes to 2.88 million bytes of information.

Hard Disks
Hard disks are much faster and hold more information than floppy disks. In most computers today, a hard disk is the main type of secondary storage.

Magnetic Tape
Magnetic tape, one of the oldest storage media, stores data in sequence on a tape similar to that used in a cassette player. Magnetic tape is still popular because tape can store large amounts of data at a low cost.

Optical Disks
Optical disks, the newest storage device, resemble compact disks (CDs). Optical disks can hold hundreds of millions of characters. They are particularly useful for storing large bodies of data that do not change (for example, encyclopedias or historical databases).

Punched Cards
The punched card was one of the earliest secondary storage media. On each card the computer read information written by only two codes, punched holes and no punched holes, combinations of which represented different letters and numbers. Punched cards have been largely replaced by the other secondary storage media discussed previously.

Output Devices

Output devices permit the computer to display or deliver data from the computer to the user. The main output devices are:

- **The Cathode Ray Tube (CRT)**: the CRT is the display screen most commonly used as monitors and screens. On the screen, a cursor, box or a line (usually blinking) indicates the position at which the next input will be entered.
- **Printers:** there are three types of printers:
1 Laser printers provide fast, high resolution, high quality output.
2 Impact printers such as dot matrix printers, actually make an impression on the page.
3 Nonimpact printers, such as ink, jet or thermal (heat sensitive) printers, do not make an impression on the page (only the ink itself contacts the page).
- **Voice Output**: this is a simulated audio response, often heard via telephone. People with a voice impediment can 'speak' by typing the words onto a small laptop computer which provides a voice output.
- **Plotters:** these are output devices that draw figures and graphs for presentations.

Input devices

Input devices permit users to enter or input data into the computer. The main input devices are:

- **The keyboard:** the computer keyboard, the most frequently used input device, is similar to a typewriter keyboard.
- **The mouse:** this is a hand held device that is moved on the desktop, directing the cursor around the screen as the mouse is moved, allowing users to point to and select commands very quickly (by simply clicking a button on the mouse).

- **The touch screen:** this enables users to select options given on the screen by placing a finger on the appropriate option. Touch screens are often used when the information is limited, for example, in a tourist information office.
- **Bar codes:** these are symbols (in bar form) read by a laser device to obtain price and stock level information. The Universal Product Code (UPC) on foodstuffs and other consumer merchandise is the most popular bar code.
- **Scanners:** scanners pick up images from a printed page and transmit those images into the computer.
- **Voice input:** voice input enables users to input instructions into a computer by speaking to the computer. Programs are available for users to dictate letters or books to a computer, which automatically 'types' these words together with punctuation commands.

Computer Software

Computers are controlled by software stored within the computer's main memory. *Software* refers to all the different kinds of computer programs, sets of instructions, procedures and rules that tell a computer what to do. Systems software and applications software are two broad categories of software.

Systems Software

Systems software does the detailed work of managing the computer and running the hardware. An *operating system*, the best known piece of systems software, performs a variety of tasks: allocating primary or secondary storage space, distributing the computer's resources among multiple users and controlling peripheral devices.

Applications Software

While systems software operates the computer, applications software are special programs that perform a particular function or application for the end user. Many applications software programs are available in ready made packages, including word processing, database management, spreadsheet and financial analysis packages. In addition to ready made packages, applications software can be written by a computer programmer for specific end users. For example, a company may have special software written for its particular reporting needs.

Computer Languages

Software can be written in different languages, but computers read and understand data and programs only in machine language. All data and programs written in other languages must be translated into machine language.

Machine language is in binary format, which is not easy for humans to read. In binary format, only two digits (0 and 1) are used in various combinations to represent any character. Each digit in a binary number is called a *bit* and eight bits make up one byte of information – that is, eight bits represent one character.

Computer languages have evolved greatly. Among the computer languages that programmers use today are assembly language, COBOL, C and BASIC.

Computer Applications

In the broadest sense, computer applications are only limited by the imagination of the programmer or user. Among the most widely used business applications are batch processing, on-line interactive systems, remote terminals, time sharing, networks and electronic communications.

Batch Processing

In batch processing a number of tasks or transactions are saved; when a sizeable collection of tasks is gathered, they are then processed together in a batch. Processing payroll checks is a typical example of batch processing.

On-Line Interactive Systems

On-line interactive computer applications allow multiple users to access the system through terminals. An example is an airline ticket reservation system, which allows agents from around the world to book tickets for the same flights at the same time. The airline ticket reservation system interacts with: (i) the agent at the terminal, inputting the passenger's personal and payment information; and (ii) a central data bank securing the reservation, issuing the ticket and updating the central data bank.

Remote Terminals

In many computer environments where the computer system is centrally located and system users are scattered in different locations, users access the system through remote terminals. Remote terminals are the same as other terminals except that they are connected directly to the computer through various long distance channels.

Time Sharing Servicing Systems

Since the cost of maintaining mainframe computer systems can be very high, a number of companies co-own large computers and share them with other companies or users. These shared systems are called *time sharing systems*, since they share the time the computer can be used. Time sharing enables small firms and individual users to access large databases that they otherwise could not afford.

Networks and Electronic Communications

Computer networks allow computers to communicate with one another. A network is a communication system that links computers, allowing them either to operate independently or to communicate with, and share the resources, of other devices linked to them. The most common type of network is called a *local area network* (LAN), which links computers in a small geographical area, for example, in one building. Networks allow users to gather information from other locations, manipulate it on their own computers and store the information for future use. Users can also transmit their information elsewhere. A *modem* is a communications device that allows computers to transmit and receive information over ordinary telephone lines.

Computers in the Workplace

The use of computers has spread very rapidly in the workplace. Computers speed up otherwise time-consuming processes, assume many tedious tasks and allow quick and easy access to vital information. At the same time, the widespread use of computers poses a number of special problems. These and other issues related to computers in the workplace will be addressed in this section.

Communication Technologies

Computerisation has led to the development of a variety of communication technologies, including the following:

- **Electronic mail,** 'E mail' for short, allows 'written' memos, letters and documents to be sent from one person's computer 'mail box' to another person's mail box.
- **Voice mail** is similar to E Mail, but stores 'oral' messages (the same kind as left on an answering machine), which can be answered (by computer if necessary) whenever it is convenient.
- **Teleconferencing** and electronic meetings enable participants from different locations to 'meet'. By way of teleconferencing, data can be written on a conference board in one city and appear on a screen in another city, together with an image of the presenter. Teleconferences can be international.
- **Facsimile (or FAX)** machines permit documents in both text and graphic form to be transmitted via telephone lines to another FAX machine or computer anywhere in the world. FAX machines have revolutionised the speed of transacting business.

Challenges of Computers

Computers are transforming the workplace, making it less monotonous and more attractive. However, computers pose several challenges which will be discussed below.

Job Security and Training

Computers and automation have displaced many people from their jobs and have caused massive restructuring in modern business. To meet the challenges presented by computers and automation, the business world must redesign many jobs to incorporate computer technology, and train employees to meet the new and varied tasks that arise in the computer environment.

Management Structure

The role, and the size, of middle management is changing as information technology and computer systems make it possible to manage large enterprises with a smaller middle management. A computer system can give top managers access to information at all levels and in all parts of the organisation; information that would previously have been provided by lower levels of management. As middle-management levels shrink, some traditional incentives are disappearing, for example, aspiring for a promotion to middle management.

Employee Privacy

Computers can monitor the amount of time employees spend on the telephone, measure how many orders a telephone salesperson receives, measure productivity on a work floor and even measure quality. As a result, some employees are intimidated by computers, fearing that computers have the power to gather information that management can use against them.

Customer Privacy

Computers allow integration of files from many sources and quick retrieval of data. Many people fear the possibility that information collected and stored by employees, tax offices, banks, insurance companies, credit agencies and numerous other agencies and companies could easily be accessed by employers, the police department, banks and so on despite promises that confidentiality will be maintained and privacy respected.

The Data Protection Act (1985)

The Data Protection Act in the UK applies to computer stored personal information which identifies a living individual. All users and bureaux dealing with such personal information have to apply to the Data Protection Registrar to be registered users, giving full details of the information, where and why it is stored, who uses it, and where it can be transferred. Individuals have the right to ask for details of any information stored about themselves. Heavy penalties, including imprisonment, can be issued to offenders. Certain information such as mailing lists and internal payroll details are exempt from the Act.

User Health Problems

The possibility of health hazards to computer users is in question for several reasons. Poorly designed workplaces (chairs too low or computer screens too high) can cause back and neck problems. In addition, users' constant focusing on a close screen can cause eye-muscle spasms and lead to myopia. Many other possible problems have been suggested and await firm clinical evidence.

Impact of Computer Errors

For many different reasons, computer output often includes errors. The most simple reason is, of course, that the input included errors, supporting the old saying 'GIGO' (garbage in, garbage out). Workers and managers who would have routinely checked manual calculations and reports often fail to check computer generated calculations and reports; as a result, minor input errors could result in major problems, for example, in lost profits.

Efficiency

Computers have been able to take over a number of applications, which were considered to be repetitive and mundane. However, questions have arisen as to whether businesses perhaps complicate simple procedures in order to computerise them, thus losing efficiency in the process.

Implementing Computer Systems

To implement a computer system requires the same planning, organising, leading and controlling skills that any other management task requires. The specific steps necessary for implementing a computer system effectively are:

1 **Requirements analysis:** define the need for the system and clarify the purpose of the system.
2 **Feasibility assessment:** establish the feasibility of the project on three levels:
    - Technical feasibility: is the equipment available? Can the software needed be purchased, or must it be developed?
    - Economic feasibility: what are the costs of the hardware, the software, maintenance and supplies?
    - Operational feasibility: is the equipment easy to use? Will the current system be disrupted? Will a new system help users? Will it displace workers? Will there be much employee resistance?
3 **User requirement analysis:** get the programmers and the analysts to determine how the system works now and identify the problems. This stage involves a lot of discussion between the system's developers and the users, to establish exactly what is needed.
4 **Logical system design:** define the system specifications, for example, on line or batch, when reports should be made, the size of files and records and so on.
5 **Physical system construction:** have the system's technicians built the system?
6 **System testing:** test the program throughout various stages of system development to ensure that the system is functioning properly before it is implemented.
7 **Implementation and evaluation:** introduce the system to the users and train them. There are various ways to implement a system: (a) parallel implementation, running the old and new systems side by side to ensure accuracy; (b) phased implementation, introducing the new system gradually, in phases; and (c) complete replacement, when the new system is introduced and the old system is removed simultaneously.

8 Maintenance: maintain the system effectively after it has been introduced. The maintenance function encompasses correcting any errors that may arise, implementing any improvements required and introducing any useful new technology that becomes available.

Future Trends and Developments

Tomorrow's computers will be smaller and faster and will have greater storage capacity. They will also continue to decrease in price, thus being used in a wider range of product areas and becoming even more prominent in everyday life than they already are. Instead of people adapting to how computers operate, in the future computers will be designed to adapt naturally to the way people work. Communication systems and networks will continue to expand. Voice communication will become an integrated part of computer use, and continuous dictating machines will be improved.

Many computers are now able to recognise handwriting. The newest of these systems is called a *tablet-based system*, and do not have keyboards. Instead, users handwrite their input with a pen on a pad-like input/output display screen, which could sit on the user's lap or on a desk.

More computer applications will make use of artificial intelligence (AI), that is, the ability to simulate human intelligence with a computer. The principal business application of AI is in *expert systems*, computer applications designed to mimic the thought process of an expert in a particular field. Expert systems are used for a variety of purposes, for instance, diagnosing disease, predicting changes in the weather and monitoring nuclear power plants.

Homes, too, will become more computer controlled. Computer sensors have the potential to direct light and heat only to rooms where and when they are needed. Computers will be embedded into everyday appliances. Just as computers are now used in cars to monitor the oil level, control the air intake and make the engine operate more efficiently, computers will be embedded into washing machines and dishwashers to provide the optimum water flow depending on the contents, and to evaluate whether the enclosed items are still dirty. Household appliances and home electronic equipment will be integrated so that the push of one button will automatically tune in your TV or stereo, switch on the oven or dishwasher and open or close the blinds, all in one step. Computerised medical monitoring equipment in a patient's home will enable doctors to monitor a patient's health without an office visit.

SUMMARY

Computers are the most significant invention of the century. They have radically changed the way we view the world today, the way we work and the way we live. Computer technology has successfully been applied to many fields: business, banking , accounting, finance, marketing, telecommunications, manufacturing and medicine. Yet computers are only as effective as their input. As computers become faster and more powerful, society will be increasingly challenged to find positive uses for computers.

SELECTED READING

Gunton, Tony. 1994. *The Penguin Dictionary of Information Technology.* Penguin.
Gibson, Glenn. 1991. *Computer Systems: Concepts and Design.* Prentice Hall.
Gosling, Peter. 1994. *Mastering Spreadsheets.* Macmillan.
Hammond, Michael. 1993. *Handling Data with Databases and Spreadsheets.* Hodder and Stoughton.

Part 7

Financial Management

19

Money, Banking and Credit

Money

Money is defined as anything used by a society to purchase goods, services or resources. Today, most countries use metal coins and paper bills, but items as varied as gold and silver, beads, wampum and clam shells have been used as money.

Functions of Money

Money is used to purchase (that is, used in exchange for) goods, services or resources. The power to purchase or exchange is the basis of money's three principal functions, described below.

Medium of Exchange

A medium of exchange is anything accepted as payment. The key word is 'accepted'. At one time, barter, the trading of goods for other goods, was the only method acceptable. Money permits the selling (rather than trading) of goods and using the money received in exchange for desired goods. As long as sellers are willing to accept money from buyers, this medium of exchange function is being fulfilled.

Measure of Value

Because the value of all products and resources are stated in terms of money, money provides the means to compare value. Money serves as the standard for the measure of value.

Store of Value

Money does not need to be spent immediately; instead, money can be saved and spent later. Thus the value of money can be stored, and storing value allows wealth to be accumulated. However, this stored value is not constant. The value of money fluctuates with the economy, losing value in periods of inflation and gaining value in periods of deflation.

Characteristics of Money

Money must meet certain criteria in order to be acceptable. The five most important characteristics of money are:

- **Portability:** money must be portable, that is, small enough and light enough to be carried easily. Paper money is easier to carry in large amounts than coinage.
- **Divisibility:** money must be divisible into smaller units to permit purchases of less than one pound and purchases in odd amounts over one pound. To make such purchases possible, coins in fractions of one pound are circulated.
- **Stability:** money should be stable, retaining its value over time. In periods of very high inflation, people may tend to lose faith in their money; as a result, they may try to store value in assets such as gold, jewels or property.
- **Durability:** whether it is in coin or paper form, money should be durable enough to withstand reasonable usage without disintegrating.
- **Authenticity:** part of the trust which people put in their money lies in the difficulty of counterfeiting it. If currency were easy to counterfeit, even authentic or genuine currency would lose value.

Types of Money

'Money' exists in several different forms, as discussed below.

Currency

Currency comprises not only paper money and coins issued by the government but also money orders, travellers' cheques, personal cheques and bank cheques issued by banks against secure bank funds. All these forms of currency are acceptable for payments. A cheque is a written order to a bank or other financial institution to pay a stated amount to the person indicated on the face of the cheque.

Current Account

A current account shows the funds on short-term deposit with the bank, or the state of an agreed overdraft. Funds can be withdrawn at any time by writing a personal cheque, by authorising a 'Switch' transfer or by withdrawal from an automatic teller machine (ATM) or 'cash point'.

Other Cheque Deposits

There are a number of other cheque deposits, deposits against which cheques can be drawn. NOW accounts (Negotiable Order of Withdrawal), function like demand deposits, but pay interest provided that users maintain a minimum balance.

Time Deposits.

Time deposits, such as certificates of deposit and money-market certificates, are savings accounts that require notice prior to withdrawal.. Cheques cannot usually be written against time deposits. While the funds are not instantly available, as they are for demand deposits, time deposits earn a higher rate of interest. If there is an opportunity for instant withdrawal facilities, then interest earned over a known time period will have been lost.

Money-Market Funds

Money-market funds pool the funds of many individual investors. The funds are used to buy short-term, low-risk financial securities in large denominations – for example, from seven to 120-day notes from banks or from the Treasury with a promise to pay a fixed interest. A minimum deposit of £30,000 or more will probably be required.

Savings Accounts

Savings accounts are traditional time deposit passbook accounts (e.g., Post Office Savings Account). Savings accounts of this type have declined in recent years because of the greater flexibility offered by NOW accounts (a cheque-based savings account with associated ATM facilities).

Plastic Money

Plastic money, or credit card purchasing, has become a major factor in purchasing goods and services. Although credit cards serve as a substitute for money, they are, as their name implies, really an extension of credit, not money.

Money Supply

The overall supply of money helps determine its value. If there is too much money in circulation, its value or purchasing power drops, leading to inflation. However, it is difficult to measure the amount of money in circulation.

In the UK, three specific measurements of the money supply – M1, M2 and M3 – are used:

- **M-1:** this is a measure of money supply that includes only the most liquid forms of money. M-1 measures currency, demand deposits and other cheque deposits (i.e., deposits against which cheques can be drawn without notice).
- **M-2:** this includes M-1 plus other types of money that can be easily converted to spendable forms, namely time deposits, money market funds and savings deposits. It includes deposits of £100,000 or less which have a maturity of one month or less.
- **M-3:** this includes M-2 plus deposits over £100,000 held by UK residents,

including all foreign currency deposits held by UK banks or by the UK private sector.

The UK Banking System
Financial Institutions

Many forms of money, especially deposits withdrawable on demand (demand deposits) or invested for a fixed time (time deposits) depend on the existence of commercial banks and other financial institutions.

Commercial Banks

A commercial bank is a privately owned profit-seeking organisation which is in the business of lending money at a higher rate than it pays to depositors. These banks have extensive branch networks and are referred to as 'clearing banks' because of the millions of transactions they carry out daily, clearing cheques between one commercial bank and another. They ensure that an account in one branch of a bank is credited with the funds drawn on another account of another branch of another bank. Business is not confined to cheques; many transfers are carried out by direct debits, credit cards, standing orders, ATMS (automatic teller machines or cash points) and other electronic methods (e.g., Switch). There are about 15,000 commercial bank branches throughout the UK, but this number is shrinking because of amalgamation, staff reductions and direct home banking methods using home computer systems.

Discount Houses

Discount houses are unique to the UK. They form a very important role in banking, borrowing money from the commercial banks for relatively short periods, for a maximum of 91 days and as little as 'overnight', and lending to other commercial banks which may have short-term cash requirements. The discount house does this by using most of the money it collects to buy Treasury Bills which are sold by the government through the Bank of England at a lower price than the face value. When the bill matures, the holder gets a higher sum.

Building Societies

Building societies receive money from millions of medium to short-term savers, and then lend the money to house buyers for longer periods, normally 25 years. Building societies have to balance the savings interest required by its depositors and the mortgage repayments affordable to its borrowers, which is again dependent on the state of the housing market, government dictated inter-bank lending rates and tax concessions to borrowers.

Finance Houses

Finance houses number around 40 in the UK and specialise mainly in hire purchases for periods of one to three years. Finance houses get their money mainly from the banking and insurance institutions and partly from the public.

Retailers are often the main agents for finance houses, but the public can also approach them directly. Interest rates for borrowers are usually fairly high to reflect the higher risks undertaken.

National Savings Bank

The National Savings Bank operates mainly through the Post Office. There is a wide range of investment accounts which are often tailored for specific needs (e.g., a children's saving account). The National Savings Bank also operates Premium Bonds of indeterminate return!

The Merchant Banks

Merchant banks are used solely by commercial organisations. Such banks assist firms to raise money on the stock market by issuing and underwriting new shares. They also assist firms to maintain cash flows by accepting *commercial bills*: a promise to pay a certain sum by a certain date, possibly a large invoice which is guaranteed. The merchant bank buys this bill at lower than the face value, which is dependent on the underlying interest rates, and sells it to another party for a higher sum as maturity approaches. This is similar to treasury bills used by discount houses.

Foreign Banks

The continuing centralisation of EC banking systems has led to the appearance of a large number of continental European banks in the UK, in addition to other foreign banks (e.g., Japanese banks) in order to participate in international trade. These banks act as a link between holders of foreign currency and those with a need for foreign currency. Sometimes the operations of these banks is purely to gamble on currency exchange rates.

The Role of the Bank of England

The Bank of England was set up in 1694 and became part of the government's banking system in 1946. The Bank of England supervises and controls the monetary sector on behalf of the government.

The Supreme Bank

All recognised banks in the UK must deposit some of their funds with the Bank of England in addition to all licensed deposit takers. The Bank of England is the only new banknote-issuing bank in England and Wales; it also takes old notes out of the system.

All the clearing banks, the commercial 'high street' banks, settle daily accounts between themselves by using their Bank of England accounts. The Bank of England may also lend money to other banks, usually via the discount houses, and acts as a commercial bank to the privilege few whose private accounts need to be held in tight security.

The Government's Bank

The Bank of England is the government's bank, taking in all the monies collected by taxes and distributing money to government departments such as the Ministry of Defence. When government money runs low, the Bank of England arranges for loans by issuing treasury bills of varying repayment dates which are purchased by commerce and also by private individuals (gilts). These individuals are then paid interest by the Bank of England.

There is a close working relationship between the Bank of England and the government. Decisions about the level of basic interest rates are usually decided by mutual agreement although, unlike the German equivalent (the Bundesbank) the Bank of England cannot act independently.

Foreign Exchange

The Bank of England supervises the gold and foreign currency reserves of the government, acting to stabilise exchange rates by buying and selling foreign currency. A stable foreign exchange rate is essential for international trade to be profitable.

Monetary Supervision

The Bank of England constantly reviews the monetary system in the UK and acts, usually through directives to the clearing banks, to regulate or to stimulate borrowing and investment. The Bank of England can act to regulate the money supply (i.e., M-1, M-2, M-3).

Credit

Credit provides immediate purchasing power in exchange for a promise to repay the total amount, with or without interest, at a later date.

Credit Transaction

Borrowers take loans to get immediate purchasing power, that is, the ability to buy something at a time when they do not have the available funds to make the purchase. The lender (a bank or a business) supplies the credit.

A bank is in the business of lending money; its profit is the interest it receives on its loans. Businesses also extend credit, either to compete with other firms that extend credit or to increase their customer base by attracting customers who cannot pay the entire purchase amount in one payment, but can make smaller payments over a period of time.

Credit Management

The primary purpose of a business is to earn a profit by selling goods or services. As part of its sales effort, a business extends credit to customers, thus taking on the responsibility of credit management.

The Five Cs of Credit

In extending credit, a business is aware of, and accepts but tries to limit, the risk that some of its customers will be either unwilling or unable to pay for their credit purchases. One way lenders try to limit credit losses is by setting standards for lending based on the five Cs of credit: character, capacity, capital, collateral and conditions. The first tool lenders use to determine how likely the borrower is to repay the loan is the borrower's credit application. From this completed form and from other key sources, the lender can learn critical information about the five Cs.

- **Character:** this refers to the borrower's attitude toward his/her debts. Have past debts been repaid in a timely fashion? Have other lenders been forced to request payment repeatedly, to threaten to sue or to actually sue, all in order to obtain payment?
- **Capacity:** this is the borrower's financial ability to meet the scheduled payment obligations in the credit agreement. An individual's capacity is reflected, in part, by his/her salary statements and other sources of income. A company's capacity can be measured (again, in part) by its income statement. In both cases, of course, other factors (i.e., outstanding obligations and expenses) must be considered.
- **Capital:** this refers to the borrower's assets or net worth. Capital can be determined from a company's financial statements (those prepared by a certified public accountant) or from an individual's credit application.
- **Collateral:** this is readily liquidated assets (such as shares, bonds or property) pledged as security that the loan will be repaid. If the borrower fails to live up to the terms of the credit agreement, the collateral can be sold to satisfy the debt. A loan that is backed by collateral is more secure than other loans; often, the borrower will be charged a lower interest rate if the loan is backed by collateral.
- **Conditions:** lenders know that general economic conditions can affect a borrower's ability to repay the loan or other credit. In a falling economy or in a recession, for example, loans for expensive consumer items carry an added risk.

Cheque Credit Information

Credit applications must be checked for accuracy. For a business, credit information can be obtained from several sources. National credit reporting agencies or local credit reporting agencies supply information for a fee. Other sources of information are industry associations and other firms that have dealt with the applicant. For individuals, many credit bureaux supply credit information on a fee basis.

SUMMARY

Successful small businesses work in partnership with financial advisors, often the local bank manager. The bigger the business, the greater the need to seek financial advice and help from larger institutions. Although these institutions are often involved with many different banking activities, often on a world wide scale, money is only generated by trading goods and services, which are provided by those 'needy' businesses. Therefore, it is a pity that recent publicity on speculative money activities and the collapse of long serving banks has tended to obscure the fact that banks and financial institutions exist to help businesses to grow and become more profitable.

SELECTED READING

Howells, Peter. 1990. *Finance Markets and Information*. Longman.
Durham, Kenneth. 1992. *The Naked City*. Macmillan.
Whiting, D. P. 1994. *Mastering Banking*. Macmillan.

20 The Securities Market

Securities, such as fixed interest securities and shares, play vital roles both for companies and for investors. Securities are bought and sold in the securities markets, which are important to both companies and individual investors. For companies, the markets make possible the establishment and growth of business by supplying the capital needed to fund their operations. For individuals, the markets provide opportunities to earn interest, dividends and capital gains.

The Role of Securities and Securities Markets

In this chapter we will examine what securities are, distinguish among the most common types of securities, witness the process of buying and selling securities, and discuss the need for securities from both the company's and the individual investor's point of view.

The Investor's View

Many millions of people invest in UK company securities, either directly through ownership of fixed interest securities and shares, or indirectly through a pension fund or insurance company. They range from the proverbial 'old lady' who wants maximum security, to the speculators whose aim is to make a short-term killing. When approaching the stock market, one must decide if he/she is an investor or a speculator. The investor buys shares in a company hoping to make a reasonable profit. The greater the uncertainty and risk, the greater the profit or risk of loss. The speculator accepts this greater risk in the hope of making a greater and quicker profit.

Income describes the money that investors receive through dividends paid to them as shareholders. Many companies have long, uninterrupted histories of paying regular quarterly dividends year after year, making their shares more desirable to the investing public.

Capital gains describes the profits, if any, that an investor realises by selling a security at a price higher than the investor's purchase price.

The Company's View

The securities markets supply two essential services for companies. First, the securities markets sell original new issues of company securities, thereby supplying the capital for companies to launch a new business or expand an existing one. Second, the securities markets also provide the marketplace for investors to buy and sell previously issued securities. Original issues are sold in what is called the *primary market*; previously issued securities are sold in the *secondary market*.

The Primary and Secondary Markets

The Primary Market

Companies raise funds in the primary market with the help of an investment banking firm; a company that underwrites the offering of fixed interest securities or shares on behalf of the company. An investment bank is a firm that acts as an agent or intermediary between the issuer of securities (the company) and the investing public (each individual investor). Underwriting the new issue means that the investment bank buys the new shares or stock (paying the company for the securities) and then sells them to the public through dealers and brokers. In practice, more than one investment banking firm underwrites a new offering because of the large sums of money involved.

As underwriters of the new issue, the investment banks assume a risk and make a profit. Their profit is the difference between the price paid to the issuing company and the price received from the public offering price. The underwriters attempt to sell the new issue of shares or stock to institutional investors (large organisations such as insurance companies, pension funds or mutual funds) and to brokerage companies, which in turn resell the securities to individual investors. To promote sales, the underwriters will advertise the new issue in the financial sections of major newspapers and list all the firms underwriting the issue.

The Secondary Market

Investors finance first the birth, then the growth and success of companies with the money they invest when buying securities. Investors are willing to buy and to risk only if they will be able to sell their securities if and when they decide to do so. If investors were not able to sell their shares or stock they would probably have not bought them in the first place. The ability to sell a security is provided by the secondary market.

In the secondary market, previously issued stock and shares are bought and sold. In the UK, the secondary market is provided mainly by the London Stock Exchange, which issues very strict rules on the securities traded and the traders using the market. Other markets with less strict rules do exist for securities in smaller or riskier companies.

Types of Company Securities

The most common types of company securities are fixed interest stock, ordinary shares and preference shares. Each category has a number of variations. Many companies issue all three types of securities.

Fixed Interest Securities

Companies issue fixed interest securities (stock) to provide them with needed capital. A fixed interest security is a loan contract between the issuer (the company) and the buyer (the investor). The amount of loan is the purchase price of the security. In return for the loan, the company promises to make regular interest payments in specified amounts for a specified period of time, the end of which is the security's maturity date. At the maturity date, the company repurchases or redeems the loan at the specified price. There are basically two different types of fixed interest securities issued by companies:

- **Debentures:** these are secured fixed interest loans. The debt is secured on specific assets (fixed charge) or, if the company is fairly large and is constantly selling and buying new assets, the debt is charged on any available assets (floating charge). Debenture holders are protected by a trust deed which specifies their rights and the conditions of the loan. A debenture for several million pounds can be divided into millions of 'shares' so that many different investors can buy and sell part of the debenture on the Stock Exchange.
- **Loan stock:** this is unsecured and less protected than debentures. In the event of a default, loan stock ranks with other unsecured creditors such as suppliers to the company. Loan stock, unlike debentures, is usually sold in blocks, of £100 for example, and not divisible any further.

Bonds

A bond is similar to loan stock but usually of a higher value such as £5,000,000. Individual bonds are often traded in the financial futures market mentioned later.

Junk Bonds

Junk bonds are high fixed interest paying securities, issued by less secure companies which are forced to pay higher interest rates in order to attract investors and compensate them for accepting a higher risk.

Fixed Interest Securities Rating Services

Investors evaluate fixed interest securities on the basis of two criteria: risk and return. Risk is the possibility that the issuing company will not meet its obligation, whilst return refers to the rate of interest payments. The higher the risk, the higher the return. The lower the risk, the lower the return.

To help investors evaluate risk of fixed interest securities, two organisations, Standard & Poor (S & P) and Moody's, publish ratings. These ratings, which are nearly identical, start at 'AAA' for the very best quality investment (government-backed securities), and so down to 'C' for an extremely poor risk. The coding goes from 'AAA' to 'AA', 'A', 'BBB', 'BB', 'B', 'CCC', 'CC', and finally 'C'. Certain types of institutions, such as pension funds, are not allowed to purchase securities with a rating of 'BB' or lower. Junk bonds are rated at 'BB'.

Ordinary Shares

Ordinary shares represent the most basic form of corporate ownership. Holders of ordinary shares are the owners of the company. The total number of shares held by all the investors represents the total ownership of the company (the rights of shareholders are discussed in Chapter 4). Shares have no maturity date and can be held permanently or sold, as the owner chooses.

As owners of the company, common shareholders are entitled to a share of the after-tax earnings, if any. When distributed to these shareholders, the earnings are called *dividends*. A company is not legally required to pay dividends.

Companies may also reward shareholders with noncash dividends. A share distribution gives shareholders additional shares of stock in proportion to the number of shares they own. For example, the company's board of directors may elect to issue a 10 per cent share dividend, which gives shareholders one additional share for every ten already owned. Under a share split, the company may issue one or more shares to shareholders for each share they currently own.

Preference Shares

A preference share is a cross between a fixed interest loan and an ordinary common share, having some features of both. Like a debenture or loan, a preference share pays a fixed income payment or dividend, but in the case of preference share the dividend represents a distribution of profit, not a payment of interest on a debt (as bond dividends represent). Preference share dividends must be paid before ordinary share dividends, if any, are paid. However, nonpayment of preference share dividends does not put a company in default. Preference shares have no maturity dates.

If a firm is liquidated, the order of priority for payments is fixed interest bondholders first, followed by preference shareholders and then ordinary shareholders.

A cumulative preference share pays cumulative dividends, that is, if the dividend is not paid one year, the dividend is carried over to the next year. Again, ordinary share dividends cannot be paid until all money due the preference shareholders has been paid. Convertible preference shares, similar to convertible loans, may be exchanged for ordinary share at a specified conversion price, allowing preference shareholders to take advantage of a price rise in the ordinary share.

Although preference shares pay dividends in the form of interest payments, the Inland Revenue classifies the dividend as part of the earnings, that is, after tax is paid by the company. This tax disadvantage has led to the decline of preference shares as a source of company funds. For example, if a company pays say 5 per cent on a preference share, it has to earn, before tax at 45 per cent, a profit of about

8 per cent per share to cover the 5 per cent 'dividend'. However, preference shares do have an advantage to corporate investors since the tax paid on the preference share dividend can be offset against their own tax bill. Hence, most preference share owners are, in fact, corporations.

Investment Trusts and Unit Trusts

Investment and unit trusts provide a vehicle for many small investors to combine their funds and act like one large investor. Investors buy shares in funds, and professional fund managers then invest the money accumulated (the types of investments will vary from one fund to another). The major advantages to individuals are the ability to buy a widely diversified range of shares through the trust and to have professional management oversee the investment. Investment fund managers buy and sell shares in extremely large quantities, making up a substantial portion of the institutional market. The difference between investment and unit trusts depends on whether they are closed-end or open-end.

Closed-End Funds

A closed-end fund sells shares in the fund only when the fund is first organised, at which time only a specified number of shares are made available. Once all the shares are sold and the fund is closed, an investor can buy or sell shares only from other investors (that is, on the secondary market) where the share price is based on the net asset value (NAV). The NAV is computed by dividing the total value of all shares owned by the fund, by the number of shares outstanding. The selling price will vary above or below the NAV, depending on the future outlook for the fund's holding.

Open-End Funds

Open-end funds issue and sell shares to any willing investor. As investors purchase shares in the fund, the fund manager utilises the additional cash to buy more securities. The value of each share in the fund varies according to the value of the fund's total investment portfolio. An open-end fund is always willing to repurchase all or any of the shares a fund owner wishes to sell, a feature that contributes to the wide popularity of open-end funds.

Investment Goals of Investment and Unit Trust Funds

Fund managers tailor their portfolios to their investment goals, which are either to achieve growth, to provide income or a combination of both. Such funds have grown to the point that funds now cover all types of investments from the most speculative to the most conservative. Specialised funds exist that invest only in government stock, utilities, specific industries, specific countries, gold, growth companies or in high-income securities. There is a fund to meet almost every investment preference.

The Exchanges

Shares and stock are bought and sold through share exchanges. The New York Stock Exchange is the largest exchange in the world, followed by the Tokyo Exchange. The London Stock Exchange ranks third.

The London Stock Exchange

The London Stock Exchange provides both a primary and a secondary market where securities can be traded for as long as they are viable. In the case of shares, this means forever, or until the company is liquidated or merged with another company. The London Stock Exchange operates a dual capacity – that is, people dealing in shares on behalf of investors and sellers (called stockbrokers) can either be agency brokers or broker dealers. A *broker dealer* acts as a market maker, buying and selling shares. The profit is on the 'turn', the difference between the 'bid' price (buying price) and the 'ask' price (selling price). The broker dealer has to commit himself to quoting a bid and ask price continuously during the trading hours. This bid-ask spread is only conditioned by the maximum number of shares which the broker will be committed. *Agency brokers* act on the instructions of buying or selling clients and charge a commission on the deal.

Since computers and telephones are used extensively by brokers, the trading floor of the Stock Exchange, once the place of frantic activity, no longer exists. The frantic activity now takes place in a number of private trading rooms where maybe up to 100 million shares are traded daily

The London Stock Exchange not only contains the trading activity of the UK quoted shares, but also contains a very significant percentage of European trading activities. London is still the centre for a large proportion of the world's investment business.

Buying and Selling Securities

Buying and selling any good or service, including securities, requires a buyer, a seller and an agreed upon price. However, for shares the price is not set by the seller alone.

The Stockbroker's Role

The stockbroker can perform a number of functions and services for investors. Full service brokers supply research material, analysis and advice. Discount brokers only execute buy and sell orders (they offer no other services), allowing discount brokers to charge lower commission and transaction fees. To place a client's order to buy or sell securities on an exchange, the agency stockbroker places the order with a broker dealer, who may also work for the same organisation as the agency broker.

Orders and Lots

Agency brokers receive various instructions or orders for buying and selling shares.

Orders

Most orders are market orders which authorise the sale or purchase at the best possible price at that moment, generally very close to the price of the last trade for a particular share. A limit order, however, limits the agency broker to buy only at a specified price or lower, or to sell only at a specified price or higher.

Lots

Shares are typically traded in *round lots*, that is, in multiples of 100 shares. A transaction of fewer than 100 shares, (for example, a buy order for 52 shares) is called an *odd lot*. Finding a seller who wants to sell precisely 52 shares is not always possible. An odd lot broker gathers and combines several odd lots to make up a round lot, which can then be sold at once.

A Typical Transaction

Let us follow a typical transaction. Say Mr A wishes to buy 1,000 shares in a UK-based oil company. He either approaches his local agency broker who finds the prices offered by a number of market makers (broker dealers), or he approaches his 'high street' bank, which probably is a market maker in its own right through a merchant banking subsidiary.

If Mr A goes through his small agency broker, this broker will tell him the lowest quoted price for the shares from the computer screen. There may be a number of close offers, each one giving a code of the maximum number of shares available. A telephone call to the broker dealer will make the contract to buy the shares. For small quantities of shares, the broker dealer could trade automatically at the best price by computer without making a telephone call.

A similar procedure is followed if Mr A is selling shares. If Mr A dealt directly with the broker dealer, this market maker's bid price is offered rather than the lowest available. However, share trading takes place with computer screens showing all share dealings and contracts, and the near perfect marketplace ensures that buying and selling prices are similar for the same share.

Settlement Period

When the contract between buyer and stockbroker has been struck, the broker will send the buyer a contract note giving full details of the transaction, together with notification of the settlement date. The settlement date is the date by which the stockbroker receives the money, and is nowadays ten business days after the day of trade. This means that several transactions relating to the same shares could take place before any money changes hands. An investor could buy and sell shares within the trading period and, if successful, be paid the profit without having to purchase the shares at all. Only on the settlement date is the owner of the shares recognised and recorded by the company's share registrar.

The Derivatives Market

Derivatives are speculative activities based on the future trading prices of bonds (fixed interest securities) and shares, and are of two types – financial futures and options.

Investors can also minimise their risks, called *hedging*, by buying futures and options, the rights to buy or sell at a later date, say up to six months later. Although initiated in the 1970s to minimise the short-term risk of share values falling, speculators have made the process 'liquid', that is, a market was established to buy and sell the futures and options themselves. High level speculators deal exclusively in the high risks of the derivatives market and sometimes come unstuck, as has been seen in the Barings Bank collapse of March 1995.

Financial Futures

A financial futures contract is a deferred spot contract, where a spot contract is the normal purchase or sale of a security for settlement at the end of the accounts period. Financial futures are differentiated from commodity and currency futures which are part of other markets.

If an investor thinks that there will be a 'bear' market (i.e., prices will fall over the short term) he will possibly make a futures contract with a broker to sell a security at a fixed price at a certain date, assuming that he will be able to buy the security later at a lower price nearer the sell date. This contract, however, can be sold via a 'trader' in the futures market at a profit, if the buyer feels that the risk is acceptable and that the initial 'gamble' is more than likely to pay off. In the end, the contract must be met and at the agreed date, the shares must be sold. The futures exchange exists to hold the risk of default of buying or selling by receiving a deposit from both parties who buy and sell futures. Traders in futures have to be recognised by the futures exchange as competent to carry out business.

Options

Options give the holder the right, but not the obligation, to buy or sell a specified share at a specified price for a specified period of time. The option, which may cost only a small amount, represents only the right to buy; it does not represent ownership.

A *call* is the right to buy a specified share at a specified price for a specified period, for example, three months. The person selling the option is called the *writer*. Assume that a speculator has purchased a call (that is, a right) to buy 100 shares of Company A at £5 a share. If the price of Company A share rises to £6, the investor can exercise his/her right to purchase the share at £5 or, if the investor prefers, sell the option which now has a greater value and can be sold for a profit to someone who wishes to buy the share at this special price. Either way, the call will realise a substantial profit for the investor.

But remember, the option expires at the end of a specified period. If the share has not risen or has fallen in price at the end of the option period, the speculator allows the option to expire. The speculator's loss is then the fee paid for the option. The writer's profit is the option fee received.

A *put* is the right to sell a specified share at a specified price for a specified period. Because a put is the right to sell, its value increases as the price of the share falls. If the price of the share rises above the stated price, the put expires without being exercised.

Reading the Financial News

Nearly every newspaper has a financial section that offers financial news and long tables of small print. A few papers are devoted entirely to business news. In addition, several periodicals supply general economic news as well as detailed financial information about companies. Besides newspapers and periodicals, there are many other sources of financial news and advice. Full-service brokers prepare detailed analyses including buy and sell recommendations, and they make these analyses available to their customers. Companies issue half-yearly and annual shareholders' reports that are available to the general public. Investors may also subscribe to services that provide financial information and advice to their readers for an annual subscription fee.

Listed Shares

Companies, listed by the Stock Exchange, which have shares available for purchase by the public (plc's), can for a price (over £1,000 per year in the *Financial Times*) have their share values printed as an initial source of information for the investor. A typical extract from *The Times* newspaper is shown in Figure 20.1. Shares are printed in a number of different categories; the one illustrated in Figure 20.1 is for engineering, vehicles. We will examine the printed listing for Trinity Holdings for Saturday 11 March, 1995.

High/Low

The first two columns show the highest and lowest price for the share unit over the past 12 months. A share unit is usually 25p. The highest price is 333p and the lowest 263p.

Price

The price quoted, 327p, is the middle price calculated from the last ask-bid prices (selling, buying prices) recorded at the time trading stopped on the last day of business, Friday 10 March.

Change +/−

The change, −1p, is the difference between the current price, 327p, and the last price reported. The last price reported must have been 328p on Thursday 9 March.

Yield %

The yield percentage, 2.5 per cent, is the dividend paid to shareholders for each

Figure 20.1

1994/95			Price		Yld		
High	Low	Company	(p)		+/-	%	P/E
19	8½	Villers Grp	9½		...	...	...
531	451	Vinten	508	–	1	2.0	13.3
805	661	Vosper Thorny	741	–	1	3.2	16.0
527	444	Wagon Ind	447		...	5.1	22.7
354¼	222	Weir	230		...	3.6	13.7
46½	36	Wellman	39½		...	3.2	64.5
548	365	Whatman	453		...	2.9	16.6
264	90	Whessoe	122		...	2.4	...
ENGINEERING, VEHICLES							
66	31	AAF Inds	39		...	...	...
160	108	Airflow Stream	157		...	3.2	15.4
639	440	Avon Rubber	445		...	4.6	16.0
236	173	BBA	195	+	2	3.1	...
86½	49½	BSG	56	+	1	7.1	35.0
18½	8½	Benson Group	8¾	-	¼	5.1	11.8
306	180	Bostrom	298		...	2.5	17.0
28½	17	Boustead†	22		...	5.7	*
22	10	Caverdale	11½		...	1.6	11.7
357	275	ERF	356		...	1.4	...
400	296	First Tech	396		...	1.7	22.8
660	510¼	**GKN**	594	+	15	4.6	17.7
4387½	2337½	General Mtr†	2550	+	37½	2.0	...
1239	918½	Honda Motor	970¼	-	22¾	0.5	...
432¼	304	Laird	315		...	4.3	15.2
360	233	Loades	360		...	...	...
239	158	Lucas	188½	+	½	4.6	...
64	50	Mayflower	58½	-	½	3.0	23.8
124	61	Midstates	70		...	...	9.7
178	149	Syltone	166		...	3.8	18.4
261	140	T & N	161	+	†	8.6	*
333	263	Trinity Hldgs	327	-	1	2.5	23.7
FOOD MANUFACTUERS							
611	499	**AB Food**	575	+	6	3.5	11.9
368	223	Acatos & Hutch†	247	-	1	4.6	9.4
74	40	Albert Fischer	40		...	11.6	11.8
270	200	Banks (S C)†	200		...	6.1	9.3
387	305	Barr (AG)†	340	-	5	2.9	*
72	15	Bensons Crsp	16		...	...	...
481	374	Booker	383	+	1	7.2	14.1

Source: *The Times*, 11 March 1995

share held divided by the current price quoted, multiplied by 100. Yield reflects the dividend policy of the company rather than the profitability. The printed listings show a variation in yields from 0.5 per cent through to 8.6 per cent.

P/E Ratio

The P/E ratio is the current price quoted per share, divided by the earnings per share. The earnings per share is the total earnings (profit) of the company after tax and interest charges have been met on loans and any preference shares, divided by the number of ordinary shares. For Trinity Holdings, the P/E ratio is 23.7. Put another way: if all the earnings of the company were paid to ordinary shareholders (none retained in the business), then it would take 23.7 years to repay the shareholder the current cost of the shares.

Stock Market Indices

The market for securities comprises the total number of securities which could be traded which amount to about 3,000 on the London Stock Exchange. This is a clumsy number to get a quick ‘feel’ of current performance, and therefore various samples of securities are taken to get information about various sectors of the market.

FT–SE 100 Index

The *Financial Times*, Stock Exchange 100 Index is the most popular index containing the top 100 companies, based on their capitalisation or total value of all their shares. The index is the weighted arithmetic average of their quoted share prices. This index is also used by investors and traders in the futures market as a basis for future share value speculations.

SUMMARY

A business which is publicly quoted must understand that it is open to a lot of professional analysis by people who care more for the value of the share than the activities of the business. Statements made on the performance of the business share valuation can be carried by news media, and adverse comment may affect the business' ability to borrow funds at reasonable rates. Thus, the knowledge of the money market is important to all businesses, especially when there is a need to borrow money for investing in new activities.

SELECTED READING

Andrew, John. 1990. *How to Understand the Financial Press.* Kogan Page.
Kaufman, Perry. 1994. *Smarter Trading: Improving Performance in Changing Markets.* McGraw-Hill.
Gough, Leo. 1994. *Investor's Guide to How the Market Really Works.* Pitman.
Mott, Graham. 1993. *Investment Appraisal.* Pitman.
Fabozzi, Frank et al. 1994. *Foundations of Financial Markets and Institutions.* Prentice Hall.

21 Financial Strategies: Short and Long-Term Financing

Money is required both to start a business and to keep it going. Ideally, the original investment is sufficient to get the company started; then income from operations pays for continued operations and provides a profit.

The Need for Financing

In actual practice, income and expenses might vary from season to season and from year to year, forcing the company to seek temporary funding during such periods to finance opportunities for expansion or to take advantage of an opportunity to purchase a new facility. Corporate expansion is most often financed through borrowing.

The decision to borrow money does not mean the firm is in trouble. Astute financial management uses regular responsible borrowing to meet needs. Some firms limit their growth or miss profitable opportunities by not borrowing or by borrowing too little. In any case, financial planning and control is critical to the success of any firm.

Financial Planning and Control

Every business, regardless of size, has concerns about money – how to get it and how to use it – and these concerns fall on the financial manager, the person responsible for planning and controlling the acquisition and dispersal of the firm's financial assets and resources. The financial manager's overall goal is to increase the value of the firm by increasing its profits and, in so doing, to increase shareholders' wealth. To achieve this goal requires a financial strategy, which is reflected in the manager's financial plan.

A *financial plan* is a plan for obtaining and using the money needed to implement the organisation's goals. The financial plan controls spending in line with the firm's priorities, ensures the availability of financing and controls the efficient use of financial resources. The plan establishes priorities that are compatible with the organisation's objectives.

A financial plan has four basic steps.

1 Establishing Valid Objectives
Financial objectives are specific, realistic statements detailing financial goals for a specific period.

2 Budgeting Income and Expenses
A budget is a statement that projects income and expenses over a specified future period. The budget process begins by constructing individual budgets for each area of activity – for example, production, sales and promotion – and then by combining these budgets into a master budget. With the master budget, the financial planner can determine whether outside funding will be required, and if so, when it will be required.

3 Identifying Sources of Funds
Financial managers identify funding sources in advance so that they are sure the funds will be available when needed. The four basic sources of funds are sales revenues, sales of assets, equity capital and debt capital.

Sales revenue is the income from future sales and is the primary source of funds for a firm. *Sales of assets* that are no longer needed by the firm can be a source of capital. If the company has no other source of funds, it may need to sell assets that are still utilised; a drastic, but sometimes necessary step. *Equity* and *debt capital* will be discussed later.

4 Monitoring and Evaluating Financial Performance
Financial plans must be monitored on an ongoing basis to ensure they are being properly implemented. By comparing reports of actual sales and actual expenses with budgeted sales and budgeted expenses, managers can often uncover minor problems before they become major problems.

Short-Term Financing

Financial managers use a variety of short-term and long-term strategies to finance the company's operations. *Short term financing* describes money that will be used within a year or less and then repaid. A company's need for short-term financing is closely related to its cash flow, the movement of money into and out of a firm. Ideally, the company wants to have enough money coming in during any period to cover expenses for that period, but this is not always possible.

For example, if the company has not yet received payments for its credit sales, it may need short-term financing to pay its bill while it waits for its customers to pay their bills. Slow sales or unexpected expenses may also cause a cash flow problem. Short-term financing may also be needed to support inventory. Holding inventory incurs a considerable expense for many businesses. Because inventory is often manufactured well in advance of the actual sale, manufacturers need short-term financing to buy materials and pay for production. Wholesalers and retailers need short-term financing to pay for the inventory they must have on hand to make sales. In both cases, manufacturers and wholesalers will repay the money when sales are made.

Sources of Unsecured Short-Term Financing

Most firms have a close working relationship with their short-term lenders. Generally, the shorter the term of the loan, the less risk to the lender. Short-term loans are usually for smaller amounts than long-term loans and are generally unsecured; the borrower is not required to pledge collateral. The major sources of unsecured short-term financing are trade credit, promissory notes, bank overdraft, commercial paper and commercial drafts.

Trade Credit

Trade credit is a payment delay that a firm grants to its customers. When a business buys a product from a supplier, the business receives a bill stating the supplier's credit terms. If the bill is paid on time, the supplier charges no interest. To encourage prompt payment, suppliers often offer a cash discount. Typically, the invoice can say that the customer may take a discount of 2 per cent off the total if the bill is paid within ten days, or else the total amount (without a discount) must be paid within 30 days.

Promissory Notes

A promissory note is a borrower's written pledge to pay a certain sum of money to a creditor at a specified future date. Unlike trade credit, promissory notes carry interest. In addition, a promissory note is legally enforceable.

Promissory notes are negotiable. The lender can sell the note, at a slight discount, to the lender's bank who in turn, then advances the money to the lender and collects the full amount of the loan from the borrower when the note becomes due. The discount becomes the bank's profit.

Bank Overdraft

Unsecured bank loans are offered by 'high street' banks to their customers at interest rates that vary according to the firm's credit rating. Most firms are granted an overdraft limit which is prearranged between the local bank manager and the client. Loans can be taken without notice up to this limit and interest is charged on a daily basis. Repayment can take place at any time, and so the 'average' interest charged is relatively low. Currently, most bank managers seek clients to reduce their overdraft to meet short-term needs and not to maintain it as a longer-term, low interest loan.

Commercial Drafts

Commercial drafts are written orders requiring the customer (the payee) to pay a specified sum to a supplier (the drawer) for goods or services. Commercial drafts are used when the supplier is unsure of the customer's credit standing.

Sources of Secured Short-Term Financing

Borrowers that cannot obtain enough capital through unsecured loans may be required to pledge collateral, most often inventory and accounts receivables (debtors), to secure their loans.

Inventory Loans

A company's inventory can be used to secure an inventory loan. As part of the loan agreement, the lender may require that the inventory be stored in a public warehouse, with the lender holding the warehouse receipt. The lender releases the merchandise only when the loan is paid.

Accounts Receivables (Debtors)

A firm may pledge its accounts receivables as collateral. The lender establishes the quality of the receivables and then advances 70 – 80 per cent of the value of the accounts receivables to the borrower. When the borrowing company receives accounts receivable payments, it must give that money to the lender in payment of the loan.

Factoring

A factor is a firm that specialises in buying receivables at a discount. Factoring, the selling of accounts receivable (debtors), is basically a variation of pledging receivables. By selling its receivables, the company receives money immediately, although it receives less than the face amount of the receivables. Then, when the account is due, the company pays the full amount of that receivable to the factor. Although the selling firm receives less than the face value of the account receivable, it does not have to wait for payment but instead gets the cash at once.

Long-Term Financing

Long-term financing describes money that will be needed longer than one year. Long-term financing might be needed for starting a business, for new product development, for long-term marketing activities, for purchasing or replacing capital assets, or for mergers and acquisitions. All of these activities require large amounts of money; too large to be repaid within the year.

Sources of Long-Term Financing

Sources of long-term financing vary according to the size and type of business. For a corporation, equity financing includes selling shares and retaining earnings. Debt financing includes long-term loans and the sale of corporate bonds. Shares and bonds (debentures) were discussed in Chapter 20.

Equity Financing

Equity financing marks the beginning of every business – sole proprietorship, partnership or corporation. Sole proprietorships and partnerships acquire equity when the owners invest their own money to start the business. Corporations acquire equity when stockholders buy shares in their corporations.

Equity financing has two main advantages for companies. First, equity financing does not have to be repaid (see Chapter 20); thus, issuing new shares of stock is one way a corporation can finance its long-term operations. Second, the corporation is under no legal requirement to pay dividends (distributions of earnings to stockholders).

The corporation may issue new shares of stock to provide equity financing. In many cases, existing shareholders are invited to purchase additional shares before the remainder are offered to others. Sometimes the shares are offered at a discount.

Retained earnings are the portion of a business' profits that is not distributed to stockholders. These funds are reinvested in the business and are considered a form of equity funding. Stockholders gain because this reinvestment tends to increase the value of their stock. By retaining earnings for future operations, the corporation does not have to pay for the use of equity capital.

Debt Financing

Debt financing is accomplished through long-term loans and issuing bonds. Small businesses are usually limited to long-term loans, whereas large corporations may also issue bonds.

Long-term loans are available from commercial banks, insurance companies, pension funds and other financial institutions. Long-term loans run from three to seven years and call for regular quarterly, semi-annual or annual payments. Interest rates and other terms depend on the credit rating of the borrower. The loans are generally secured by real estate, machinery or equipment.

A debenture is a corporation's written pledge to repay a specified amount of money at a specified date at a specified interest rate. Often, a debenture is shared by many lenders and each portion can be sold to other parties.

Interest Factors

The interest rates companies pay to borrow money are determined by many factors, the most important of which are the financial health and credit record of the firm, the risks involved in the investment, general level of interest rates in the country (as reflected in the Bank of England's inter-bank lending rate) and the overall economic outlook.

The prime rate is the lowest rate charged by a bank for a short-term loan to its best customers, usually large corporations with the highest credit ratings. Less sound or smaller firms will pay higher rates, depending on the amount of risk to the lender and the collateral pledged. Except in periods of high inflation, the longer the time for repayment, the higher the interest rate charged.

SUMMARY

The golden rule about borrowing is to match the life of the investment with the life of the loan. For example, borrow long term for long life assets, whilst borrowing short term for short life assets. Borrowing is not a sin; it is an essential business activity, especially as a business often cannot supply all the funds it needs from its own profits. However, the magnitude and duration of the interest charges and eventual repayment of the loan have to be carefully analysed, and must be less than the extra profits earned from the investment.

SELECTED READING

Williams, David. 1994. *Running Your Own Business.* Brealey Publishing.
Jones, Ernest. 1994. *Financial Times Guide to Business Finance.* Pitman.

22 Risk Management and Insurance

For businesses, risk is part of every decision. The essence of business decisions is balancing the risk and potential gains involved in any course of action. Insurance cannot guarantee safety, but it can limit the financial damage of an accident or misfortune. This chapter deals with insurance and other techniques available for managing risk.

The Nature of Risk

Risk is the possibility that a loss or injury will occur. The greatest risk exists not when the odds are very high but when they are unknown, because there is no way to insure against or manage an unknown risk. For an individual, risk is involved in driving a car, investing in shares or bonds or skiing. For a business, risk is part of every decision. Risks can be classified as either speculative risks or pure risks.

Speculative Risk

A speculative risk is accompanied by the possibility of earning a profit. Investing in stocks or bonds involves risk, but investments also have the possibility of making a profit. Business decisions, such as whether to market a new product, involve speculative risks. If the new product is successful, the business reaps profits; if not, the business suffers losses. We have seen in Chapter 20 how speculators minimise risk by using the futures and options market.

Pure Risk

A pure risk involves the possibility only of loss; it offers no possibility of profit or gain. Hurricanes and fires present pure risks: there is no gain if they do not occur, but there is certain loss if they do.

Risk Management

Risk management is the process of identifying exposure to risk, identifying possible ways to handle each exposure and acting to establish protection against the risk. The responsibility for managing speculative risks belongs to the entire management team. The responsibility for managing pure risks in most firms lies with specific individuals, generally called *risk managers*. Their concerns are property risks and liability risks.

Property risks include fire, flood and other damage to property. Liability risks are related to the firms' liability for losses suffered by an individual or another company as a result of, for example, an accident or product liability.

Techniques of Risk Management

The four basic methods for handling risk are risk avoidance, risk assumption, risk transfer and risk reduction. The risk manager chooses the appropriate technique or combination of techniques.

Risk Avoidance

Risk avoidance recognises that not all risks are avoidable and that the costs of attempting to avoid all risks might be high. A company can avoid the risk of product failure by not introducing new products, but such a course would ensure eventual failure. A firm can, however, attempt to avoid engaging in activities that lead to an exposure to risk. For example, many companies avoid operating in politically volatile countries to avoid risks associated with political instability. Jewelry shops place their merchandise in vaults at night to avoid losses through robbery.

Risk Assumption

Risk assumption describes a company's acceptance of responsibility for loss resulting from a particular risk. Knowing and accepting that risks are part of doing business, a firm may reasonably assume risks in certain situations, for example:

● If the potential loss is too small to be of concern.
● If effective risk management has reduced the risk.
● If insurance coverage is either very expensive (too costly in relation to the potential cost of the loss) or unavailable.
● If there is no other way of protecting against loss.

One kind of risk assumption is self-insurance; a company's attempt to protect itself against the risk of loss by establishing a fund to cover a loss. Self-insurance is practical only in situations where the company is large enough to spread the cost over a large operation. For example, rather than pay insurance premiums for truck repairs or damages, a large trucking company may opt instead to pay any damages itself, using the money it sets aside each year as part of its self-insurance.

Risk Transfer

Risk transfer, the most common method of dealing with risk, consists of transferring the risk to an insurance company. The insurance company estimates the potential loss of a given risk and assumes the financial responsibility for that specific risk, in return for which the insurance company charges a fee called a *premium*.

Risk Reduction

Risk reduction assumes that since risk cannot be avoided, perhaps it can be reduced. For example, a company may sponsor employee safety programmes and provide safety equipment in an effort to reduce risk of injury to its workers. It may also install fire alarms, smoke alarms and sprinkler systems to reduce the risk of fire loss.

Insurance and Insurers

An insurance company is a business whose product is protection from loss. An insurance policy is a contract between the company and the insured that reduces the risk of loss to the insured.

Principles of Insurance

An insurance policy requires the insured to pay a fee, called a *premium*, in return for which the insurer will pay a specified amount to the insured should an event occur that has been identified in the policy. Insurance generally works on five basic principles, discussed below.

The Law of Large Numbers

The law of large numbers is a statistical principle that states that, as the number of units in a group increases, predictions about the group become more accurate and certain. While insurance companies cannot predict whether a particular house will burn down within the year, they can project within close range how many houses will be destroyed by fire in a 12-month period. By using the law of large numbers, probability and statistical analysis, insurance companies can reduce the risk for an entire class of insured entities (for example, single family wood homes) and profitably offer protection at a reasonable cost.

Indemnification

The principle of indemnification requires the insurer to pay only for the actual cash value of the loss. This is usually established by independent organisations called *loss adjusters*. The standard property insurance policy, for instance, will pay only the purchase price of an item less its depreciation. A building may be insured for £200,000, but if its value is only £150,000, then the insurer will pay only that amount. It is possible to purchase replacement-value insurance, but since the replacement cost of used property is usually higher than its current cash value, the cost of the insurance is higher. In life insurance, the value for a life lost is difficult to determine, so life policies pay a specific predetermined amount at the death of the insured.

Uninsurable Risk

An uninsurable risk is one that few, if any, insurance companies will assume because of the difficulty of calculating the probable loss, and also the probability of the loss happening.. Market risks such as price or style change, and political risks such as revolution or war, are generally considered uninsurable risks.

Insurable Risk

Insurance policies can be purchased only for insurable risks, risks that are financial, measurable and predictable. Emotional or sentimental values are not insurable. Insurable risk must generally meet the following requirements:

- **Losses must be under the control of the insured:** an insurance company will not pay for the damage that was intentionally caused by the insured party. A building owner cannot collect damages for a fire deliberately set by the owner.
- **Losses must be measurable:** property insured must have a value measurable in pounds, not in sentimental or emotional value, because insurance firms reimburse losses with money.
- **The insured hazard must be widespread:** the insurance company must be able to write many policies covering the same hazard throughout a wide geographic area. Unless the insurance company spreads its coverage in this way, a single disaster in a particular area (a hurricane, for example) could cause it to pay out on all its policies at one time.
- **A sufficiently large number of similar situations must have previously occurred:** the probability of loss, using the law of large numbers, can then be calculated to arrive at an accurate estimate of risk due to a specific cause.

When the insurable risk is too large, an insurer will utilise a process called *reinsurance*, that is, sell off portions of the coverage to other insurance companies. In this way, insurance companies too transfer risk. Therefore, reinsurance is actually an insurance policy limiting the potential loss to the insurance company.

Insurable Interest

In order to purchase insurance, an individual or company must have an insurable interest – that is, the individual or company must be the one to suffer a measurable monetary loss. Thus, an individual cannot, for example, purchase insurance on a house owned by a neighbour hoping to profit if that house suffers a fire.

Government Insurance

Although we do not think of the government as being in the insurance business, it is sometimes the only source of many types of insurance. In the UK, all employers, employees and self-employed persons are required to pay National Insurance contributions which are generally collected by the tax office as agent for the government. The contributions and benefits vary depending on specific circumstances and level of contributions. Hospital care is provided free of charge under the National Health Service. Benefits, including retirement pensions, are paid by the Department of Social Security. Other benefits include:

- **Unemployment benefit:** this is paid to individuals who are out of work but capable of, and actively seeking, full-time work with an employer.
- **Crisis loans:** these are loans paid to people who cannot meet their short-term expenses following an emergency where there is serious risk to the health of themselves or their family.
- **Industrial injuries disablement benefit:** this benefit is paid to employees, and those self-employed, who are disabled following an injury at work.

Private Insurance

The insurance industry is very large in the UK and is internationally recognised as probably the major force in world insurance. However, in the late 1980s and early 1990s, parts of the insurance business dealing mainly with disaster type insurance (such as earthquake cover, fire risk to off-shore oil platforms, aircraft crashes, pollution) suffered multiple high claims which brought many groups of insurers to bankruptcy. High risk insurance can bring very high profits but rather like dealing in speculative shares, some sort of 'hedge' is required. Prudent insurers in high risk areas will reinsure and place much of the risk over the market as a whole.

Insurance companies are of two types: limited companies, such as the Guardian Royal Insurance plc; and mutual businesses which are owned by their policy holders and in which profits earned go towards reducing premiums. The Norwich Union is a mutual organisation.

Types of Insurance Coverage

Effective risk management ensures that insurance coverage is adequate. Considerations include the hazards to be insured against, the cost of the coverage and the risk management techniques that can be utilised. There are many classes of business insurance; some are compulsory and others are tailored to meet the needs of a specific business.

Compulsory Insurances

In the UK, compulsory insurance is required by employers to cover the employer's liability, part of any road vehicles owned, and some engineering activities.

Employer's Liability Insurance

The Employers Liability (Compulsory Insurance) Act, 1969, puts a duty on all employers to take out an insurance policy providing cover for their legal liability when the employee sustains illness or injury arising out of his/her employment. The proof that the insurance is in force is a certificate of insurance which must be displayed on the premises.

Motor Insurance

Under the Road Traffic Act, 1930 and later, it is compulsory for owners of motor vehicles to insure themselves against third party claims. This covers death or injury to any person and damage to another person's property.

Engineering Insurance

Under the Factory and Workshop Act, 1901, and subsequent legislation, inspections of certain types of plant and machinery have to be carried out regularly. Insurers provide cover for three main types of inspected plant: boilers and pressure vessels; electrical and mechanical plant; and lifting equipment. Statutory inspections are often an integral part of the cover provided, that is, the insurer is competent to inspect.

Non-Compulsory Insurance

Advisable but not compulsory insurance includes public and product liability, buildings and assets including stock, and interruptions to business.

Public and Product Liability

Public liability policies cover for the insured's legal liability in the event of accidental injury to third parties, or loss or damage to their property. Product liability covers the same claims but due to goods sold, distributed, repaired or by services undertaken by the insured.

Computer Insurance

Computer insurance can be divided into two areas: computer damage insurance and computer business interruption. Cover for business interruption includes loss of gross profit and any other costs following the breakdown of the computer system. All computer insurances require that computer maintenance agreements are in force.

Contractor's All Risk Insurance

Contractor's 'all risks' insurance covers loss or damage which occurs during construction. Cover can also be provided for loss or damage to plant and materials.

Latent Defects Insurance

Latent defects insurance covers the owners of new properties which have been surveyed and passed as fit, only to find that a hidden or latent fault was present and discovered at a later date, sometimes resulting in the collapse of the building.

Property Damage Insurance

Property damage or material damage is essential cover for all businesses. The cover includes loss, and damage to all buildings, contents and stock. Many other types of special insurances can be included within this policy often resulting in a less expensive premium. An 'all risks' premium will also cover theft, accidental damage and subsidence.

Business Interruption

Business interruption insurance covers the same risks as those for property damage, with usually both business interruption and property damage being included in one policy. Business interruption insurance covers loss of gross profit, and the claim will meet the actual agreed loss in gross profit. In addition, cover is usually extended to cover increased working costs, such as the temporary hiring of buildings and equipment.

Theft

A person is guilty of theft if he/she dishonestly appropriates property belonging to another with the intention of permanently depriving the other of it. Theft is a crime which appears to be increasing every year, and premiums for cover continue to rise. Theft insurance is either full cover or limited to forcible or violent entry into or exit from the premises.

Other Insurances

Other insurance cover includes: money insurance such as wages 'in transit'; personal accident assault during a robbery; glass insurance; goods in transit; fidelity insurance (theft by employee); book debts following the loss or destruction of credit records; legal expenses insurance in defending prosecutions and professional indemnity insurance. These are all areas which should be examined, and the losses of not being insured must be balanced against the premiums required.

Medical Insurance

Extra 'private' medical insurance can be taken individually or by a group of employees. Often, as an employment benefit, a percentage of the costs will be paid by the employer. Group insurance rates are usually much cheaper than individual rates.

Life Insurance

Key staff in a business are often insured by the company against death. The insurance company will pay a lump sum to the business or surviving partner(s). Often major loan organisations will require that an individual takes out a life policy so that any loan can be settled rather than having an additional burden on the estate.

Claims

In the event of a claim being made, there are certain duties imposed on the insured. The law requires that the insured should act as if he/she were not insured and take all necessary steps to minimise loss. Claims must also be made within a time period specified in the contract, and proof must be made available to the insurers that a loss has been incurred.

SUMMARY

All business involve a degree of risk. Frequently, part of this risk can be transferred to a specialist who can manage it more efficiently than the business. Some risks have to be covered legally by a business, such as employee protection, but other risks are either carried or transferred. Owners of businesses, and also key employees, match their own perceptions of risk to those of the business. Risk takers are unlikely to work in Local Government, whilst risk avoiders are unlikely to own a local theatre.

Part 8

The Challenge of the Future

23	# International Business

In the earliest days of society, trade was carried on within a village, then expanded to neighbouring villages. As states and countries emerged, this expansion process included larger and larger areas of trade. Today, trade crosses all borders and oceans.

The Foundations of International Trade

International trade, trading between countries, has long been established. But the globalisation of business – multinational businesses operating worldwide – is a newer, important factor in international trade, and it will grow in importance in the years immediately ahead. About half of the total revenues of Exxon, Mobil, Texaco, IBM, ICI, Shell and many other companies already come from operations outside their 'home' countries. The key factors in international business are discussed below.

Specialisation

Natural resources, populations, climate and navigable waterways are not evenly distributed throughout our planet. As a result, a country that is better equipped to produce certain goods or services, compared to other countries, has an opportunity to specialise in that good or service. Specialisation may give that country an absolute or comparative advantage.

Absolute Advantage

Two countries that provide excellent examples of specialisation because of their huge reserves of valuable natural resources are Saudi Arabia (oil) and South Africa (diamonds). In the United States, California and Florida have a climate that is perfect for growing citrus fruit, while Scotland has an ideal climate and abundant pure, fresh water for producing malt whisky. Each country or region has an absolute advantage as regards that specific product, allowing it to produce that product more efficiently than any other region.

Comparative Advantage

A country has a comparative advantage when it can produce a specific product more efficiently than it can produce other products. Taiwan, for example, can produce electronic goods more efficiently than it can produce wheat. It is therefore advantageous for Taiwan to concentrate on electronics, using the income from electronic products to purchase wheat from a country that has a comparative advantage in wheat production.

Exporting and Importing

For a number of reasons, in today's world no country is self-sufficient. Because of the demands of contemporary life styles and other key factors, a country buys (imports) goods from countries that have a comparative advantage in the production of those goods. In turn, the importing country sells (exports) goods in which it has a comparative advantage to other countries. This exchange between countries forms the basis of importing and exporting. For each international transaction there is an importer and exporter.

- **Importing:** consists of purchasing goods or raw materials from other countries and bringing the goods into the home country.
- **Exporting:** consists of selling and shipping goods or raw materials from the home country to another country.

Balance of Trade

This is the difference between a country's total imports and its total exports (both measured in monetary values) over a given period.

A *trade deficit*, or an unfavourable balance of trade, exists when the value of the imports exceeds the value of exports. A *trade surplus* or a favourable balance of trade, results when the value of exports is greater than the value of imports.

Balance of Payments

Another measure, the balance of payments, is much broader than the balance of trade. The balance of payments includes not only the imports and exports that make up the balance of trade but also money invested by foreigners, money spent by foreign tourists, foreign investment by UK citizens, and money spent overseas by UK tourists. The balance of payments also includes payments by foreign governments, aid given to foreign governments, and any international payments and receipts.   The UK usually has an increasingly unfavourable balance of payments.

Exchange Rates

In international trade the value of any currency, or money, is expressed in terms of another currency; this value is its exchange rate.   The United States trade deficit has resulted in a less favourable exchange rate for the US dollar, the most popular and exchangeable currency in the world.

Exchange rates respond to the law of supply and demand, and rates vary from day-to-day. Until 1971, the world economy operated on a fixed rate of exchange set by each country.   In 1971 most countries abandoned the fixed rates because they no longer reflected economic reality.   Instead, the exchange rate was allowed to fluctuate or float.   Today, very few countries retain fixed exchange rates.   In 1989 the exchange rate of the Russian rouble was officially fixed at over $1.50.   On the unofficial and illegal black market however, which realistically reflected supply and demand, the rouble had a value of less than ten cents.   It continues to fall.   One major problem that Russia and the former Soviet states face as they try to convert to a free market economy is realistically making the rouble convertible to other currencies, while at the same time avoiding internal economic chaos.

Adjusting Currency Values

A continuing imbalance of trade will cause the value of one currency to decline and the other to rise.   There are two artificial solutions to the problem: devaluation and revaluation.

● **Devaluation:** an arbitrary downward adjustment of one country's currency in terms of another country's currency.
● **Revaluation:** an arbitrary upward adjustment of one country's currency in terms of another country's currency.

Balancing Payments

To attain a desired balance of payments, the Soviet Union in the past set a fixed rate of exchange and enforced the rate by law.   The free market solution is to increase exports from the nation with the unfavourable balance to its trading partner with the favourable balance.   For example, to reduce its trade deficit with Japan and bring payments back into balance, the United States tries to sell more of the goods and services in which it has a comparative advantage to Japan.

The 'free' market however, is not completely unrestricted.

Restrictions of Trade

In 1776 in the *Wealth of Nations*, Adam Smith argued that specialisation and free trade with no artificial barriers would eliminate trade imbalances. His theory has been tested ever since. Although over 200 years have passed, Smith's ideal of a free market has yet to be realised. Among the obstacles has been protectionism.

Protectionism

Protectionism describes the creation of artificial barriers to free international trade. These barriers are designed to protect domestic industries and jobs, or to equalise the balance of payments. In new industries, such as information technology, a country may try to protect a fledgling domestic industry from the established might of a similar foreign industry.

Protectionism can take many forms. Proponents of protectionism are found among labour unions, business managers in certain industries, farmers, fishermen and others who feel threatened by foreign competition. Types of protectionism are discussed below.

Tariffs

Nations have historically used tariffs to protect their industries and balance of payments. Protective tariffs are taxes imposed on imported goods. By making the goods more expensive, protective tariffs limit the sales of the imported goods and therefore protect domestic industries.

Import Quotas

Import quotas limit the quantity of a particular good that can be brought into a country during a specified period of time. In the 1980s, the UK government agreed a 'voluntary' import quota with Japan on Japanese cars.

Embargoes

An embargo is a government law or regulation forbidding either the importing or the exporting of certain specified goods. An embargo is designed to protect technology or to punish another nation, not to protect domestic business and industry. As a national defence measure, for example, the United States embargoes the export of nuclear related technology. As a punishment, following the Gulf War, the United Nations has imposed an embargo on the import of oil from Iraq.

Bureaucratic Red Tape

Bureaucratic red tape, the colourful name given to describe the complicated web of government regulations and procedures, is perhaps the most widely used and most effective trade barrier. Either deliberately (as a result of policies) or accidentally, the regulations and paperwork involved in import export transactions in many countries produce delays, confusion and frustration. Among the international barriers encountered are laws that require permits, licenses and item-by-item inspections, as well as business practice laws that in some cases make the payment of bribes legal and permit cartels to control prices.

Foreign Exchange Controls

Foreign exchange controls restrict the amount of a particular foreign currency that can be bought or sold, in effect limiting the amount of goods an importer can purchase with that currency. Critics of foreign exchange controls point out that the cost of these restrictions can be considerable, that these costs are passed on to the consumer in the form of artificially higher prices, and that controls restrict consumer choice, causing resources to be misallocated.

International Trade Agreements

In spite of the protectionist barriers cited above, there has been a strong movement toward encouraging international trade. Virtually every country has trade agreements with other countries or groups of countries for the specific purpose of encouraging international trade.

General Agreement on Tariffs and Trade (GATT)

The General Agreement on Tariffs and Trade (GATT) signed by 92 countries shortly after the end of World War II, is both a treaty and an organisation (based in Geneva, Switzerland) to administer the treaty. GATT offers a forum for settling international trade disputes and for negotiating tariffs. GATT has sponsored a number of international meetings, called *rounds*, intended to reduce trade restrictions. The Kennedy Round (begun in 1964) and the Tokyo Round (begun in 1977) succeeded in reducing a number of both tariff and non-tariff barriers. One of GATT's aims was to reduce import taxes to 5 per cent worldwide; however, this aim has been ignored by most signatories.

United National Agencies

Two agencies of the United Nations help finance international trade, although they are not involved in either reducing tariffs or pricing goods. They are the International Monetary Fund and the World Bank.

The International Monetary Fund (IMF)

The IMF uses contributions from UN member nations to make loans to nations with balance of trade problems. The IMF ties certain economic changes to loan approvals often including, for example, cuts in social programmes designed to reduce inflation; as a result, some countries are unwilling to accept IMF loans.

The World Bank

The World Bank makes loans to less developed countries in order to help them improve their production capacity.

International Economic Communities

The aim of GATT is to remove barriers on a global scale. On a more modest scale, several groups of countries have joined to promote common economic polices and the free movement of products and resources among their members. The major organisations are discussed below.

The European Community (EC)

The European Community (EC) or Common Market was formed in January 1958 to encourage free commerce among its members. Initially the EC comprised of six members, but by 1986 this had risen to 12 including: France, Germany, Italy, Belgium, Netherlands, Spain, Luxembourg, Portugal, UK, Ireland, Denmark, and Greece.

Since 1958 many trade restrictions among members have been abolished. The EC now trades with the rest of the world as a single economic unit and in many ways as a single political unit with a common tariff policy. The political and economic unification, however, is a tortuous path and means to many the unacceptable loss of national sovereignty. In addition, a large number of Eastern European, Scandinavian and Mediterranean states are seeking full or associated membership of the EC; this could increase the number of members to 28 or so by the year 2000.

The Latin American Integration Association (LAIA)

The Latin American Integration Association, successor to an earlier Latin American Free Trade Association, includes the following member countries: Argentina, Mexico, Bolivia, Paraguay, Brazil, Peru, Chile, Uruguay, Colombia, Venezuela, Ecuador. To date, the LAIA has achieved only limited economic integration.

The US/Canada Free Trade Agreement

The US/Canada Free Trade Agreement went into effect in 1989. When fully implemented, and after a gradual removal of trade barriers, the result will be a North American marketplace resembling that of the EC.

The Organisation of Petroleum Exporting Countries (OPEC)

OPEC is an international economic organisation of a different kind. OPEC was formed in 1960 not to reduce trade barriers but to control and regulate the price and production of crude oil.

Although members do not always cooperate fully, OPEC has succeeded in raising and maintaining the price of crude oil well above pre-OPEC levels.

Levels of Involvement in International Trade

Businesses that decide to enter the international trade arena must decide on their level of involvement. Several approaches, discussed below, are available to companies.

Licensing

Licensing, a basic level of entering international trade, is a contractual agreement in which one firm permits another to produce and market its product or to use its brand name in return for a royalty or other compensation. Licensing permits a company to expand into a foreign market with little investment. However, since the licensee is in charge of the operations, the licensing firm gains no first-hand foreign marketing experience. Another disadvantage is the risk that the licensee may not maintain quality levels, thereby damaging the product's image.

Exporting

A higher level of involvement is needed when a firm decides to export manufactured products for sale in foreign markets. The exporting firm may use its own salesforce, or it may sell its products to an import/export merchant firm, a merchant wholesaler that assumes all the risks of product ownership, distribution and sales. The import/export firm may even purchase the goods in the manufacturer's home country and take all responsibility for export.

As an alternative, an exporting firm may use an import/export agent, who is a resident of the foreign country and represents the firm's products in that country. Import/export agents have the necessary market knowledge, sales knowledge and contacts in that particular environment. Agents are paid on the basis of their sales and represent a low-cost entry into exporting.

The reputation of the agent is an important consideration. Since the manufacturing firm has no office in the foreign country, the agent is the only recourse for customers who have problems with product quality, defects or service.

Joint Venture

Under an international joint venture, a domestic firm forms a partnership with a foreign company in order to produce and/or market the domestic firm's product abroad. Unlike a licensing arrangement, both parties put resources and capital into the new venture and share in the profits.

Joint ventures have become an increasingly popular way to move into international trade. In some countries, joint ventures are almost the only way to start an international business; many countries have laws requiring that firms making an investment in the country have a local joint venture - a partner. Although an international joint venture supplies a partner with local knowledge and expertise, it also removes some of the domestic company's control.

Direct Investment

Many major corporations and some smaller ones have chosen to make direct investments overseas by establishing plants or other facilities, or buying an existing firm in a foreign country. A substantial portion of the total assets of companies, such as Exxon, IBM, General Motors and Dow Chemical, is represented by direct investment overseas. The decision on the part of Japan's Honda to become a partner with the previously known British Leyland Group, to build Japanese designed cars in the UK, is another example. Nissan's high investment in the North East Development area of the UK provided much needed jobs, but also gave Nissan a 'toehold' on the EC car market which it found difficult to penetrate directly because of protectionist activities.

Although direct investment requires higher costs, it makes the company a part of the business life of the foreign country. Benefits include access to information, tax advantages and exemption from import duties, regulations, and laws governing outside firms. Because of the size of the investment involved, errors concerning the marketability of the product can be costly. In addition to the economic risk of direct investment, there can be political risks in some counties, for example, the risk of nationalisation or seizure of the company's assets by the foreign country.

International Firms

An international firm does business overseas by selling goods designed and manufactured domestically. It may have plants overseas, but its headquarters are domestic. Domestic marketing and manufacturing are the company's main concerns.

Multinational Firms

A multinational firm designs products and markets them in many countries. It operates on a worldwide scale, without ties to any specific nation. It does not have a domestic division or an international division, for example, but instead gears its planning and decision-making to one international level, regardless of where its headquarters may be. Unilever, Royal Dutch Shell and Nestlé are all truly multinational firms.

There are many advantages to multinationalism, including local management, the ability to buy raw materials locally, local R&D, and some protection from international currency fluctuations. Overseas operations for multinational firms are important independent enterprises.

SUMMARY

This chapter has addressed the globalisation of business, a new fact in international trade which is growing more important every year. Every day meetings at many levels are under way for the specific purpose of trying to reduce or limit trade barriers, to find ways to finance international trade, and to move toward a free market economy. Governments worldwide are increasingly involved with commercial diplomacy, encouraging and promoting international trade and a world economy.

24 Careers

What is a 'Career'?

There is an important difference between a *job* and a *career*. Your job belongs to your employer. It is a specified function, a set of tasks that an organization needs a person to perform. If you do not do it, someone else will.

Your career belongs to you. You will have many jobs, even if you only have one employer, and these jobs will make up your career. Each job is a step toward establishing a satisfying and successful career. One job is 'better' than another only if it moves you toward that goal.

This chapter will help you attain your personal definition of success by identifying information about yourself and by gathering information about organisations that are most likely to have career opportunities for you.

Choosing a Career

Some people choose their career. In other cases, careers choose people, that is, their careers happen by chance. Some wait for an opportunity, recognise it and take advantage of it as best they can. Some accept the recommendation or advice of parents, friends or counsellors.

The people who take charge of their future forge their own careers. In some cases, the path is a straight line; once the career decision is made, the individual may spend a lifetime in that chosen occupational field. Most times, however, interests and needs change, as do business environments. As a result, an individual will choose to, or be forced to, shift jobs, locations and careers.

In any case, a career is a journey and not a destination. Career decisions are part of a broader set of decisions that include lifestyle, family and other personal matters. As important as career decisions are, they are not made on a one-time permanent basis. Rather, they are part of a continuing lifelong process. There is no set route. The only constant is change. The better the understanding you have of yourself, work tasks and environments, and career paths, the greater control you will have of your own career.

Choosing a career is an information gathering process involving a series of steps and searches. The process starts with self-assessment, moves to an assessment of the business world, and then finds the best 'fit' between you and the organisations that need you and offer the kinds of jobs you want. Let us begin, then, with the first step in the process, self-assessment.

Understanding Self-Assessment

The first step in choosing a career is self-assessment. Before you can choose a career, you need to know who you are, what skills you have, what motivates you and what you find satisfying. The process of self-assessment is based on your examination of your own personal characteristics – your interests, personality characteristics, skills and abilities, values and lifestyle.

Interests

Interests are anything you enjoy doing. It can relate to work or play, to career or hobby. The Strong Interest Inventory is frequently used to elicit a person's interest or attitudes. It does not measure intelligence, aptitudes or skills. Rather, it produces a profile based on the work of John Holland, a career-development theorist who classified six broad career categories marked with simple letters:

- **R** – Realistic occupations, which deal with things rather than with ideas or people. Examples include computer repair and construction.
- **I** – Investigative occupations, which centre around science and scientific activities to better understand the physical world. Examples include medical research and oceanography.
- **A** – Artistic occupations, which provide many opportunities for self-expression. Examples include commercial art and acting.
- **S** – Social occupations, which are concerned with the welfare of others. Examples include social work and nursing.
- **E** – Enterprising occupations, which require persuading others. Examples include sales and advertising.
- **C** – Conventional occupations, which are highly ordered. Examples include secretarial and accounting.

Personality Characteristics

Personality characteristics determine to a large extent who you are. The Myers-Briggs Type Indicator (MBTI), based on the theories of Carl Jung, examines the preferences that determine your personality predispositions. The categories are arranged in scales representing opposites in four dimensions.

- **The Extraversion-Introversion scale** describes where one likes to focus attention; the outer world of people or one's own inner world.
- **The Sensing-Intuitive scale** describes the opposite ways a person perceives or acquires information. A sensing person depends on physical senses (e.g., hearing, seeing) while an intuitive person relies on feelings.
- **The Thinking-Feeling scale** describes how a person reaches conclusions or makes decisions once he/she has appropriate information.
- **The Judging-Perceiving scale** describes one's adaptation to the outer world. A

judgemental person likes things planned and in place, while a perceptive person is more spontaneous.

The MBTI divides people into 16 combinations of these distinguishable personality types, identifying preferences in jobs and work arrangements that will provide people with the opportunity to express and use those preferences.

Skills and Abilities

Skills and abilities are your talents. Academic skills, mechanical aptitude, dexterity, language fluency and social skills all contribute to the total picture. These skills may already be present, but they can be developed or enhanced through education and training.

Values

Values are the principles or standards that represent what is important to you. Life values include, for example, financial independence, family, religious freedom and marriage. These values are influenced by people such as your parents, teachers and peers, and by social, cultural and economic factors. Work-related values include recognition, security, challenge, meaningful job tasks, commitment to quality and working conditions.

Lifestyle

Lifestyle describes the way a person chooses to live. The interrelationships of your work, leisure and interpersonal relationships make up your lifestyle. You can choose to be part of a family or not, to live in a flat or a single family house and so on. Lifestyle decisions include choices such as the geographical location of where you live, for example, urban, suburban or rural. Lifestyle goals can change as personal needs and circumstances in life change.

The Job Seeker

There are several standardised tests that can help you with the process of self-assessment and with determining vocational interests. The Myers-Briggs Type Indicator and the Strong Interest Inventory have already been mentioned. Others are the Jackson Vocational Interest Survey and the System of Interacting Guidance and Information Plus (SIGI Plus), a computerised career-information system.

Conscientiously executed, the self-assessment process is very informative and develops a great deal of data. In addition to an inventory of skills, the process will give you a good idea of the workstyles you prefer. You will learn whether you:

● Like to work alone or in teams.
● Prefer to have autonomy or work on clearly defined tasks.
● Would rather organise or execute.
● Prefer to work with detailed analyses or with broader ideas.

You will also have an understanding of the sort of environment you prefer, what pace of work you like, how much variety you require and the other aspects of work that are important to you.

Understanding the Business World

In order to make an intelligent choice, you must know what the options are. The process starts with the broad choice of industry, narrows to the occupation and finally to the job. All three areas are discussed below.

Industry

The examination of career opportunities begins with a broad view of industries, which can be classified as either goods-producing or service-producing industries:

- **Goods-producing industries:** these are divided into four main categories: manufacturing, agriculture, construction or mining. In recent years, the number of jobs in goods-producing industries has not grown appreciably, due partly to automation and partly to improved productivity resulting from better trained workers.
- **Service-producing industries:** these comprise retail and wholesale trade, government (local, state and federal, including education), repair and maintenance services, transportation and public utilities, finance, insurance, real estate, advertising and health care. Service-producing industries have shown continuing growth in recent years.

Occupations

Occupations can be divided into four groups: white-collar, blue-collar, service and farm. In evaluating any of these groups, you should consider whether it shows a trend for growing or contracting.

- **White-collar:** white collar jobs or non-factory jobs include professional and technical workers; for example, teachers, engineers, doctors, accountants, clergy, managers and administrators, sales workers and clerical workers. Managers and administrators are increasingly in demand as firms come to depend on trained management specialists more and more. Because of needs in electronic data processing, the demand for computer-literate clerical workers is rapidly expanding. Sales workers – people selling goods and services for retail, wholesale, insurance and real estate firms – also represent a growth area.
- **Blue collar:** blue collar workers include craft workers, semi-skilled workers and labourers. Craft workers include carpenters, machinists and electricians. Semi-skilled workers assemble goods, operate machines in factories and drive vehicles such as trucks or buses. Labourers perform unskilled work and include truck loaders and stock clerks.

● **Service occupations:** service occupations workers are employed in service fields such as health care, appliance maintenance and service, and a wide range of personal-services occupations (for example, beauty shops). Many white-collar workers such as secretaries are employed in service industries, but the term service occupations refers only to those who perform the actual services.

● **Farm:** farm occupations include farmers, farm managers and farm supervisors. As mechanisation of farms continues, the number of farm occupations is shrinking.

Jobs

Ultimately, an individual works at a job within an occupation in an industry. This book will help make you aware of the diverse jobs existing in business, help you understand the nature of some of those jobs, and assist you in identifying career opportunities that are appropriate for you. Therefore, we will discuss representative job titles of occupations as they were presented in this book.

Part 1: The Challenge of Government Business
Job opportunities include analysts, advocates and lobbyists, economic geographers, government inspectors (including health inspectors), food and drug inspectors, meat and poultry inspectors, wage and compliance officers, and bank economists. Old concepts regarding the challenge of government-type business jobs are now mostly obsolete, as a new 'market driven' culture takes over.

Part II: Business Formation
Job opportunities include lawyers specialising in government regulatory work; litigation, labour law, equal employment opportunity, banking, criminal law, the environmental, bankruptcy and corporate law, and product liability law.

Part III: Management of the Enterprise
Job opportunities include work supervisors, analysts, management consultants, hotel managers, hotel assistants, health services administrators and medical records administrators.

Part IV: Managing People and Production
Job opportunities in managing people include personnel specialists, recruiters, trainers, wage and salary compensation specialists, recreational safety and health workers, labour relations specialists, labour union business agents, and interviewers in employment agencies.

Job opportunities in production management include computer assisted manufacturing production supervisors, manufacturing inspectors, engineering technicians, industrial planners, purchasing agents and technical writers. Drafters and industrial designers are employed in product development. Production and operations departments are headed by a director of operations at the top management level, and a plant manager in middle-level management.

Part V: Marketing Management

Job opportunities include: special events coordinators; retail, wholesale and manufacturers' sales workers; retail buyers, displayers, promotion assistants; public relations workers; advertising space salespeople; product or brand managers and assistants; account executives; market research analysts, interviewers and statisticians.

Part VI: Management Tools

Job opportunities include book-keepers and accounting clerks, credit managers, internal and external auditors, public and corporate accountants, tax accountants, controllers, data processing clerks, computer operators and programmers, application support workers, computer service technicians, customer services representatives, computer designers, computer engineers, documentation specialists, statisticians and operations analysts.

Part VII: Financial Management

Job opportunities include: bank tellers, bank branch officers and/or managers; trust and estate administrators; loan counsellors; credit analysts; claims adjustors; insurance agents, brokers and actuaries; securities sales workers or stockbrokers; financial analysts; underwriters and treasurers.

By researching the job description for a particular job title, you will gather much valuable information. For example, in most occupations, jobs will require different levels of skill and responsibility. The job description details the responsibilities for a particular job. The job specifications outline any requirements for training, education and prior work experience needed to perform the responsibilities; at entry level, people with good general skills and the ability to learn are sought. The job outlook describes the anticipated future for a particular job.

Opportunities for getting a particular job depend on the relationship between the number of openings and the number of qualified people for that job. At any time, economic forces, government programmes and geographic imbalances can cause a shortage or a surplus for a particular job. In general, jobs in the future will require increasing levels of training and education.

Making the Match

Once you have identified a job that matches your interest, abilities and career goals, your next step is to identify companies where you would like to work and that have, or will have, job openings, and then persuade them to hire you. You begin this stage by leaning more about specific companies.

The Company and its Culture

Just as people have individual identities, so do organisations. The 'personality' of an organisation can be seen in its *corporate culture*. Corporate culture evolves from many aspects of each corporation's environment: the way people dress, the way they act, the management style, the expected number of work hours. Some firms encourage independence, some emphasise close adherence to established procedures and policies. All these factors, and more, contribute to a company's corporate culture.

Different areas of business have different cultures; for example, advertising agencies and accounting firms tend to have very different cultures. But even within the same industry (e.g., in advertising) different firms have different styles.

Gathering information on an industry, and on a specific firm within an industry, involves research. Libraries have a variety of useful directories that describe industries by company, location, sales volume and other characteristics. Do not hesitate to contact the library counter staff at your local library, college or university. They can usually point you in the right direction and save you considerable time in looking for the information you want. Many libraries now have CD-ROM (compact disk read only memory) computer accessed data systems which enable you to browse through vast quantities of data for the information you want very efficiently.

As you narrow your choice to specific companies, much information can be gathered by looking at copies of the latest financial statements using CD-ROM FAME issued by the British Institute of Management, and also by looking up all references to the specific business in 'quality' newspaper files on computer. These methods are very applicable to larger companies but limited as regards smaller, privately owned companies.

The Match

Armed with job and career goals, and having a sense of what companies you might want to work for, your next step is to find a good match. Sometimes you will find a position that seems perfect for you, but the company may not be interested in you, or it may have other candidates it prefers. Sometimes you will find a company which is interested in you but does not offer the work environment, salary or opportunity that you want. Neither of these situations is a good match. A good match is a job opportunity that meets your requirements in a company you like and has a need for someone with your qualifications.

The Job Search

Newspaper classified advertisements are one good source of position openings. College placement offices, newsletters, trade publications and specialised job 'shop' services also list openings. In the UK, your local Training and Enterprise Council (TEC) will also hold information on career and career retraining opportunities. A job search can be a numbers game: the more people you contact for jobs or leads, the wider your contact list becomes and the more likely it is that your search will be successful.

Networking

Networking, a proven effective strategy, is the process of using contacts to make more contacts. The key to networking is to develop contact lists. Write lists of the names of businesspeople you know, people in companies you are interested in, people in professions of interest, and friends and relatives who might provide the names of additional contacts or information about industries, companies or jobs. Then select from your list the names of those people who can most likely provide you with help in the form of additional contacts, company information, career objectives and so on.

Before you call, develop a short sample presentation in which you introduce yourself, explain how you acquired the person's name and state the purpose of the call. Note that your purpose is not to ask for a job; you must make this clear immediately. The purpose is to get information about their fields, companies, contacts and the labour markets. You are calling to schedule a brief meeting, an informational interview, at a convenient time to discuss career opportunities.

Before the meeting, prepare your key questions. At the meeting, ask for suggestions for your job search and for names of others who might be of assistance. Respect the person's time: keep the meeting brief, as you promised. In using this approach, you present yourself as a knowledgeable person who has a professional manner.

The more people you meet for an informational interview, the greater your chances of obtaining job leads and expanding your contact list; there lies the strength of networking, getting referrals from each person you contact. Sometimes you learn about job opportunities during the informational interview. If you act on any suggestions given to you, be sure to inform the originator of the suggestion about the results.

Employment Offices

Employment offices are operated by city, state and federal governments, and by private agencies. They list job openings and charge no fee to either the employee or the hiring company.

Employment Agencies

Employment agencies, which include both private employment agencies and executive recruiters, do charge fees. Many employment agencies specialise in a single industry (engineering or marketing, for example). Agency fees may be paid by either the company or the individual. Employment agencies are more useful for those who already have some work experience.

Direct Mailings

Direct mailings to companies can also result in interviews, although according to estimates, you may need to send 100 letters to generate five interviews. Including a customised cover letter with the CV (curriculum vitae - a summary of your qualifications, training, and experience) is more expensive and time consuming, but it is also more effective than sending the CV alone. Direct your mailings to a specific person, preferably one in a position to hire you.

Your Curriculum Vitae (CV)

Your CV represents you. Thus, the information it contains and its physical form are very important and deserve your careful attention. In addition to saying what you want about yourself, your CV should present the information your prospective employer will want to know about you. The best CVs are directed to a specific audience for a specific purpose. If your job search covers several industries or occupations, you may need to develop a CV for each target audience.

There is no single correct way to design a CV, but there are guidelines. Neatness counts, as do spelling and grammar. Use white or off-white paper and a matching envelope. If possible, limit the CV to one page; certainly not more than two pages unless you have years of experience. The reader will scan your CV quickly, for about 20 seconds, so use a format that guides the reader to the key words that address the reader's needs.

The CV should contain the following information.

- **Personal data:** include your personal data; your name, address and telephone number.
- **Career objectives:** state your career objectives in a way that does not limit possible jobs.
- **Potential:** demonstrate your potential. Highlight the skills, talents and capabilities that give you an advantage compared to other applicants. Stress your accomplishments and achievements.
- **Experience and education:** list information related to your experience and education that are pertinent to the position sought. Use action words such as 'accomplished', 'demonstrated', 'increased', 'managed' and 'initiated'.
- **References:** do not include the names of references in your CV, but prepare a list for those employers who request references. In your list of references, include the names of teachers and previous employers. Before you list any names, however, be sure to get each person's permission.
- **Other information:** try to differentiate yourself from other applicants. Add information about activities, language skills, travel or personal interests related to the specific job. Remember your purpose is to convince the prospective employer to grant you an interview.

Many books have been written about writing effective CVs. Writing a CV is not a light undertaking; it is hard work. Write, rewrite, refine and polish your CV, both its content and its format, until you are proud to have it represent you.

The Cover Letter

Never mail a CV without a cover letter; a letter whose purpose is to accompany the CV and highlight key points of information that are pertinent to the job. No matter how you find out about a job opening, learn as much as you can about the employer and the job, and use this information in the cover letter. Its appearance, form, style and content all contribute to the message you convey. The letter should be on the same type of paper as your CV.

Here is a brief outline for a cover letter:

1 In the first paragraph, clearly identify the specific job you are applying for and why you are interested in that job. If you have been recommended by an individual, mention his/her name. If you are replying to an advertisement, mention the source of the advertisement.

2 In the second paragraph, discuss your qualifications, expanding on the experience described in your CV. Make clear your knowledge and interest in the company and the particular job.

3 In the closing paragraph, express your interest in meeting with the employer to discuss the requirements of the job and your qualifications.

The cover letter and CV have one purpose – to get an interview. They should convince the prospective employer to grant you an interview.

If you do not hear from the prospective employer in a reasonable length of time (say two weeks), telephone the person you wrote to and inquire how the search is progressing. This will indicate your continuing interest and could lead to an interview.

The Interview

Dress according to industry practice. If you do not know, visit the company in advance to see how people dress. Your dress should underscore the impressions you want to make and the image you want to project: neat, clean, enthusiastic, capable, motivated and responsible.

Think of the interview as a conversation with two purposes: to sell yourself to the interviewer, and to get information about the company and the job. Be prepared for that conversation.

To prepare, find out everything you can about the company (and if possible the job) in advance, and anticipate the kinds of questions you can expect the interviewer to ask. The interviewer will, of course, want to know about your work experience. Be prepared to answer questions about whether you can do the job, why you are interested in that specific job, what skills or experience you have that specially suit you for the position, why you have chosen this field and what your career objectives are. Do not be afraid to ask questions. You might ask questions related to the self assessment-information you gathered through the Myers-Briggs Type Indicator or the Strong Interest Inventory. For example, you might ask whether you will have the opportunity to apply your specific skills and talents, and whether you will work alone or in a group.

The information exchanged in an interview is not all verbal. In addition to your appearance, your manner, your voice and your presence communicate too. Make eye contact. Be friendly, honest and sincere. Try not to answer all questions with just 'yes' or 'no', but at the same time do not do all the talking.

After the interview, write to the person who interviewed you, expressing your thanks for his/her time and your continued interest in the job. If you omitted any pertinent information in the interview, mention it in your letter.

SUMMARY

The job search process is not easy. Gathering the information needed will take much time and effort, and the job search may not have instant success. But because your work constitutes a major part of your life, finding a satisfactory job and career is well worth the effort. Best of luck!

Glossary

A

absolute advantage A country's or a region's inherent superiority in producing a product more efficiently than any other country or region.

accounting Systematic collecting, analysing, classifying, recording, summarising, reporting and interpreting of business transactions.

accounting equation Assets = Liabilities + Owners' Equity

accounts payable Amounts owned by a company and payable in one year or less (see Creditors)

accounts receivable Amounts owed to a company to be received within one year or less (see Debtors)

accrual basis Methods of recording revenues and costs in the year they are incurred.

acid-test ratio Financial measure found by dividing quick assets by current liabilities.

advertising Paid messages communicated through a mass medium to a wide general audience by an identified sponsor.

advertising campaign Detailed advertising strategy organised in stages.

advertising platform Summary of key selling points or features that are to be incorporated into the advertising campaign.

agent Person who acts for, and in the name of, a second person who is known as the principal.

applications software Special-use computer programs that perform a particular function.

arbitration Procedure in which a neutral third party hears both sides of a dispute and renders a decision.

assembly-line production Transformation of resources by moving materials through a series of work areas, where different groups of workers perform specific assembly operations.

assets Anything of value, either tangible or intangible, owned by a firm.

autocratic leadership Style describing managers who make decisions without consulting employees, then announce their decisions and expect or demand compliance.

automated teller machine (ATM) Machine that allows users to make common banking transactions electronically without human assistance. (alt. cash point)

automation Production that maximises the use of mechanical operations and minimises human involvement.

B

balance of payments A country's payments to other countries minus payments received from those countries.

balance of trade A country's total exports minus its total imports.

balance sheet Financial statement summarising all accounts and showing the financial position of the firm on a specific date, as a balance between owners funds and total net assets.

bankrupt A person or business being declared insolvent by a court and assets administered for the benefit of creditors.

bartering Exchanging goods and services for others' goods and services, not for money.

batch processing Saving, gathering, then processing a number of tasks or transactions in one lot.

beneficiary Individual or organisation named in a life insurance policy to receive payments in the event of the insured's death.

binary Use of only two digits - 0 and 1 - in various combinations to represent any character (number, letter, or symbol).

bit Digit in a binary number.

bond Long-term loan contract between a business, national, or local or government corporation or municipality and investors

bonus Compensation in addition to wages, salary or commissions.

book-keeping Record-keeping of accounting and financial information.

boycott Agreement not to do business with a particular firm.

branch Merchant wholesale firms that are owned by the manufacturer and stock only that manufacturer's goods.

brand Name, term, or symbol that identifies one seller's products and distinguishes them from competitors' products.

breach of contract Failure of one party to fulfil the terms of a contract.

breakeven point Number of units that must be sold at a given price to cover both fixed and variable costs.

broker Intermediary who executes clients trades for a securities firm.

budget Financial plan that projects income and expenses over a specified future period.

business-interruption Insurance that protects a business against loss of income from interruptions caused by fire, storm or other natural disaster.

buying on margin Buying stock by borrowing part of the money from a broker using the borrowed stock as collateral and then repaying the broker with interest.

byte Eight bits, which represent one character.

C

call Right to buy a specified stock at a specified price for a specified period.

callable bond Bond that may be redeemed before the maturity date.

capital Money or funds needed to operate a business; buildings, machinery and tools owned by a business.

capital gains Profits realised by selling an asset or a security at a price higher than the purchase price.

capitalism Economic system that relies on free markets.

cash basis Method of recording revenues or costs in the year they are received or paid.

cash discount Price reduction offered to customers who make cash payments.

catalogue showroom Outlet that features a wide assortment of merchandise, samples of which are displayed in the showroom.

centralised organisation One in which most of the decision-making authority is retained by upper level management.

central processing unit Part of a computer that controls the computational aspect of the computer system.

chain of command Flow of authority within an organisation, from the topmost level through all lines of authority.

chain store Group of retail establishments owned by one individual or one company.

channel of distribution Route that a product travels from producer to consumer.

cheque Written order for a bank or other financial institution to pay a state amount to the person indicated on the face of the cheque.

closed shop Workplace that requires an employee to be a union member as a condition of employment.

collective bargaining Process of negotiating a contract between labour and management.

commercial bank Profit-making organisation that accepts deposits, makes loans and supplies related services to its customers.

commercial paper Short-term promissory note issued by large corporations and secured only by company reputation

commission Payment based on a percentage of sales revenues.

common law Law based on precedents established by prior decisions.

common stock Certificates that represent ownership in a corporation.

comparative advantage A country or region's greater efficiency in producing certain products as compared to another country or region.

compensation Monetary payment employees receive in exchange for their labour.

computer-aided design (CAD) Use of computer technology to design and produce drawings, sketches and various other kinds of product specifications.

computer-aided manufacturing (CAM) Use of computer technology to analyse product design as part of the manufacturing process.

conglomerate Corporation that operates in widely diverse fields.

consideration Something of value that each party must receive in order for a contract to be legally binding.

consumerism All activities intended to protect consumers in their dealings with business.

consumer market People who buy products for their personal use or consumption, not for profit.

contract Legally enforceable agreement between two or more parties.

convenience goods Low priced products the consumers purchase frequently with little shopping effort.

convenience store Retail outlet that offers customers limited convenience goods at higher prices than supermarkets charge.

convertible security Convertible preferred stock or convertible bond, which may be exchanged for common stock at a specified conversion price.

co-operation Non-profit corporation owned collectively by its members to supply services for the distribution, marketing and purchasing of goods.

copyright Exclusive rights to publish, perform or sell an original book, article, design, illustration, computer program, film or other creation.

corporate culture Personality and environment of an organisation.

corporation Organisation that is formally and legally chartered as a business and has the rights of an individual, that is to own and sell property, borrow money, and be sued.

correlation analysis Statistical technique that measures the relationship between two or more variables.

cost of living adjustment Automatic employee wage increases intended to keep pace with inflation.

cottage business Business operated by an individual who works in his or her home.

craft union Early union made up of workers with specialised skills, such as carpenters.

critical path method (CPM) Technique for scheduling complicated production processes that focuses on the one step, activity or "path" that requires the longest time to complete.

currency All paper money and coins issued by the government plus money orders, travellers cheques, personal cheques and bank cheques or cashier cheques.

current assets Cash and other assets that can be quickly converted to cash.

current liabiiities Debts that will be paid within one year.

current ratio Measure of liquidity found by dividing current assets by current liabilities.

D

data Raw facts and figures. (singular: datum)

debenture Bond not backed by the issuer's assets. Usually divided into units for 'sale' to investors.

debit card Plastic card used to deduct money electronically from the customer's account at the time of sale. (known at 'switch' in the UK)

debt financing Borrowing through long-term loans or the selling of corporate bonds.

debt-to-assets ratio Measure found by dividing total liabilities by total assets.

debt-to-equity ratio Comparison of equity supplied by creditors with equity furnished by the owners; found by dividing total liabilities by owners' equity.

decentralised organisation One in which authority is delegated to lower management.

decision-support system MIS system that is specifically designed to support complex decision-making.

deed Written document transferring ownership of real property.

deflation General decline in the prices of goods and services.

demand Willingness of purchasers to buy specific quantities of a good or service at a given price at a given time.

demand deposit Bank account funds that can be withdrawn at any time.

demography Statistical study of the characteristics of human populations.

departmentalisation Grouping jobs into manageable work units, or departments, usually based on function, geography, product or service, customer, process matrix or a mixture or combination of these.

department store Large, service-oriented retail establishment that offers a wide range of merchandise.

depreciation Method of distributing the cost of devaluation of fixed assets over a period of years.

deregulation Reduction of the complexity and quantity of regulations that affect business.

devaluation Arbitrary downward adjustment of one country's currency in terms of another country's currency.

direct mail Advertising through letters, fliers, cards and so on, sent directly to consumers' homes or their places of business.

disability income insurance Insurance that protects an employee against loss of income while he or she is disabled as a result of illness or accident.

discount store General-merchandise outlet that offers products at reduced prices.

discretionary income Disposable income less savings and expenditures on necessities.

disposable income Personal income less all personal taxes.

dividends Earnings distributed to shareholders

double-entry book-keeping System in which each financial transaction is recorded as two separate accounting entries.

E

earnings per share Net profit after taxes divided by the number of shares outstanding.

embargo Government law or regulation

forbidding trading in a specified good or with a certain country.

entrepreneur Person who assumes the risks, accepts the responsibilities and takes the steps necessary to create a business and make a profit.

equilibrium Point at which supply and demand are in balance.

equity financing Selling stock or retaining earning rather than seeking secured loans. Implies a lessening of control of the business because of more 'owners'.

exchange Giving something of value to another individual as part of a transaction for a good or a service.

exchange rate Value of a particular currency expressed in terms of another currency.

exchanges National, regional and other associations established for the specific purpose of trading securities.

exclusive distribution Distribution by only one retail outlet in any one geographical area.

expenses Costs involved in creating and selling products or services and operating a business.

exporting Selling and shipping goods or raw materials from the home country to another country.

external data Data that originate from sources outside the company.

F

factoring Selling the firm's accounts receivable at a discount in order to secure capital.

factors of production Resources from which all goods and services are produced, namely, land, labour, capital, information resources and entrepreneurs.

financial accounting Reporting accounting information to inside users such as stockholders, potential investors, the government or lenders.

fixed assets Assets that will be held or used longer than one year.

fixed costs Costs that remain constant within a significant range of the number of units produced. Fixed costs tend to change with time and also when the range is exceeded.

flat organisation One with few levels of management, greater decentralisation and greater delegation of authority.

floppy disk Magnetised portable disks used to store computer data.

form utility Value of products to consumers resulting from transformation of inputs into finished products.

four Ps Four elements of the marketing concept: product, price, promotion, and place (distribution).

franchise License to sell another company's products or to use another company's name or both.

franchisee Person or company that buys the rights to another company's logo, methods of operation, national advertising and products in exchange for fees and payments.

franchisor Company that sells a license to use its name or products.

free-enterprise system or free market system Economic system in which individuals (not governments) control all or most of the factors of production and make all or most of the production decision.

frequency distribution Table in which possible values of a variable are grouped into classes and the number of times a value falls into each class is recorded.

G

Gantt chart Scheduling device in bar-graph format that shows what has been done and what remains to be accomplished.

general expenses Costs incurred in running a business other than production costs and selling expenses.

general-partner Co-owner who bears full liability for the debts of the business.

globalisation Trend among businesses to operate worldwide, as multinational organisations.

goals Measurable steps in a plan, sometimes 'milestones'.

goods Tangible products (such as cars and shoes).

governmental market That part of the industrial market (namely, federal, state and local governments) which buys goods and services for internal operations or to provide citizens with motorways, water or other services.

grievance procedure Formal process for resolving employees' complaints against management.

gross national product (GNP) Total value of all goods and services produced in a particular economic system during a one year period.

H

hard disk Sealed, magnetised disk used to store massive amounts of computer data.

hardware Computer equipment and components.

high-growth venture Small business that has the potential to grow into a large company.

holding company Corporation organised to own stock in and manage another company.

horizontal merger Combination of two direct competitors in the same industry.

human resources management (HRM) Management of personnel, including planning, recruiting, hiring, training and development, performance appraisal and compensation.

I

importing Bringing in goods or raw materials from other countries.

income statement Summary of revenues and expenses for a certain period of time.

index number Percentage showing the degree of change between a base number (such as cost or price) in one period and the current number in the current period.

industrial market Organisations that buy products for use in day-to-day operations or for making into other products to sell for profit.

industrial products Products sold to private business firms or public agencies for use in the production of their goods or services.

industrial union Organisation made up of workers in a particular industry, regardless of skills or jobs.

information Data transformed and presented in a meaningful form.

information sector That part of the service sector which includes people employed in the computer and information processing technologies.

institutional market That part of the industrial market which includes institutions such as churches, schools, hospitals and clubs.

insurable risks Risks that are financial, measurable and predictable.

intangible assets Assets having financial value because they grant legal rights, advantages or privileges.

intensive distribution Distribution to all intermediaries or retailers willing to stock and sell the product.

internal data Data available from the company's records.

international trade Trading between countries.

inventory control Maintaining inventories of inputs at the lowest levels necessary to meet customer demand.

J

job analysis Detailed study of the jobs to be performed and the specific duties entailed in each job.

job description Key tasks and responsibilities of each position, as well as the relationship of one job to another.

job specification Statement summarising the knowledge, skills, education and experience required to perform a job.

joint venture Separate corporation owned by two or more corporations and established for the purpose of working on a specified project or in specific markets.

junk bonds Bonds offering higher yields because they are issued by less-secure companies.

just-in-time inventory control (JIT) Technique for reducing inventories by delivering materials "just in time" to be used in the manufacturing process.

K

key-executive insurance Insurance that protects the company against the financial impact of the death or disability of a key employee.

L

labour union Workers' organisation formed to achieve common goals in the areas of wages, hours and working conditions.

laissez-faire Economic system that calls for private ownership of property, free entry into markets and an absence of government intervention.

laissez-faire leadership Style describing managers who allow employees to make decisions.

law of demand Principle stating that people will buy more of a product at a lower price than at a higher price.

law of large numbers Statistical principle stating that as the number of units in a group increases, prediction about the group become more accurate and certain.

law of supply Principle stating that producers are willing to produce and offer for sale more goods at a higher price than at a lower price.

leadership Ability to influence organisation members to attain the organisation's objectives.

lease Agreement for the temporary transfer or use of property from owner to tenant.

leveraged buyout (BLO) Purchasing a company by borrowing money, using the company itself as collateral.

liabilities Firm's debts and obligations to others.

licensing Contractual agreement in which one firm permits another to produce and market its product or to use its brand name in return for a royalty or other compensation.

life-style business Modest business operation that has little growth potential but provides the owner(s) with modest income.

limited partner Co-owner whose liability is limited to the amount of his or her investment in the firm.

line management That part of the chain of command with direct responsibility for achieving the organisation's goals.

line of credit Loan approval for a specific total amount before the money is needed.

liquidation In bankruptcy cases, selling the assets of the business.

liquidity Ease with which an asset can be converted to cash.

loan fund Mutual fund that charges investors a sales fee.

lobbyist Representative for a special-interest group who attempts to influence legislators to approve legislation favourable to the group and oppose legislation that is not.

local area network (LAN) Communication system that links computers in a small geographical area, for example in one building.

lockout Company's refusal to allow workers to enter the workplace.

long-range plan Covers actions over a two to five year period, sometimes longer.

long term liabilities Debts that will come due in one year or more.

low contact service Service that does not directly and closely involve the customer (for example, lawn care and television repair).

M

M1 Money supply that includes currency, demand deposits and other checkable deposits.

M2 Money supply that includes M1 plus time deposits, money-market funds, and savings deposits.

mail-order retailing Selling merchandise by mail.

mainframe computer Large, general purpose system that has the capacity to serve hundreds or thousands of users.

management Process of working with and through people and other organisational resources to achieve organisational goals and objectives.

management accounting Reporting accounting information to people within the firm.

management development Specialised form of training, designed to improve the skills and talents of present managers or to prepare future managers.

management information Information that is vital to decision-making.

management information system (MIS) All the tools and procedures that transform data into information that can be used for decision-making at all levels within an organisation.

margin requirement Percentage of total purchase price an investor is required to put down to buy stock on margin.

market Group of individuals, organisations, or both that have needs for a given product and have the ability, willingnesss and authority to purchase the product.

marketing The process of planning and executing the conception, pricing, distribution, and promotion of ideas, goods and services to create exchanges that satisfy individual and organisational objectives.

marketing concept Principle stressing the need for the entire organisation to achieve customer satisfaction while achieving the organisation's goals.

marketing mix Combination of the four Ps in a particular marketing strategy.

marketing orientation or customer orientation Business approach that focuses primarily on customer needs and wants and developing goods and services to meet those needs and wants.

market order Client's authorisation to a broker to buy or sell at the best possible price at that moment.

market research Gathering, recording and analysing data concerning a particular marketing problem.

market segmentation Division of a market into various smaller groups or target markets.

market share Percentage of total industry sales.

mark-up Amount added to the total cost of a product to determine its selling price.

materials handling Transporting, handling and inventorying goods.

materials-requirements planning (MRP) Computer-based co-ordination system that ensures the availability of needed parts and materials at the right time at the right place.

mean Sum of all the items in a group divided by the number of items.

mechanisation Replacement of human labour with machine labour.

median Midpoint of a group of numbers, when arrayed in ascending or descending order.

media plan Detailed description of media, ads, schedules and costs.

mediation Use of a neutral third party in

management - labour negotiations.

merchant wholesale Intermediary who takes title to goods in large quantities and resells them to retail and industrial users in smaller quantities.

merger Combination of two companies in related industries.

microprocessor Processing unit that combines many of the functions of a CPU into just one chip.

minicomputer Computer of intermediate size and cost; scaled-down version of a mainframe computer.

mission Company's broad, general business purpose.

missionary selling Long-term sales strategy that emphasises the company's positive image.

mixed economy Economic system that shares some of the features of both the market economy and the planned economy.

mode Number that occurs most frequently in a group of numbers.

modem Communications device that allows computers to transmit and receive information over ordinary telephone lines.

money Anything used by a society to purchase goods, services or resources.

money-market fund Mutual fund that invests in short-term, low-risk securities.

monopoly Company control of a market, industry or area.

multinational company Corporation that operates on a worldwide scale.

mutual fund Company that sells shares to investors and uses the combined funds to make specific investments (as in stocks or bonds).

mutual insurance company Company owned by its policyholders.

N

national bank Commercial bank chartered by the US government.

national monopoly Monopoly permitted and regulated by the government.

negotiable instrument Any form of business paper used instead of cash - for example, cheques, bank drafts, certificates of deposit and promissory notes.

net income Profit earned (or loss suffered) by a firm during an accounting period.

net profit margin Measure of how effectively sales are transformed into profits, found by dividing net income after taxes by net sales.

network Communications system that links computers and other devices.

networking Process of using contacts to make more contacts for a specific purpose, such as obtaining a job.

no-load fund Fund that charges no sales fees.

nonprofit or not-for-profit corporation Corporation set up for charitable, educational or fraternal purposes.

nonstore retailer Retailer that does not maintain conventional store facilities.

O

objective Statement of how an organisation plans to achieve its mission.

oligopoly Market dominated by only a small number of very large firms.

open shop Workplace where union membership has no affect on hiring or firing.

operating expenses Costs other than costs of goods sold.

operations planning Determining the types and amounts of resources needed to produce specified goods and to plan for the purchasing, routing, scheduling and dispatching of these resources.

opportunity cost Value of a resource as measured against the best alternative use for that resource.

option Right to buy or sell a specified stock at a specified price for a specified period of time.

order processing All activities involved in receiving and filling customers' orders and in shipping, billing and granting credit.

organisation chart Blueprint of a company's structure, showing all components, their relationship and the chain of command.

orientation Process of acquainting new employees with the company, its policies and procedures and its personnel.

over-the-counter (OTC) market Network of dealers who trade stocks.

owners' equity Difference between assets and liabilities; amount that would remain for the firm's owners if the assets were used to pay off the liabilities.

P

partnership Business owned and managed by two or more people.

patent Exclusive rights to a machine, a process or other useful invention.

penetration pricing Strategy of setting a low price in order to garner a large market share.

performance appraisal Formal program comparing employees' actual performance with expected performance.

personal property Property other than real property.

PERT (Program Evaluation and Review Technique) chart Chart showing activities to be done, time required for each activity and relationships among the different activities.

physical distribution functions Functions that involve the flow of goods from producers to customers.

picket March by striking employees in front of their workplace holding signs notifying the public that a strike is in progress.

place utility Value of a product to consumers resulting from the product's availability at a place where a customer wishes to purchase it.

planned economy Market system in which the government controls the factors of production.

planning Process of establishing objectives and then setting policies, procedures and a course of action to accomplish these objectives.

point of purchase displays Product displays designed to catch customers' attention at specific, prominent locations.

policy Broad, general guidelines for making decisions and taking actions.

positioning Establishing in consumers' minds a clearly identifiable image for a product.

possession utility Value of a product to consumers resulting from transferring the title or ownership of the product to the customer.

preference shares Equity shares in a business which pay a fixed dividend to the shareholder.

preferred stock Stock that shares some features of both corporate bonds and common stock.

primary data Data gathered through original research.

prime rate Loan rate that banks give to their most creditworthy borrowers.

principal Person whom an agent represents.

private accountant Accountant employed by a specific organisation.

private corporation Corporation formed by private individuals or companies and chartered for a specific business purpose.

producer market That part of the industrial market that buys products for the purpose of manufacturing other products.

product differentiation Process of developing and promoting differences between one company's product and all the other similar products that are available.

product line Group of related products.

product mix All the products that one firm offers.

production Transformation process for converting resources into goods or services.

production and operations management Business approach that focuses primarily on improving manufacturing efficiency.

productivity Measure of efficiency that compares the total amount of outputs and the resources needed to produce them. More exactly, a ratio of the actual usage of resources to the best use of the resources.

product life cycle Four key stages of a product's life: introduction, growth, maturity and decline.

profit Selling price less production and marketing costs.

profit margin Difference between selling price and total cost.

promissory note Borrower's written pledge to pay a certain sum of money to a creditor at a specified future date.

promotion All persuasive techniques designed to induce customers to buy products or services.

promotional mix Combination of specific methods a firm uses to market its products or services.

property Anything tangible or intangible that can be owned.

prospecting Process of finding and identifying potential customers ('prospects').

protectionism Creation of artificial barriers to free international trade.

prototype Working model of a product.

psychographics Profiles of consumers according to their motives, attitudes, activities, interests and opinions.

public corporation Corporation set up by Congress or a state legislature to provide a specific public service.

publicity Nonpersonal, unpaid mass media

messages about an organisation, its products or services or its personnel.

public relations Company-influenced publicity.

pull strategy Promotional technique that relies on mass advertising to convince consumers to buy goods.

purchasing Operations-planning function that deals with all aspects of buying raw materials or components.

pure competition Situation in which a large number of small firms are producing identical or nearly identical products.

pure risk Risk that involves only the probability of loss with no possibility of profit or gain.

push strategy Promotional technique that encourages wholesalers and retailers to push products to customers.

put Right to sell a specified stock at a specified price for a specified period.

Q

quality circle Small voluntary group of workers that meets regularly to solve problems related to quality.

quality control Process of ensuring that final quality meets planned quality.

quantity discount Price reduction to buyers who purchase in large quantities.

quasi-public corporation Corporation with a government-granted monopoly to provide certain services to the public.

R

random sample Sample in which any person or item in the population has an equal chance of being selected.

real property Land and anything permanently attached to it, such as housing or other structures.

recruiting Process of finding and attracting

sufficient qualified job applicants.

regulatory law Business law formed by the decrees and regulations of government agencies.

reserve requirement Percentage of a bank's total deposits that the bank is required to maintain on hand.

resume Summary of a job applicant's work experience, education and other relevant information. (Curriculum vitae, or CV in UK)

retailer Business that sells directly to consumers.

return on investment Measure of how much income is generated by each dollar of equity, found by dividing net income after taxes by owner's equity.

revaluation Arbitrary upward adjustment of one country's currency in terms of another country's currency.

revenues Gross sales, all receipts from customers purchases.

risk Possibility that a loss or injury will occur.

risk management Process of identifying potential risks and ways to protect against each.

round lot Stock transaction in one-hundred share multiples.

S

salary Compensation at a specified rate regardless of time worked or output.

sales agent Commission sales representative for one or more manufacturers within a specific territory.

sales office Manufacturer owned office that acts as agent, selling both the manufacturer's products and other products that complement the manufacturer's product line.

sales promotion Activities or materials designed to influence customers to buy products or services.

sample Small group that ideally is representative of a larger group.

savings account Traditional demand deposit passbook account.

scrambled merchandising Offering an odd mix of unrelated merchandise in addition to a store's traditional merchandise.

seasonal discount Price reductions offered in the off-season.

secondary data Data that originate from sources outside the company.

selection Process of identifying appropriate job applicants and selecting from among each geographic area.

selling expenses Costs related to marketing, advertising and promotion.

selling price Total cost plus mark-up.

selling short Selling stock borrowed from a broker and replacing the borrowed stock later, when the price is anticipated to be lower than the current price.

serial bonds Bonds in a single issue that mature on different dates.

service Intangible item, such as professional advice and assistance.

service business Business that does not produce goods, but instead, provides intangible professional assistance or advice.

shopping goods Products that consumers shop actively for, comparing prices, values, features, quality and styles before finally making a purchase decision.

shop steward Person elected by union members to represent them at a particular work location.

short-range plan Covers one year or less.

sinking-fund bond Bond for which the issuer regularly makes payments into a fund in preparation for payment at maturity.

situational leadership Style of managers who adapt as appropriate to each specific situation and to the people involved in that situation.

small business Business that is independently owned and operated for profit and is not dominant in its field.

small medium enterprise (SME) A small business employing up to 400, but usually reserved for small businesses with less than 100 employees.

socialism Economic system in which the government controls key industries and major natural resources.

software Computer programs - sets of instructions, procedures and rules - that tell a computer what to do.

sole proprietorship Business that is owned and managed by one person.

specialist Intermediary who works on the floor of an exchange for the purpose of making a market (trading) in a particular stock.

specialisation Division of labour into smaller work tasks.

specialty store Retail establishment that sells a limited line of merchandise.

speculative risk Risk accompanied by the possibility of earning a profit.

staffing Supplying the organisation with the human resources it needs through recruitment, selection and employee orientation.

statement of cash flows Statement describing the company's cash receipts and payments for a specific period.

statistics Figures that summarise and represent factual data.

statutory law All laws enacted by central government legislation.

stock average or stock index Adjusted average of stock prices of selected companies, used to measure performance.

stockbroker Person who executes clients' orders to buy and sell securities and receives a commission for services rendered.

stock insurance company Insurance company owned by stockholders and operated for profit.

stock split Issuing one or more shares of additional stock to stockholders for each share they currently own.

strike Work stoppage by employees.

subsidiary Corporation that is owned by another corporation and operated as a separate entity.

supercomputers World's fastest, most expensive computers.

supermarket Large retail food outlet.

supply Amount of output of a good or service that producers are willing and able to make available to the market at a given price at a given time.

survey Method of eliciting opinions and attitudes and/or gathering facts by means of questionnaires or telephone interviews.

syndicate Group of firms operating together, usually on one large project.

systems software Instructions that manage the computer and run the hardware.

T

tall organisation One with many levels of management, greater centralisation and less delegation of authority.

target market Group of people with similar wants and needs.

tariff Tax imposed on imported goods.

telemarketing Personal selling that uses the telephone for any or all steps.

Theory X Management theory that employees can be motivated only be fear (of job loss for example).

Theory Y Management theory that employees can be motivated by better challenges, personal growth and improved work performance and productivity.

Theory Z Management theory that employees

should be involved, should participate, and should be treated like family.

time deposit Savings account that requires notice prior to withdrawal.

time series analysis or trend analysis Statistical technique for observing changes in data over time and basing forecasts on those observations.

time sharing service system Co-ownership of large computers for the purpose of sharing costs and computer time.

time utility Value of a product to consumers resulting from the product's availability when the customer wants it.

tort Noncriminal injury to person or property.

trade credit Credit granted by a supplier to a business.

trade deficit Negative balance of trade.

trade discounts Price reductions offered to wholesalers and distributors.

trademark Brand legally protected from use by anyone except the trademark owner.

trade show Exhibit sponsored by an industry or association to promote sales.

trade surplus Positive or favourable balance of trade.

transportation Moving products through the channels of distribution to the ultimate consumers.

U

unemployment benefit Insurance funded by the government from National Insurance contributions from employers and employees, to provide partial, temporary income replacement to eligible workers who become unemployed.

uninsurable risk Risk that presents an incalculable loss.

unsecured loan Loan not backed by collateral.

utility Power of a good or service to satisfy a need.

V

value-added tax Tax assessed at each level in the chain of distribution.

variable In statistics, a factor that changes in a situation.

variable costs Costs that change as more goods or services are produced.

vertical marketing system Integration that results when two or more members of a channel of distribution are joined under a single management.

vertical merger Combination of two companies in the same chain of supply.

W

warehouse store Minimal-service outlets that carry large inventories of merchandise.

warehousing Activities that ensure the availability of products when needed.

warranty Seller's promise (either expressed or implied) that a product meets certain standards of performance.

wholesaler Business that buys and then resells products to other businesses.

Z

zero-based budgeting Method of budgeting that starts with no base from the preceding budget period.

zero-coupon bond Bond sold at a deep discount from its face value and redeemed at full face value.

Index

A

ACAS (Advisory, Conciliation,and Arbitration Service), 81
accounting cycle, 142
  equation, 142
  institutions, 140
acid test ratio, 151
administrative order, 45
  receivership, 45
advertising, 128, 13
  agencies, 134
  campaigns, 133
  media, 131
  message types, 131
  regulators, 134
  advocacy, 131
agents, 12, 44, 115
AI (artificial intelligence), 177
air miles, 137
airfreight, 126
applications software, 172
appointment scheduling, 91
arbitration, 80
Arkwright, Sir Richard, 8
Articles of Association, 28
ASA (Advertising Standards Authority), 134
assets, 142, 143
ATM (automatic teller machine), 180
auditing, 140
automation, 84
AVCO (average cost method), 148
average, 163

B

balance of payments, 214
balance of trade, 10, 214
balance sheet, 143
bank overdraft, 200

Bank of England, 183
bar charts, 162
bar code, 172
Barings Bank, 194
BASIC language, 173
batch processing, 173
bear market, 194
billboards, 132
bonds, 189
book-keeping, 142
brand insistence, 106
  loyalty, 106
  name, 105
  preference, 106
  recognition, 106
  types, 106
branding, 105
  strategies, 107
breakeven analysis, 111
breakeven point, 111
British Code of Advertising Practice, 134
brokers, 120, 192
budgets, 153, 199
building societies, 182
business ethics, 46
  cottage, 34
  niche, 34
  retail, 36
  wholesale, 36
Business Expansion Schemes (BES), 37
Business Link, 36
buying, 99

C

CAD (computer aided design), 84
cafeteria approach, 76
call (financial), 194
CAM (computer aided manufacturing), 84
capital budget, 154
capital gains, 187

capitalism, 4
cargo ships, 126
carriers, 126
cash budget, 154
cash flow statement, 149
CBI (Confederation of British Industries), 81
CD (compact disk), 171
Central Statistical Office, 157
Chartered Association of Certified Accountants, 140
Chartered Institute of Management Accountants, 140
Chernobyl, 18
closed-end funds, 191
Coca-Cola 'Classic', 105
collective bargaining, 79
commercial banks, 182
commercial draft, 200
commission merchants, 119
common law, 39
communism, 4
community shopping centres, 123
Companies Act (1980), 27
Companies Act (1985), 140, 143
Companies House, 141
company, conglomerate, 31
  holding, 30
  joint venture, 30
  private limited (ltd), 30
  public limited (plc), 29
  subsidiary, 30
competition, 5
  monopolistic, 6
  pure, 6
Competition Act (1980), 22
computer generations, 168
  languages, 172
consumer channels, 115
Consumer Credit Act (1974), 18

Consumer Protection Act (1987), 18, 107
contingency approach, 51
contract law, 41
contract of employment, 71, 74
CSHH (Control of Substances Hazardous to Health Regulations) (1988), 19
controlling, 55, 87
convenience goods, 97
copyright, 43
corporate culture, 226
correlation, 165
cost based pricing, 110
cost of goods sold, 147
couriers, 127
courts, County, 41
    Crown, 41
    European, 41
    High, 41
CPM (critical path method), 86
CPU(central processing unit), 170
creative selling, 135
credit cards, 182
credit management, 184
creditors, 141, 145
critical path, 86
currency, 180
current assets, 144
current ratio, 151
Customs and Excise, 141
CV (curriculum vitae), 229
cyclical changes, 14

D

data, 156
    collection, 157
    types, 157
Data Protection Act (1985), 175
debenture, 189
debt financing, 202
debtors, 141, 144, 201
debtors turnover, 151
decision making, 58
decision support systems, 160
delegation, 65
demand, 5
demographic factors, 100
demography, 14
department stores, 120
Department of Social Security, 207
Department of Trade and Industry (DTI), 36
depreciation, 145, 147, 148

derivatives, 194
development, 15
direct labour costs, 147
direct mail, 132
Disabled Persons Act (1958), 18
discount houses, 182
discount pricing, 113
dispatching, 87
dissatisfiers, 66
distribution channels, 115
distribution methods, 117
dividends, 190
door-to-door retailers, 122
double entry book-keeping, 142
Douglas, McGregor, 57
downsizing, 70
Drucker, Peter, 58
DTI (Department of Trade and Industry), 36

E

EC (European Community), 17, 218
economics, 2
    variables, 13
    electronic mail, 174
embargoes, 216
employee benefits, 75
Employers Liability (Compulsory Insurance) Act (1969), 208
employment, full, 9
Employment Act (1990), 19
Employment Acts (1980-1990), 78
Employment Protection Act (1978), 19, 72
entrepreneur, 1, 2, 35
Environmental Protection Act (1991), 17
EPS (earnings per share), 153
Equal Pay Act (1970), 18, 75
equilibrium, 5
equity financing, 201
error cause removal, 88
ethics, business, 46
European Community, 17
exchange rates, 215
expenses, 147
expert system, 177
exporting, 214, 219

F

factoring, 201
factors of production, 2
Factory and Workshop Act (1901), 209

Fair Trading Act (1973), 22
FAX, 174
Fayol, Henri, 49, 64
feedback, 12
FIFO (first in, first out method), 148
financial accounting, 139
    futures, 194
    ratios, 150
    statement analysis, 150
fixed assets, 144
fixed costs, 110
floppy disks, 170
foreign exchange, 184
franchising, 37
free enterprise, 7
    markets, 215
freight forwarders, 126
frequency distributions, 161
Friedman, Milton, 16
FT (Financial Times) Index, 196
futures market, 194

G

Gantt, Henry, 49, 86
GATT (General Agreement on Tariffs and Trade), 23, 217
gearing, 152
general ledger, 143
generating ideas, 103
GIGO (garbage in, garbage out), 176
Gilbreth, Frank and Lillian, 49
GNP (Gross National Product), 9
government deficits, 10
Gross National Product (GNP), 9
Guardian Royal Insurance, 208

H

hard disks, 170
hard information, 156
hardware, 169
Hawthorne studies, 50
Health and Safety at Work Act (1974), 19
hedging, 194
Hertzberg, Frederick, 66
high street banks, 183
hygiene factors, 66
hypermarkets, 121

I

IMF (International Monetary Fund), 217
import quotas, 216
importing, 214
independent variables, 166
Independent Broadcasting Authority, 134
index numbers, 165
Industrial Revolution , 8
inflation, 10
Inland Revenue, 141
inputs, 12
insolvency, 44
Insolvency Act (1986), 45
Institute of Chartered Accountants, 140
Institute of Public Finance and Accountancy, 140
institutional advertising, 130
insurance premium, 206
intangible assets, 145
intellectual property, 43
interest rates, 202
international business, 220
interviewing, 230
inventory control, 124
    loan, 201
investment trusts, 191

J

JIT (just in time), 88
job analysis, 69
    description, 70
    specification, 70
    types, 225
joint venture, 219
judicial precedence, 39
junk bonds, 189

L

labelling, 107
LAIA (Latin American Integration Association), 218
LAN (local area network), 174
laser printer, 171
law of agency, 44
layoff, 74
leaders, autocratic, 55
    laissez-faire, 56
    participative, 55
leading, 55
leverage buyout, 31
liabilities, 142, 145
licensing, 219
lifestyle, 15

LIFO (last in, first out method), 148
limited company, 28
line graphs, 161
liquidation, 46
liquidity, 143
    ratios, 151
loan stock, 189
long term financing, 201
    term loans, 152
loss adjuster, 206

M

M-1/2/3, 181, 184
Maastricht Act (1992), 40
magazines, 132
mail order, 122
mainframe computers, 169
management development, 71
    information, 158
    line, 64
    staff, 64
Management by Objectives (MBO), 57, 58
managerial accounting, 139
manpower planning, 69
mark-up, 110
market coverage, 117
    economy, 3
    research, 98
    segmentation, 95, 96
    types, 95
marketing concept, 97
    functions, 94
    intermediaries, 117
    mix, 98
Marx, Karl, 4
Maslow, Abraham, 50
Maslow's hierarchy of needs, 57
materials handling, 125
Mayo, Elton, 50
McDonalds, 89
mean, 163
median, 164
mediation, 80
Memorandum of Association, 28
merchant bank, 183
merchant wholesalers, 119
merger, horizontal, 31
    vertical, 31
MIS (management information system), 156, 159
mission statement, 54
missionary selling, 136
mixed economy, 4
mode, 165

modem, 174
money, 179
    supply, 181
    types, 180
Monopolies and Mergers Act (1965), 22
Monopolies and Restrictive Practices Act (1948), 21
Monopolies and Restrictive Practices Commission, 21
monopoly, 6
Moody's, 189
mouse, 171
MRP (materials requirements planning), 87
multinational business, 220

N

NASA, 64
national savings, 183
National Insurance, 207
negative correlation, 166
negligence, 44
neighbourhood shopping centres, 123
Nestles, 118
net profit margin, 153
new product development, 103
newspapers, 131
NIFO (next in, first out method), 148
Norwich Union, 208
NOW (negotiated order of withdrawal), 180

O

objectives, business, 54
occupations in business, 224
Office of Population Censuses and Surveys, 157
oligopoly, 6
on-line computing, 173
OPEC (Organisation of Petroleum Exporting Countries), 218
open-end funds, 191
operating expenses, 149
opportunity cost, 3
optical disk, 171
options, 194
order processing, 124
orders and lots, 193
ordinary shares, 190
organisation, centralised, 64
    chart, 61
    decentralised, 64

matrix, 62
organising, 54
outputs, 12
overdraft, 145
overtime, 80
owners equity, 142, 145

P

packaging, 107
Partnership Act (1890), 26
partnerships, 26, 27
party selling, 122
patents, 43
PC (portable computer), 169
PE (price earnings) ratio, 196
penetration pricing, 112
performance appraisal, 73
personal selling, 128, 134
PERT (program evaluation
    and review technique),
    86
picketing, 80
pictographs, 163
pie charts, 163
pipelines, 127
planned economy, 3
planning, 53
plotters, 171
poison pill, 31
political climate, 16
political process, 16
pollution, 17
POM (production and
    operations
    management), 82, 89
positive correlation, 166
preference shares, 190
prestige pricing, 113
price lining, 113
    skimming, 112
pricing methods, 110
    objectives, 109
    strategies, 111
    tactics, 112
primary demand advertising,
    130
primary market, 188
principles of insurance, 206
printers, 171
probability, 160
process, batch, 83
process, continuous, 83
product differentiation, 101
    flow, 83
    liability, 44
    life cycle, 102
    line, 101
    mix, 102
    types, 97
production layout, 85

line, 84
    processes, 82
    types, 84
productivity, 10, 84
profit and loss account, 146
profit before tax, 149
profit margin, 110
profitability ratios, 153
promissory notes, 200
promotional methods, 128
    objectives, 128
    strategies, 129
property law, 42
protectionism, 216
psychological factors, 100
    pricing, 112
public relations, 137
publicity, 128, 137
pull strategy, 129
purchasing, 85
purchasing power, 99
pure risk, 204
push strategy, 129
put (financial), 195

Q

quality circles, 88
    control, 87
    improvement team, 88
queuing theory, 91
quick ratio, 151

R

Race Relations Act (1976), 18,
    76
radio, 132
railways, 126
recruiting, 71
reducing value method of
    depreciation, 148
redundancy, 74
regional shopping centres,
    124
reinsurance, 207
Resale Price Act (1964), 22
research, applied, 15
    basic, 15
resignation, 73
Restrictive Trade Practices
    Act (1956), 21
Retail Price Index, (RPI), 10
retailers, 120
retirement, 74
return on equity, 153
revenues, 147
risk assumption, 205
    avoidance, 205
    management, 204
    reduction, 206

transfer, 205
Road Traffic Act (1930), 209
robotic production, 84
routing, 86

S

Sale of Goods Act (1979), 18,
    107
sales promotion, 128, 136
sampling, 158, 161
satisfiers, 66
savings accounts, 181
scarcity, 3
scheduling, 86
scheduling service
    operations, 91
scrambled merchandising,
    121
seasonal variations, 165
secondary market, 188
selection, 71
selective advertising, 130
separation, 73
service characteristics, 90
    production, 89
    quality control, 92
    site location, 90
settlement period, 193
Sex Discrimination Act
    (1986), 18
share prices, 195
shareholders, 141
shareholders equity, 152
shop stewards, 78
shopping goods, 97
short term financing, 199
Single European Act (1987),
    40
site selection, 85
slowdown, 80
social values, 15
Social Chapter, 18, 76
socialism, 4
soft information, 156
software, 169
sole trader, 25
sources of funds, 199
span of control, 66
speciality goods, 97
speculative risk, 204
SSAPs (Statements of
    Standard Accounting
    Practice), 143
St.Michael brand, 106
stability, economic, 9
stakeholders, external, 13
    internal, 13
Standard & Poor, 189
statistical analysis, 163
    quality control, 88

stock control, 88
  turnover, 152
  valuation, 147
Stock Exchange, 192
straight line method of
    depreciation, 149
strategic plans, 54, 154
strategy, accommodation, 17
  defence, 17
  denial, 16
  proactive, 17
  reaction, 17
strike, 80
Sunday markets, 124
supply, 5
Supply of Goods and
    Services Act (1982), 18
systems, closed, 13
systems life cycle, 176
  open, 13
  software, 172
  theory, 12
  approach, 50

T

tactics, business, 54
tariffs, 216
tax, 145
Tax, Corporation, 23
  Income Personal, 23
  Value Added, 23
Taylor, Frederick, 49
telecommunications, 127
teleconferencing, 174
telemarketing, 136
television, 132
television marketing, 123

test marketing, 103
Thatcher, Margaret, 16
Theories X and Y, 57
threshold pricing, 113
time deposits, 181
time series analysis, 165
tort law, 43
total costs, 110
touch screen, 172
trade credit, 200
  deficit, 214
  shows, 136
  surplus, 214
trade unions, 77
Trade Descriptions Act
    (1968), 18, 107
Trade Union Act (1984), 79
Trade Union and Labour
    Relations Act (1974), 77
trademarks, 43, 105
traders, 194
Trades Union Council, 81
training, 71
Training and Enterprise
    Councils (TECs), 36
transportation methods, 126
Treaty of Rome (1957), 40
trend, 165
trial balance, 143
trucks, 126
Tupperware, 116
types of non-compulsory
    insurance, 209

U

Unfair Contract Terms Act
    (1977), 108

unions, craft, 77
  general, 77
  industrial, 77
  staff, 78
unit trusts, 191
utility, 82, 93

V

variable costs, 110
vending machines, 123
VMSs (vertical marketing
    systems), 116
voice mail, 174

W

wage structure, 75
wages, 75
warehousing, 125
warranty, 107
Weber, Max, 49
white knight, 31
wholesaler types, 119
  services, 118
withdrawal of goodwill, 80
work in progress, 147
work to rule, 80
working capital, 151
World Bank, 217

Z

zero based budget, 154